# THE SKY IS INCOMPLETE

# The Sky Is Incomplete

## *Travel Chronicles in Palestine*

IRMGARD EMMELHAINZ

VANDERBILT UNIVERSITY PRESS

*Nashville, Tennessee*

Originally published in Spanish as *El cielo está incompleto: Cuaderno de viaje en Palestina* (Taurus, 2017).

Library of Congress Cataloging-in-Publication Data

Names: Emmelhainz, Irmgard, author.
Title: The sky is incomplete : travel chronicles in Palestine / Irmgard
  Emmelhainz.
Other titles: Cielo está incompleto. English
Description: Nashville, Tennessee : Vanderbilt University Press, [2023] |
  Includes bibliographical references.
Identifiers: LCCN 2023002344 (print) | LCCN 2023002345 (ebook) | ISBN
  9780826505651 (paperback) | ISBN 9780826505668 (hardback) | ISBN
  9780826505675 (epub) | ISBN 9780826505682 (adobe pdf)
Subjects: LCSH: Emmelhainz, Irmgard—Travel—Palestine. | Palestinian
  Arabs—Politics and government—21st century. | Palestine—Description
  and travel.
Classification: LCC DS107.5 .E4513 2023  (print) | LCC DS107.5  (ebook) |
  DDC 915.69404—dc23/eng/20230124
LC record available at https://lccn.loc.gov/2023002344
LC ebook record available at https://lccn.loc.gov/2023002345

Map of Palestine by Léopold Lambert / *The Funambulist* (originally in 2014,
and regularly updated since then). Source of data includes, among others, the
United Nations Office for the Coordination of Humanitarian Affairs (OCHA),
Palestine Remembered, Zochrot, and the United Nations Relief and Works
Agency for Palestine Refugees in the Near East (UNRWA). This version was first
published in the *The JVC Palestine Portfolio* 20, no. 2 (August 2021).

*To Lizzy, Layla, Roberta, Thea, Bruno, Vaqui, and Rita,*
*my interspecies life companions, with love*

# CONTENTS

# INTRODUCTION TO
# THE ENGLISH EDITION

Many things have changed, and others have intensified or worsened since I last visited the Occupied Palestinian Territories in 2015 and the Spanish version of this book was published in 2017. On the ground, there is de facto annexation of the West Bank and East Jerusalem through the expansion of illegal Jewish settlements.[1] The international community has failed to call out systematic violations of international law by Israel, while the organized effort of the Israeli government and its allies is shutting down criticism and intimidating opponents, accusing them of anti-Semitism and even criminalizing them.[2]

Although I was warned early on against writing anything related to Palestine and Palestinians—especially because I am not Arab, Muslim, or Jewish—I had never met censorship like I did in April 2022, when I submitted a text I had written about a contemporary Palestinian artist whose work was showing at a prestigious museum in Norway. I was asked to eliminate the following sentence: "Israelis have told Palestinians again and again they don't exist." Earlier in 2022, when commissioned to write another text, this time about a film made by a Palestinian artist shown in a German institution, I was requested not to "politicize" the text. Friends from the West, fearful of repercussions, have asked me not to use their real names in this book. I live with the fear that the book will be censored, that it will cost me entry to Palestine or the United States, and that my career will pay a price for my having written and published it.

Just as the freedom to defend or even talk about the Palestine Question has shrunk in the past few years as polarization along lines of ethnicity, belief, culture, class status, and religion has increased on social media and in real life, the conditions of Palestinians—whether in the West Bank and Gaza or in Israel—have considerably worsened.[3] Without a doubt, we are living in a neo-totalitarian era grounded in the failure of Enlightenment values to emancipate humanity from the "collateral damage" of modernity—colonialism and its evils, among them occupation, genocide, and oppression. The Israeli-Palestinian conflict, moreover, has been a twentieth-century prototype and laboratory for the technologies of war, dispossession, and population control, with Israel a global leader in the production and sales of security and war technologies. In fact, the Palestinian struggle constitutes a nexus for imperial control, as there is much at stake for imperial elites—whether ideologically, religiously, or strategically—in the occupation of Palestine.

In August 2019, Israeli forces shot tear gas, sound grenades, and rubber bullets at the Al-Aqsa Mosque, the third most sacred site for Muslims, injuring dozens of Muslim Palestinians gathered for the first day of Eid al-Adha (the Feast of Sacrifice, the most important holiday in Islam).[4] The clashes continued when Israeli authorities allowed hundreds of religious Jews to enter the sacred mosque during Eid.[5] The history of aggressions to the mosque that led to the Second Intifada in 2000, when Palestinians perceived Ariel Sharon's visit to the Al-Aqsa compound as a provocation, seems to repeat itself with increasing intensity.

As I finish revising this manuscript in 2022, a hundred far-right Jewish nationalists have entered the Al-Aqsa Mosque compound ahead of a provocative "Flag March" that could reignite confrontations between Israelis and Palestinians.[6] As Palestinian counter-protests erupted, dozens were arrested and over 165 have been injured.[7] Palestinians fear that their sovereignty over the compound is being eroded as far-right Israelis call for the mosque and the Dome of the Rock to be replaced with a Jewish temple.[8]

The Flag March is a demonstration by Israeli settlers celebrated every year to commemorate the occupation of East Jerusalem in 1967, when Israel annexed the area in a move that was not sanctioned by the international community. Every year, thousands of people belonging to far-right Israeli groups take part, waving Israeli flags and singing racist anti-Palestinian songs and slogans. Palestinians perceive the Flag March as a provocation by Jewish settlers to display their sovereignty over the occupied territory. The Flag March in 2021 even provoked rocket fire from Gaza, to which Israel responded by bombing the besieged territory and beginning an eleven-day war.[9] This was the fourth major offensive launched by Israel on the Palestinian territory in fourteen years: 261 Palestinians and 13 Israelis were killed, vital infrastructure was damaged, and more than seventeen hundred civilian homes in the Strip were partially or completely destroyed. Palestinians have not been able to rebuild because Israeli authorities restricted access to building materials in Gaza.[10]

In April, a month before the 2022 Flag March, Palestinians in Al Aqsa threw stones and firecrackers to which Israeli forces responded by arresting 60 and injuring 62 people.[11] These events preceded the death of Palestinian American reporter Shireen Abu Akleh, a veteran journalist for *Al Jazeera*, who was shot in the head while covering an Israeli military operation in Jenin, in the West Bank. She was a respected and loved presence, well-known for her coverage of the hard realities of the occupation. The latest evidence demonstrates that she was shot in a targeted attack by Israeli forces.[12]

This year, 2022, marks seventy-four years of the "Nakba," the catastrophic destruction of historical Palestine. It is also the fifty-fifth anniversary of uninterrupted military siege, dispossession, systematic oppression, apartheid, and restrictions on movement for Palestinians. We can add to this the ceaseless destruction of the Palestinians' social tissue, including the communal networks used for subsistence and survival, family networks, political structures, infrastructure, economic and territorial sovereignty. These forms of destruction happen alongside harm to the psychological well-being of Palestinians through extortion, torture, and other coercive means to seek collaboration and by means of subtle and not-so-subtle Israeli policies and laws.[13] Following Ariella Azoulay, the Israeli state apparatus governs Palestinians alongside Israelis with a different set of rights—rather, as noncitizens—or as Israeli citizens with different or fewer rights.[14] In 2020, the Knesset approved a law for "authorities of the occupation" to have the power to take away the residency rights of Palestinians living in Jerusalem if they "break their loyalty to Israel."[15] All these systemic forms of discrimination impede the normal development of Palestinians, who live under what they call "the tyranny of incertitude."

For Palestinians, any solution to the political conflict depends on ending the occupation, recognizing the national rights of the Palestinian people, and establishing an independent, sovereign, and viable state according to the 1967 borders, with Jerusalem as a shared capital. However, the political peace process and binational solution have been dead for over a decade. Instead of discussing peace and diplomacy, Israeli prime minister Benjamin Netanyahu defended something that he called "economic peace," which is an approach to the conflict based on mutual economic cooperation. Netanyahu was the first global leader to use racist hate language in the public sphere and to disseminate fake news (in the sense used by Aleksandr Dugin, who believes journalism is persuasion[16]) in social media.[17]

Netanyahu was Israel's prime minister from 1996 to 1999 and again served as prime minister beginning in 2009, winning elections in 2013 and 2015. The result of the 2019 elections was inconclusive; Netanyahu and his opponent, Benny Gantz, negotiated a coalition government from September 2019 to March 2020. During this time, it was being debated in Israel whether Netanyahu would face trial for charges of corruption, fraud, breach of faith, and other crimes. In March 2020, Benny Gantz opted to join Prime Minister Netanyahu in a new government, breaking with half of his party. Both agreed to rotate as prime minister, each serving for eighteen months. In the interim, Gantz would be foreign minister and deputy prime minister.[18]

In 2009, Netanyahu gave a speech famous for its controversial declarations at the Bar-Ilan University. He proclaimed that Jerusalem was Israeli territory and that Palestinians had to recognize Israel as a Jewish state with an undivided Jerusalem as capital.[19] This claim implicitly obliterated the possibility for Palestinian refugees to return, as the return of exiled Palestinians, including those living in the diaspora, would threaten Israel's existence as a state for the Jewish people only. Netanyahu also declared that it was not possible to stop the expansion of West Bank settlements because of "natural demographic growth" and the migration of populations.[20] It is said that with the speech, Netanyahu shut the door to any negotiation that could result in a permanent accord with the Palestinians.

Netanyahu has also been repeatedly accused of crushing truth and inciting hatred through "alternative facts" in election campaigns, social media posts, and public declarations.[21] In retrospect, Netanyahu was the prototype of a new form of government, one that has been destroying the public sphere and diplomacy by engaging in political speech rooted in racism and hatred. Netanyahu's "alternative facts" have led to millions of racist commentaries circulating on social media,[22] which in turn are reflected in recent clashes in public space at the Al Aqsa Mosque compound and elsewhere across the territories.

Since Netanyahu, moreover, the "Israeli Occupation" is no longer an occupation as defined by international humanitarian law. For the United Nations, a "military occupation" does not imply the sovereignty of the occupier over the occupied, the right to transfer citizens from the occupied land, or the right to engage in ethnic cleansing, destruction of property, collective punishment, or annexation of settlements.[23] Israel's military occupation of the West Bank is thus revealed as one of the phases of Zionist colonization of historical Palestine, a process that began over a hundred years ago and was accelerated by Trump's support of Netanyahu.

Another recent chapter in the story of the Israeli occupation is the normalization of diplomatic and economic relations between Israel and the United Arab Emirates, a deal brokered by the United States after Israel agreed to "temporarily halt" plans to annex all of the occupied Palestinian territories in the West Bank. The Palestinian Authority rejected and denounced the trilateral deal and recalled its ambassador in the UAE.[24] This open public alliance between Israel and one of the most reactionary, antidemocratic monarchies in the world is another big blow for the Palestinians: the UAE is the first Arab country to officially recognize Israel.[25] While the Palestinians have lost the support of an Arab government, Arab public opinion continues to consider Israel a great danger.[26]

The current situation for Palestinians is untenable, and they will keep on demanding equal national rights and self-determination. The fact that the Palestinian ordeal reproduces itself throughout the world makes Palestinians exemplary in their resistance against occupation, aggression, and dispossession.[27] Palestine must not be forgotten. Palestinians struggle to maintain their resistance in the face of censorship and persecution. To find strength as their self-determination falters in the face of exile, younger Palestinians are now identifying with Blackness and the struggles of First Nations in North America. This solidarity must renew their resistance and *sumud* (perseverance, dignity) as their efforts take new forms. For the moment, we can support their boycott campaign against Israel.

This book, written with love for my Palestinian friends and their land, bears witness to the scars littering the Palestinian landscape and to the painful memories embedded in the endless shaven hills of red earth, haunted by the ghosts of the long-gone pine forests, Palestinians and their old villages.

*Mexico City, May 2022*

# INTRODUCTION TO
# THE SPANISH EDITION

Les territoires occupés n'étaient que du drame vécu seconde par
seconde par l'occupé et par l'occupant. Leur réalité était l'imbrication
fertile en haine et en amour, dans les vies quotidiennes, semblable
à la translucidité, silence haché par des mots et des phrases.

JEAN GENET, *Captif amoreux* (1986)

Because I'm the size of what I see
And not the size of my stature.

FERNANDO PESSOA, *The Book of Disquiet*

*The Sky Is Incomplete: Travel Chronicles in Palestine* is a compilation of notes,
letters, and reflections I wrote during my prolonged stay and subsequent
visits to the West Bank, Palestine, between 2007 and 2015. While editing and
rewriting these notes, one of the things I had in mind was the twentieth-
century tradition of "committed literature" from Walter Benjamin and André
Gide in Moscow in the 1920s, to Susan Sontag and Juan Goytisolo in Sarajevo
in the 1990s, all of whom were grappling with the issue of how to engage with
the political processes of others, elsewhere. In order to address the issue of
representation, of speaking on behalf of the Palestinian ordeal in all its complexity, I decided to compose the book as a collage. I gathered many *textures*
of writing: a diary, letters, experimental writing, a play, poetry, art criticism,
political analysis, and short stories. I play with these genres so as to convey
a "paralactic" view of the Palestine Question. More than giving testimony or
speaking on behalf of the Palestinians, my approach is relational: *The Sky Is
Incomplete* is about encounters with friends, mentors, interlocutors, lovers,
children, activists, housewives, artists, filmmakers, and soldiers (both Israeli

and Palestinian). In that sense it is very much influenced by Jean Genet's *Captif amoreux* (1986), in which he states that he probably missed out on the Palestinian revolution because the reality of the Occupied Territories is mere drama lived by the occupier and the occupied. He claims that such a reality is the translucent and fertile imbrication of love and hate in everyday life, and I also attest to that. In addition to being influenced by Palestinian writers and thinkers like Edward Said, Hussein Barghouti, and Mahmoud Darwish, this book has also been shaped by the work of Hannah Arendt, Simone Weil, Chris Kraus, Dodie Bellamy, Elena Garro, Rosario Castellanos, Eileen Myles, Marguerite Duras, Arundhati Roy, Leanne Betasamosake Simpson, Virginie Despentes, and Maggie Nelson.

The purpose of my first visit to Palestine was to follow the steps of radical activists and creators to Palestine to find the remaining traces of Western solidarity with their struggle as expressed within the frame of Marxist-Leninist revolutionary movements in the 1960s and 1970s. I then wanted to compare this form of international solidarity to contemporary expressions of commitment to the Palestinian ordeal and to understand the discourses and practices that underlie them. By the mid-1970s, armed struggle geared at establishing socialist regimes had failed across the world, and humanitarian work became the primary frame for relating to conflict and catastrophes elsewhere. Humanitarianism presupposes that inhabitants of war zones or areas facing disaster need external help and infrastructure to achieve political self-determination and to provide basic services for the population. That is why the premise of humanitarianism—exercised by nongovernmental organizations and subsided by governments, global organizations, and corporations—is that the victims of war and oppression demand restitution and material and psychological help: as victims, humanitarianism argues, they are unable to give it to themselves.

I sought to go beyond the humanitarian dynamic to see the image Palestinians carved out for themselves as refugees, victims, or terrorists. Being neither Jewish nor Arab, I tried to be conscious of the traps of anthropology, orientalism, and colonialism and made efforts to transcend my point of view as a foreigner, as *other*, and to go beyond the traumatic shock that the hardships and pains of the situation I was experiencing had caused me. I quickly began to inhabit the bridges between Arab and Latin culture and felt at home. I also experienced extremely sophisticated, effective, and painful forms of Israeli power and repression being inflicted on my own body. During my stay, I began asking questions: What does it mean to be radical today, to go to the root of the injustice? What inspires someone to be radical? Who are the most radical in the Israeli-Palestinian conflict—the Islamists, the Zionists, the Israeli settlers, or the secular activists?

Besides seeking out remaining traces of anti-imperialist solidarity, I was also interested in questioning the discursive place that had been given to the Palestinian struggle by the instauration of "empire." By the 1990s, the Palestinians had achieved a place to voice their struggle. In the second half of the twentieth century, postcolonial theory had emerged in countries such as India and South Africa that had achieved independence from their former European rulers; their struggle opened up space for the voices of the wretched of the earth. This opening up, mainly in the English-speaking world, gave way to a cacophony of multicultural voices and images rewriting their stories, bearing witness to and denouncing their ordeals. In this way, the "others" of the West freed themselves from the narratives imposed by the colonizers and began to voice their own struggles from the discursive position of subalterns. During the glorious years of this liberal utopia of global multiculturalism, *everyone* was given a place to speak from their own point of view, whether ethnic, religious, historical, national, or gendered.

The radical potential of this discursive space ended in 2001. In March 2001, seven years after having declared war against the Mexican state, the Zapatista guerrilla movement marched toward Mexico City in a campaign of lobbying and dialogue to amend the country's constitution and achieve formal autonomy for the nation's indigenous population.[28] Instead of fleeing or hiding, as they had when Emiliano Zapata's troops arrived in the capital in 1915, the Mexican political class received the insurgents with open arms, inviting them to the Chamber of Deputies to articulate their proposal. Then president Vicente Fox had guaranteed the Zapatistas a safe passage to the capital and declared his support for their reforms.[29] Under the framework of participatory democracy, the Zapatistas and the country's right wing formed a political alliance. Sixteen years later, it is clear that the guarantees the Mexican government gave to ethnic groups, based on cultural specificity, succumbed before the new necrocapitalist, extractivist system that has displaced and repressed originary populations not only in Mexico, but all over the world.

The Zapatista Liberation Army's entry to Mexico City was allowed at a moment of antagonistic coexistence between oppressed and hegemonic perspectives, a historical period in which power guaranteed cultural autonomy to minorities in the name of tolerance and inclusivity, a time during which the Palestinians also achieved visibility in the global political field as an oppressed and occupied people. The September 11 attacks on the World Trade Center in New York, however, brought a sudden end to such forms of multicultural tolerance and visibility. The attacks intensified xenophobia and propagated intolerance and religious fundamentalism in the three monotheisms. At the same time, finance capitalism brought about a new arrangement of privilege, dividing the world's population into the 1 percent and the 99 percent, with corresponding new forms of slavery, dispossession, forced migration, war, surveillance, and control through necropolitics and neuropower. And this is when the Palestinian struggle becomes more relevant than ever: much more than being an "ethnic conflict," it exemplifies vital struggles happening across the world in defense of territory and in opposition to neoliberal policies of extraction and destruction of the commons, as in Chhattisgarh, India; the mountains of British Columbia, Canada; the Sierra del Norte, Mexico; and innumerable places across the African continent and Latin America.

The year of the 9/11 attacks also marks the moment in which the codes of Western modernism became ubiquitous globally; this is when English and corporate culture came to be established as the lingua franca of global exchange. In this manner, a form of Western modernity was instituted (in some places as the ideal of development and progress) with local specificities, while the liberalization of global commerce homogenized the consumption of material, audiovisual, and experiential merchandise as well as homogenized political goals (specifically: parliamentary democracies) and subjectivities.

We should also bear in mind that by 2001, beyond the democratic space of the "in-between" cultures that opened up in the 1990s at the eve of globalization and after the Fall of the Berlin Wall and the communist bloc, a fragile possibility emerged of considering and sympathizing with both sides in the Israeli-Palestinian conflict, creating a gray zone, a liminal discursive place that understands the ordeals of both groups. This is one of the characteristics of "cultural" or ethnic wars: cultural and religious specificities function as frameworks and goals of struggles under apparent "neutrality." Framing struggles from the standpoint of culture, religion, or ethnicity, however, means that political referents that could pluralize struggles and social movements wane beyond cultural and local specificities. That is to say, in the attempt to safeguard a territory in the name of an ethnicity or religion, cultural particularities or local specificities begin to predominate at the cost of potential pluralization of emancipation struggles, putting to rest the anticapitalist and anti-imperialist struggles that inspired solidarity with the Palestinian people in the 1960s and 1970s. After the 1990s, more or less, the Israeli-Palestinian conflict began to be thought as a war of victims against victims, both sides claiming restitution and rights over the land based on an asymmetrical cultural and religious difference between "Jews" and "Arabs."

When digging into what remains of anti-imperialist solidarity framed by Marxist-Leninism, I looked for a place from which to think about ties of solidarity beyond multiculturalism, postcolonialism, cultural specificity, and humanitarianism. And I was not on my own! Filmmakers, artists, and researchers were engaged in similar investigations. Among the films are *Ça sera beau* (2005) by Waël Noureddine, *Nervus Rerum* (2009) by the Otolith Group, *The Anabasis of May and Fusako Shigenobu, Masao Adachi and 27 Years Without Images* (2011) by Éric Baudelaire, *When I Saw You* (2012) by Annemarie Jacir. Mohanad Yaqubi and Reem Shilleh's image research, projection, and recovery platform, *Militant Cinema and the Adjudicating Gaze (Subversive Films)*, seeks to recover the film archive of Fateh (or the Palestinian Liberation Organization), lost in Beirut in 1982 during the Israeli siege. There is also Olivier Hadouchi's research on Tricontinentalism, and *Past Disquiet: Narratives and Ghosts*, a project by Rasha Salti and Kristine Khouri, who rebuilt a 1978 art exhibition in solidarity with the Palestinian struggle that included two hundred works by artists from thirty countries. Digging into the history of political struggles is a way to rethink the current fragmentation of those struggles, which suffered another blow in 2001 with the massive repression of the Globalophobic movement in Geneva, a blow from which the movement was unable to recover and from which we can draw the lesson that struggles against globalization can only be local. Such historical analysis is tied to a certain Zeitgeist of my generation seeking to rethink the current dissociation between theory and political practice, the impasses of the left, and the fracture between history and the present. It responds to the urgent need to overcome the framework of humanitarianism and human rights as the main discourses of solidarity. Part of the interest in this specific historical moment derives from a search for the knowledge lost during the depression and melancholia suffered by leftist activists during the *Winter Years* (described by Félix Guattari in his book with the same title), just at the brink of the Arab Spring, Occupy Wall Street, and other global movements whose momentary effervescence dissolved between 2011 and 2013.

Bearing in mind the Zapatista struggle, orientalist fantasies, and the incipient frame of decolonization in Latin America, I pondered the privileges that neocolonialism and globalization let us, a cosmopolitan caste of intellectuals, artists, writers, researchers, and cultural producers from all over the world, enjoy today. There is, first, the privilege of unrestricted mobility across the world and, second, the spaces for exchange and encounter sponsored by governments, corporations, and cultural organizations where we gather to discuss urgent topics from the standpoint of the defense of rights, denouncing and making visible violations of those rights. While these encounters were the rule in the Soviet Union and common in Cuba, Palestine, Vietnam, Nicaragua, and Chile, sometimes sponsored by socialist states or revolutionary movements, the current professionalization of intellectual production and its instrumentalization as a palliative for the ravages caused by neoliberal reforms and neocolonialism have created a strange, increasingly depoliticized platform to express solidarity from within the realm of culture. It does not hint at any new and necessary means of political organization or emancipation but instead, it either measures "betterment" in the short term and provides instances of dialogue and cultural exchange, or it enables concern and indignation without medium- or long-term political commitment.

I observed a strange phenomenon: cultural producers visiting the Occupied Territories exhibited and presented their academic or artistic work there, then traveled to Israel with the same objective, without being the least concerned about the contradictions of changing territories or sides. Inhabiting that gray zone of tolerance and sympathizing with both sides is definitely detrimental to real political processes. For this reason, it became urgent to question sites of privilege, pockets or bubbles for journalists, diplomats, entrepreneurs, and cultural producers where the pistons that enable the circulation of the semiotic fluxes of globalization are activated, where political realities are discussed and alternative ways to understand those realities are created with signs and symbols that at the same time remain distant from that reality.

In spite of Empire's apparent tolerance and openness, openly expressing solidarity with Palestinians began to be persecuted about ten years ago under a new McCarthyism. Pro-Palestinian activity started to be condemned in Israel, as pro-Palestinian Israelis and refuseniks began to be isolated and rejected by society; foreigners expressing solidarity with the Palestinian cause were deported from Israel. Some members of the Israeli movement Peace Now were threatened with death in 2010, and the FBI invaded the homes of seven pro-Palestinian and pro-Colombian activists from the Minnesota Anti-War Committee. Sixty agents were mobilized to confiscate documents, cell phones, computers, and personal belongings of fourteen activists who were summoned to appear before a federal grand jury.[30] In 2011, a small exhibition of drawings by Gazan children, illustrating their vision of the 2008–2009 war, was censored at the Oakland's Children's Arts Museum.[31] In the United States and Israel, full professorship has been denied to renowned researchers devoted to denouncing Israeli policies, among them Norman Finkelstein, Ariella Azoulay, Steven Salaita, and Ilan Pappé.[32] Members of the Boycott, Divestment, and Sanctions (BDS) movement, which was initiated by Palestinians in 2005 and has gained support from academic and cultural institutions and organizations globally, are also routinely harassed and persecuted and live under the threat of losing their jobs. Entry into Israel is—apparently haphazardly—denied to exiled Palestinians, Muslims in general, and Arabs specifically, as well as members of BDS, International Solidarity Movement (ISM), and other international organizations that support Palestinians. *Mavi Marmara*, one of the five boats in the Freedom Flotilla, which sailed in 2010 from different points in the Mediterranean, was brutally attacked by the Israel Defense Forces (IDF) in international waters. There were nine casualties, and everyone on board was taken to detention centers in Israel and then deported.[33] New forms of censorship and repression have emerged, characterized by the selective opening up of borders, manufactured uncertainty, racial and economic profiling, and elevated levels of oppression and precarity that Palestinians live with daily. To this, add the hardships of Palestinians living in exile or as refugees with precarious citizenship in the country in which they reside.

The recent hardening of persecution of Palestinians and Palestinian solidarity is perhaps symptomatic of what the conflict represents: what is at stake ideologically and geopolitically is a form of differentiated government over a unified territory divided into exclusive zones where citizens enjoy differential privileges. Zones are, however, interdependent and interconnected to global processes, including the right to mobility and differentiated access to commodities, services, education, and jobs. The manner in which Ariella Azoulay described the Israeli occupation of Palestine is illuminating: she explains how Palestinians are cogoverned alongside Israelis but defined as noncitizens, with an ensemble of different laws and rights.[34] This form of government is characterized by the administration of resources in favor of the more privileged populations. Such a model is characteristic of all neoliberal governments worldwide, who administer populations and resources differentially, dispossessing and displacing some groups. Under this model, the fate of the Negev Bedouins is similar to that of originary populations in the Guerrero Mountains in Mexico, which implies that they will be relocated to homes offered by the government using the justification of "modernization." As a consequence, populations are alienated from their life forms and way of making a living, impoverishing them materially and culturally in the medium term, leading eventually to their inevitable demise.

The model of oppression, militarization, and security that Israel applies against Palestinians is also exported internationally to control undesirable or redundant populations, which are disconnected from global processes of exchange. Israeli occupation of the Palestinian territories uses the most sophisticated weapons, technologies of oppression, and forms of power, which are disseminated as surveillance and war technologies to the rest of the world. For example, when after a thirteen-year-old boy, José Luis Tehuatle, was murdered by state forces during a demonstration in Puebla State, former Puebla governor Rafael Moreno Valle (who implemented the use of rubber bullets against protestors) blamed the protestors for using the child as "human shield."[35] In the Occupied Territories, foreigners act as "human shields" or as "white face defenses" for Palestinians—that is, Israeli soldiers may be more lenient toward Palestinians during a confrontation if there are foreigners present documenting their abuses. Since the Gaza attacks in 2008–2009 known as Operation Cast Lead, human shields became legitimate targets of attack under the assumption that they are defending terrorists.[36] Describing casualties in this way, however, is common rhetoric used to justify abuses of the Israeli army against Palestinians. Tear gas is another example of Israeli war technology that has made its way from its use against protesters in the West Bank to its use against protesters on Mexico. In the December 1, 2012, demonstration against the ceremony in which Enrique Peña Nieto took over as president of Mexico, the same repression technique was used. Activist and theater director Juan Francisco Kuykendall died after being in a coma for around a year due to complications of a skull fracture caused by a tear gas grenade, a common wound in protests in the Occupied Territories.[37]

It is evident that the Israeli-Palestinian conflict cannot be reduced to the frame of colonization or to the case of a people occupying the land of another people, nor can it be dismissed because the Middle East is considered to have faced conflict for millennia. This argument has enabled many the comfort of blindness before the urgency and geopolitical relevance of the Israeli occupation of Palestine. At the eve of the twenty-first century, Israeli occupation reflects a highly developed model of social control, conflict administration, resource and land dispossession, segregation of communities and families, social tissue fragmentation, implementation of mechanisms of psychological oppression that generate paranoia and self-destruction, and application of culturally specifically torture techniques. The occupation has also generated cultural and economic impoverishment for Palestinians. Israelis oppress Palestinians by administering their space-time, slowly and daily denigrating almost imperceptibly a whole people. For their part, Palestinians have been examples of resistance for their uninterrupted struggle for political self-determination, the formal establishment of the borders determined by the 1967 war, the right of return, and Jerusalem as capital of the Palestinian state. They have turned to armed struggle, such as the revolution in the 1960s and 1970s, the Intifada or uprising in the 1980s, and the Second Intifada in the early 2000s. Hamas has engaged in armed resistance by launching *qassam* missiles at civilian targets in Israel, and other Palestinians have used nonviolent strategies, such as BDS and *sumud*. *Sumud* can be translated as perseverance, steadfastness, integrity. It means firmly and patiently holding on in the face of an extremely difficult and oppressive situation that cannot be changed immediately. For Palestinians, *sumud* is an ideology and a political strategy that consists of resisting being uprooted and constantly reaffirming their presence in their land. *Sumud* is the attitude of taking action; it is the art of living, existing, and working.

*The Sky Is Incomplete: Travel Chronicles in Palestine* is the product of editing and rewriting my reflections, notes, and letters to friends, professors, and family members as well as collecting images I took or found during my prolonged stays in Palestine in 2007, 2007–2008, 2009, 2011, and 2015. The text constitutes an experiment with degrees of distance between Palestine and me, providing a collage of forms of writing, points of view, and intensities of my experiences in the Occupied Territories. I combine factual information with personal opinion, my friends' opinions, and heard histories and stolen words that seek to transfer an accumulation of perceptions codified in a diversity of formats. I seek to visualize and articulate a paralactic field of vision of the Palestine Question. By paralactic I mean that the object of focus (Palestine) varies with the speakers' position or point of view, with the purpose of offering a kaleidoscope of gazes upon the conflict from within life in Ramallah. When I rewrote these notes, the relationship between space and language became a challenge: the point of departure for writing is the distance that opens up from memory as well as my condition of dislocated expatriate. How is it possible to *speak from* any given place?

The first time I visited Ramallah I fell in love with the sound of the name of the city when pronounced in Arabic: Ram-allah. My first Palestinian hostess, Reem, had explained to me where to take the bus in Jerusalem to get to the Occupied Territories. I had been roaming in Jerusalem for exactly a week, asking people who seemed trustworthy how to get there. I got a mix of horrified and surprised stares and no answers. I was obviously completely unaware of the full context. It was not until a friend of a friend put me in touch with Reem that I got instructions to walk up to the Holy Sepulcher, along the street that leaves from the Bab Al'mud (or Damascus Gate) in Old Jerusalem. A couple of hours later, when I met Reem in person, I asked her to repeat out loud the name of the city: Ram-allah. I felt the intense desire to learn how to pronounce the city's name with the familiarity of someone who has grown up or lives there; my friend Nathalie said that to speak the word evokes the sound of a pearl necklace sliding through fingers. "A little justice: Ramallah sounds like pearls spilling from a string."[38] The spherical form of the pearls evokes the character of the promised city of Ramallah, a bubble where one can hallucinate a life of freedom under the mirage of normality. The place is inhabited by Palestinians who come from different cities, countries, and socioeconomic strata: those who came back from the diaspora with the Oslo Accords in the 1990s, 1948 Palestinians (or Israeli-Arabs, Palestinians with Israeli citizenship), and those who teach in universities or work at government, cultural, or mass media institutions. Ramallah is a cosmopolitan city where Palestinians from Venezuela, Brazil, Colombia, Tunisia, Lebanon, Syria, Jordan, France, England, Germany, and Italy live together. Ramallah is the site of the Palestinian National Authority (PNA), of consulates and cultural centers, NGOs, journals, and mass media centers from all over the world. Its society includes a global consumer middle class, owners of mortgages and credit, debtors who dream of living in condos overseeing the Mediterranean sea to which they have no access. Ramallah is the temporary capital of a state that will not come. It is a hub for the global symbolic class of executives and entrepreneurs as well as journalists, cultural producers, intellectuals, and rock stars of the globalized Left. Ramallah is the point of encounter of those who directly take part in the professional global network of economic, political, and cultural exchange.

The global relevance of the city was highlighted in June 2011 when the Van Abbemuseum, in support of a project by Palestinian artist Khaled Hourani, lent Pablo Picasso's *Buste de femme* (1943) to the Palestine Art Academy for a month.[39] The transportation of the painting to the Occupied Territories made political and cultural struggle converge. In order to transfer the Picasso to Ramallah, hard negotiations had to take place between the museum and Israeli and Palestinian authorities. The action unveiled the bureaucratic and spatial complexity of the Israeli occupation, evidencing what is at stake in the conflict: international visibility and recognition of Palestinians in the cultural realm standing in contrast with the situation of occupation, harassment, and gradual destruction by the expansive security Israeli policies.

Ramallah is also the political, media, economic, and artistic center of Palestine, enriched by all the travelers that pass through. The city is the product of an opaque political project that extends beyond itself because it functions as the capital of a country that does not exist. Is it therefore a place of resistance or a co-opted site? In all Palestinian cities, occupation makes itself present in different ways and in specific degrees of intensity that affect the collective social and psychic tissue of its inhabitants with incursions, curfews, arrests, daily attacks and harassment. The situation of the occupation is not the same in Nablus, Hebron, and Jenin, nor is it the same in the Gaza Strip and Bethlehem, Nazareth, or Haifa. How is it possible to negotiate the different points of view that emerge from diverse experiences to offer a kaleidoscopic image of Palestinians and of the conflict?

In a notable paragraph from *Memories for Forgetfulness (August, Beirut 1982)*, the Palestinian poet Mahmoud Darwish diagnosed that the image that Palestinians had built for themselves had become a problematic anchor of vision.[40] This was because such an image situated the political reality of Palestine against its own materiality, while invoking a form of representation that, when it became an image, became its own reality—what Jean Baudrillard called the "hyperreal." Through writing, I am trying to traverse the hyperreal of *that* image of Palestine. I also seek to go beyond first impressions, to show what is beyond clichés and archetypes. My collection of photographs of fedayeen (revolutionary Palestinian soldiers from the 1960s) from *Life*, *Paris Match*, and other magazines that I found in archives in Paris, Ramallah, and the Internet comes to mind. The fedayeen show themselves as idealized under the orientalizing gaze of Western reporters, portraying a masculinity linked to the weapons they are carrying. We see them in images training physically and ideologically alongside women and children who are also part of the revolutionary movement. This is the moment when the black and white *kūfiyya* becomes an icon of the liberation movement (for the PLO). The fedayeen clearly function as symbols in Western media, as threats as well as heroic idealizations.

These images contrast with the images from a photograph shown to me one day by Rabiʿ, my friend J's father. The image is a small-format Kodak impression, a little blurry, where he and his wife appear during the PLO's legendary trip on the *Atlantis* from Beirut to Tunis in 1982. The trip was subject of a short film by Lebanese filmmaker Jocelyne Saab (*Le Bateau de l'exil*, 1982) and a slide show by Lebanese photographer Fouad Elkoury (*Atlantis*, 2012), who were also on board. Despite the devastating defeat of the Palestinian Liberation movement in Lebanon, after which they were expelled, unleashing a fifteen-year-long civil war, Rabiʿ and his wife, dressed as soldiers, appear very young as they smile for the camera. Their joyful and loving smiles are framed by the out of field, which is one of the blackest episodes in the history of Palestine. What were they thinking during the trip? They are part of an educated elite who grew up in the diaspora and joined the struggle in the PLO's Information Services Bureau, commanded by Yasser Arafat. She was a secretary, and he is still a journalist. After the Oslo Accords were signed, which conferred political self-determination for Palestinians, some Palestinians in exile came back to establish themselves in the West Bank. The Camp David Accords, which enabled their return, were systematically undermined by the Israeli government, however, giving way to the eruption of the Second Intifada.

In 2007, I came to Ramallah for the first time. This was after Yasser Arafat's death under mysterious circumstances in his *muqāṭaʿ* in 2004 and the end of the Second Intifada in 2005.[41] The day of my arrival in June 2007, I encountered a lot of commotion: before my eyes, vans and military vehicles paraded with armed people wearing uniforms from different factions. I was not sure whether that was normal or not, and as I couldn't understand what was going on, I locked myself inside a cheap hotel room downtown and watched the news on TV and the Internet. I didn't feel like my physical integrity was under threat, but I was also unsure whether this commotion was dangerous for me as a foreigner. It turned out that I arrived in Ramallah during the middle of a coup. The first general legislative election had taken place in the West Bank and Gaza in January 2006 (it was the last election that has been possible in Palestine). Palestinians voted for change: frustrated with the government of the PLO, which had transformed into the Palestinian National Authority (PNA) after the Camp David Accords, the majority of Palestinians voted for Hamas, the Islamic Resistance movement founded in Gaza in 1987, shortly before the First Intifada. Ismail Haniyeh, president of the new government, took power once the interim president of the PNA, Mahmoud Abbas, quit. The day I arrived in Ramallah, the PNA, in collaboration with Israel and the United States, and after the wave of violence unleashed by the kidnapping of Israeli soldier Gilad Shalit by Hamas in the Gaza Strip, orchestrated persecution of Hamas in the West Bank.[42] Since then, Palestine has remained divided in two governments: the PNA in the West Bank and Hamas in Gaza, where it established an Islamic government. My new Palestinian friends were sad and angry about what this political rupture at the heart of their people meant. Eventually, the Palestinian National Authority would assume a more pronormalization stand toward the occupation, establishing a government with the help and following the interests of the United States and Israel, implementing neoliberal economic policies. For their part, Hamas embodies an openly hostile government at war against Israel; the siege in Gaza was imposed that same year. The cost of the exercise of democracy for Palestinians—who elected the Islamic party not because they were religious but because they were tired of the PNA—was the debilitating, catastrophic political and geographic separation of what remained of their country.

While Palestinians were undergoing these political dilemmas and the de facto governmental separation of the geographically severed Palestinian areas, I came back to Tel Aviv to attend to my Israeli friend's cousin's wedding. I don't remember why I didn't make it to the ceremony. For some reason related to enhancing the quality of my curls, at the time I had stopped brushing my hair; it fell thick on my back, and it felt as heavy at the reception as I felt invisible. I had been advised (by Israelis) to be discreet in Tel Aviv regarding my visits to Palestine and to avoid making people uncomfortable or suspicious. If I did have to discuss my travels, I had been told to justify my visits to Israel by saying that I had a Jewish grandmother. At a restaurant at Jaffa beach, the old Palestinian city in the south of Tel Aviv in the process of being gentrified, wedding guests drank caipirinhas and listened to techno music, their bodies moving under the tenuous lights of the city and the stars. The Gaza Strip, a hundred kilometers away, kept coming to my mind, as did Gilad Shalit's kidnapping. Three years later when I was in Guatemala, I would be reminded of that kidnapped soldier as I drove by a billboard on the highway from Guatemala City toward Antigua each day. What was the connection between Israel and Guatemala? Why was there a billboard demanding the liberation of the Israeli soldier? At the end of the beach wedding in Jaffa, when all the guests were intoxicated, a group of young Palestinian men appeared. Members of the population in the process of being displaced observed the guests at the party with curiosity. When people began to exchange looks, I felt a wave of tension spread and I heard the bride, speaking in English, ask the Palestinian owner of the place to ask the boys to leave the premises. I suddenly felt tired and said goodbye to my friend and walked alongside the boardwalk that connects Jaffa with the urban development in the north of the city, the Namal. After walking for about an hour, I took a cab to my friend's apartment in Dizengoff and Ben Gurion. During the ride, I observed the city on my left: older urban development coexisted with modern and new green areas, some better lit than others. The heterogeneity of the urban tissue reminded me of Mexico and Guatemala, as did the tension that always arises when two foreign yet coexisting worlds briefly come face to face, reminding each other of their mutual alienation and a muted history of colonization.

Months later I would install myself in a small apartment in Ramallah, where I realized that I was incapable of visually and aurally registering what I was experiencing. Therefore, I sought different ways of processing my perceptions. It is said that vision is characterized by being incorporeal and violent, as gaze inscribes and marks bodies. I asked myself: with whose blood will my vision be carved? *To see* became for me *the possibility of seeing,* of tirelessly rebuilding a point of view from which to process tensions, resonances, transformations, trauma, resistance, complicity and pain, frustration, submission, hatred, memory, and what Palestinians call life's "tyranny of incertitude" under the occupation. In a way, my experiences revealed to me the sensorial and corporeal aspects of vision. I began to feel what I saw and to undergo the "panic of altruism." This form of panic is an empathy loop, because there is never a separation between what I see and what I am. I saw a fragmented social tissue, sad lives, depressed and frustrated men and women, hatred embodied by an eight-year-old Israeli girl. She was the daughter of settlers occupying the old city in Hebron, one of the cities in which the occupation is most painfully and complexly lived because of the daily confrontations between Zionists and Palestinians. The anxiety of being trapped inside the loop of my own gaze translated what I was seeing into anorexia, codependency, anxiety of blindness, depression, heartbreak. And I realized that seeing is not saying, but *seeing haunted by the anxiety of blindness.* It is saying: I try to see. The sensation of incompleteness that gives consciousness to the inevitability of a partial gaze is comparable to the void left by exile and the incompleteness of the condition of the Palestinian landscape: *Fish balad. Sār fī balad?* (There is no country. Will there be a country?)

Without a doubt, this book is written with love and from heartbreak. On the one hand, I wanted to infringe women's silent vow made to heteropatriarchy: never to speak about our loves and broken hearts. In this story, Lubna is looking for her Majnuna and recovers from a heart broken by Najnun. Maybe broken hearts are not very eloquent or trendy, but I attempt to give them voice as a means to assume other forms of being and understanding. I also try to transgress the law of Western heteropatriarchy that dictates that to make a statement is to make something happen in reality. This is why I encompass emotion and affect in writing. I am seeking to name what happens between words and things, in that process of mediating between the word and what is happening. Removing the use value of language as a tool of information and communication, I write from the interstice that opens up in the abjectness of affection and emotion, parting with feminine discretion and with the idea (or fantasy that I had) that writing is not traversed by gender. In the process, I discovered that visiting a war zone is a subjective way to exteriorize internal accumulated violence rooted in gender and colonial violence, violence that is exercised by heteropatriarchal colonial society against feminine and racialized bodies. Perhaps it's similar to a breast-enhancing operation that we paradoxically choose for ourselves. Modern societies are rooted and founded in violence that implies normalizing and marginalizing what is different: gender, race, religion. Under this logic, foreigners and strangers are sometimes treated as the most precious guests, as elements of interest and curiosity; other times we become scapegoats or scapeghosts. Palestinian reality is in itself fertile in love and hate, a silent and translucent reality punctuated by words and phrases that articulate the inescapable reality of the occupation. The adventure of falling in love is a form of experiencing the real, in which the *I* can completely lose itself to then seek, rebuild, and maintain itself. Writing thus becomes the thread that marks the path in a labyrinth illuminating the way out; it registers becoming Palestinian, soaking in pain, pride, and insolence, experiencing the inescapable need to find ways to resist.

During my prolonged visit to the Occupied Territories, I decided to do away with a camera. This decision was because one of the historical effects of photography has been to expunge art and thinking from fiction and, above all, to censor the imagination. And, in general, the portrayal of Palestine for outsiders, Mahmoud Darwish posits, tends to be narrowed to show exceptional or urgent situations as clichés in the double sense of the word in French: as snapshots and stereotypes. The site from my balcony was the only image I captured with my laptop's camera during my visits to the Occupied Territories. Every morning I gazed up the hill across the valley toward the P'sagot settlement, only eight hundred meters away. I could not resist capturing that landscape, which reveals the territorial proximity of Israeli settlers and Palestinians. A walled-in settlement that looks like a U.S. suburb, surrounded by the most expensive and sophisticated barbed wire in the world. From the privileged position at the top of the hill, from the strategic and menacing military control towers, one can see the fragile and messy texture of the Palestinian urban landscape. "My neighbors," Rana, my resigned landlady, would call them as she observed with curiosity as I gazed up toward the towers, an action that in some areas could lead to a jail term: many times I watched as the IDF arrested Palestinian youth on the pretext that they had broken the rule prohibiting them from looking up at the settlements and military towers. I also remember AH's expression, a mix of masculine temerity and real fear, when he told me that during the Second Intifada bullets were raining down on his home from the towers from P'sagot. During the nightly shootings that felt endless, AH would hug his French girlfriend, who, once her thirst for heroism had been satiated by someone else's war, left him without looking back, breaking his heart forever.

*Ramallah-Tel Aviv (2007–2008, 2009, 2011),*
*Guatemala (2010), Istanbul-Salamanca (2011),*
*Ramallah (2015), Mexico City (2017–2022)*

THE SKY IS INCOMPLETE

THE PROJECT OF ISRAEL AS NATION, as an exclusively Jewish state and thus the first theocracy in the Middle East (Israelis would forcefully rebuke this and discuss the complex legislative system that makes their state a democracy, not a theocracy) is, together with what remains of Fidel Castro's Cuba, one of the two left-standing utopias of the twentieth century. In turn, Palestine is an imagined community with a diaspora of more than three million refugee Palestinians in other Arab countries, Europe, and North and South America, as well as 4.2 million Palestinians in the West Bank and the Gaza Strip, and 1.6 million Palestinians living in Israel. Palestinians living in the latter two territories live as noncitizens under an insidious apartheid regime governed by the Israeli state.[43] The year 1948 marks both the independence of Israel from British Mandate and the Nakba, or Palestinian catastrophe, when 750,000 Palestinians (out of the 1.9 million living in historic Palestine) became refuges as they were expelled from their homes and land, dispossessed of their livelihoods, and separated from their communities and families.[44] Some fled to other Arab countries that still have not incorporated them as citizens (in Lebanon, for example, seventy professions remain prohibited to Palestinians[45]); some others settled in refugee camps in the West Bank and Gaza.

In the 1960s, exiled Palestinians organized a Marxist-Leninist revolution to liberate their country: they established military training camps in Jordan, Syria, and Lebanon. Among the many factions were the Palestinian Liberation Organization (PLO, *Fateḥ* in Arabic), whose leader was Yasser Arafat, and the Popular Front for the Liberation of Palestine, under George Habash. When they lost the war against Israel in 1970, the PLO was taken in first by Lebanon, then by Tunisia. The tensions caused by the presence of the Palestinian guerrillas in Lebanon's complex multireligious context were the root of that country's civil war from the end of the 1970s until the 1990s.[46] After the Six-Day War in 1967, Israel occupied the Palestinian areas that were not annexed to Israel: the West Bank and Gaza (which had remained under Jordanian and Egyptian leadership, respectively).[47] Since then, the Israeli state began to build a network of strategically situated settlements at the tops of hills throughout the West Bank and Gaza.[48] As part of the Roadmap for Peace negotiations after the Second Intifada, Prime Minister Ariel Sharon evacuated the Gaza settlements in 2005.[49] In the West Bank, however, they kept growing, and new ones were founded by Zionist settlers supported by the State of Israel. Today, more than a half million Israeli settlers live in suburban conglomerations in East Jerusalem and throughout the West Bank that are deemed illegal by international law.[50]

The First Intifada, or Palestinian uprising against Israel, took place in 1987; it led to the Oslo Accords in 1993. Following the peace agreement the PLO became the Palestinian National Authority (PNA), a political party to govern Palestinians. In principle, the agreement stipulated that Israel would disengage from Gaza and the West Bank and that the borders that existed prior to the 1967 war would be reestablished, conferring sovereignty and self-determination to Palestinians. The PNA was created as a temporary governmental authority with a maximum term of five years, providing time to negotiate the remaining issues, which included the status of Jerusalem as binational capital, the right of return for Palestinians in exile, the establishment of borders, and how to deal with the Israeli settlements.[51] A symbolic portion of the Palestinian elite came back from the diaspora in the 1990s to build the future Palestinian state. The negotiation of the pending issues never took place, and Ariel Sharon's visit to the Al-Aqsa Mosque (one of the most important religious sites for Islam) was perceived by Palestinians as yet another arrogant affirmation of Israeli sovereignty. After this event, the Second Intifada erupted in 2000. Violence intensified in 2000 and in 2004; the Israeli army invaded Palestinian cities and destroyed homes, infrastructure, and civilian spaces. There were also deportations, murders, imprisonments, and battles across the West Bank and Gaza involving the Palestinian factions of Hamas, the Al-Aqsa Martyrs' Brigade, and Islamic Jihad. Palestinians responded to Israeli violence by launching *qassam* missiles, engaging in suicide missions, and throwing stones.

After the death of Yasser Arafat, who allegedly died poisoned in his *muqāṭaʿ* in November 2004, Mahmoud Abbas was named interim president, and the Palestinian National Authority called for an armistice. The Roadmap for Peace was established, providing a mechanism for resolving the outstanding elements of the Oslo Accords and toward a permanent two state solution.[52] The living conditions of Palestinians, however, worsened after the Second Intifada: the Israel Defense Forces (IDF) made regular incursions into the Palestinian Territories, imposed curfews in Nablus and Hebron, destroyed homes, expelled Palestinian citizens, and permitted harassment against them by settlers, who had been recently armed by the government with grenades, tear gas, and guns with rubber bullets. Israel began to build separate roads for settlers and Palestinians in the West Bank; in 2005, Israel erected a racist separation wall that completely isolated the Gaza Strip and surrounds most of the West Bank's cities, further fragmenting the territory.[53]

The Israeli army's sophistication—which is the basis of the asymmetry that characterizes this war—is difficult to describe. The form of war Israel wages against Palestinians has been named "urbicide."[54] Critical theorist Eyal Weizman described the conceptual and technical complexity of the operation conducted by Israeli army units during the 2002 attack against the city of Nablus at the peak of the Second Intifada. Palestinian refugee camps are usually made up of buildings of four or more stories and narrow alleys. As a result, the *mukhayyamāt*, or refugee camps, which were originally tent settlements, are now dense cement neighborhoods with little visibility from above or from within, thus posing a challenge as urban war sites. Brigadier General Aviv Kochavi referred to the operation against the Nablus *mukhayyam* as "inverse geometry," which he considers to be "the reorganization of urban synthaxis through a series of microtactical actions."[55] This means that during an attack, soldiers cross the city through "superficial tunnels" that are excavated through the dense and contiguous urban tissue. In other words, the military does not use streets, roads, alleys, patios, external doors, stairs, or windows—the proper syntax of a city—but instead move by through walls and blowing holes in roofs and floors. In this manner, the army transformed private spaces into public ones, transferring war to the domestic interior. Battles took place in semi demolished living rooms, bedrooms, halls, and kitchens, some with food still cooking on the stove.[56] The unexpected penetration of war to the private domain was deeply traumatic and humiliating for Palestinian citizens, evidencing the Israeli tactic of maximizing the psychological impact on the enemy.

Weizman also explains how during the Cast Lead Operation (December 2008–January 2009), one of the most violent Israeli attacks against Palestinians, Israel used experts in international humanitarian rights, the area of law that regulates military conduct during war, to argue that there were no human rights violations or war crimes.[57] In that sense, the current Israeli military operations, along with the mechanisms that rule the occupation, are legal actions. Israel uses humanitarian law to justify its atrocities against Palestinians and to increase the level of destruction. During Cast Lead, the army used a technique known as "knock on the roof," which consists of launching

false bombs designed to hit rooftops with enough strength to scare inhabitants, leading them to escape before a second destructive bomb is launched.
Another technique, "knock on the door," consists of calling homes and cell
phones to "warn" people that in a few minutes their homes will be destroyed.[58]
Due to lack of money to pay cell phone bills and lack of electricity to charge
phones, thousands of those calls are made to suspended phone lines. From
the point of view of international humanitarian law, once citizens are alerted
that their homes will be attacked, they become "voluntary human shields" if
they fail to evacuate. From a legal perspective, "human shields" take direct
part in hostilities and thus become legitimate targets. This is how Israel has
justified the death of noncombatants.[59]

Since the 1967 occupation of the Palestinian Territories, the Israeli government developed a particular spatio-legal approach to govern their coun-
terparts under as noncitizens. The objective is to expand Israeli territorial
jurisdiction by dispossessing inhabitants of the occupied zone of their citizenship. This means that the PNA is, in truth, in charge of municipal matters
like dealing with trash but Israelis exercise sovereignty in the Palestinian
territory through a nebulous yet hyper structured legal regime under a gen-
eralized military system. The rupture of the ties between people and lands is
materialized and administered through laws that isolate Palestinian villages
from each other, placing them in isolated enclaves (or Bantustans) that sever
familial, social, and economic relationships. Palestinian land is confiscated
for use as Israeli military zones, nature reserves, and illegal settlements. The
Oslo Accords consolidated extant spatial structures, reaffirming the Israeli
legal logic of temporally and spatially fragmenting what remained of Palestinian sovereignty. Three zones—A, B, and C—were established, according
to a scale based on the relationship of two categories: the more territory, the
more sovereignty.[60]

The illegal construction of settlements and the destruction of Palestinian
homes and properties have the same origin: the unbridled Israeli exercise
of power with total impunity. Most destruction occurs in area C of the West
Bank. The territory comprises more or less 60 percent of the region, and Israel maintains total control of security, planning, and zoning by managing
construction permits, demotion of residential structures, and dispossession
of residency papers if the person has a second nationality; to this is added
constant displacement of people by other causes and methods.[61]

In 2005, Israel began the construction of what they call a "security fence"
around the West Bank. Palestinians call it the "apartheid wall" or *jidār
al-ʿunṣury*, "racist wall." When it was built, Israel annexed a sizable portion

of Palestinian lands, often separating people from their own olive trees and arable land, and severing East Jerusalem from its Palestinian suburbs.⁶²

I met N and B, the daughters of the imam of Al-Aqsa Mosque, in Ramallah. When the wall was erected in 2006, their family home remained on the side controlled by the Palestinian National Authority but their workplaces were on the side controlled by Israel. (It's difficult to go from one side to the other, the checkpoint they have to cross is more like a border, and it can take more than two hours to cross.) The Israeli government gave their family the choice of where to stay. Because of their work, the imam and his wife (a reputed Qur'an scholar) had no option but to stay on the Israeli side. The daughters chose to stay in the home where they grew up; doing so required giving up their Israeli citizenship. This is part of the complex and discriminatory system of citizenship Israel has established for Palestinians: Palestinians who live in Israel, called "Arabs" in Israel, have Israeli passports and citizenship; they represent 20 percent of Israel's population. They are forbidden to travel to the West Bank and Gaza and are subject to a fine of $2,500 dollars (US) if they go. Citizens of Jerusalem, who have a blue identity card (*Jawia*) may freely go into the West Bank. Those in the West Bank with a green *Jawia*, who gave up Israeli citizenship and are "governed" by the PNA, can circulate using specific roads assigned to them (different from those roads used by the settlers) and crossing checkpoints within the territory; going to Jerusalem or any other Israeli city requires a permit from the Israeli authorities.⁶³ My friend S, who belongs to a prominent family in Ramallah, asks every two years for a permit to go shopping in Tel Aviv for a few hours. GH, my friend W's brother, member of an artists' family from Hebron, asked for a permit to spend a day in Tel Aviv where, in a tragic accident, he drowned in the ocean together with his nephew. Palestinian children are able to visit Jerusalem, the Dead Sea, or the Mediterranean without an Israeli permit if they are accompanied by a foreign adult. To travel to the rest of the world, Palestinians from the West Bank must fly from the airport in Amman, Jordan. But first they need to cross a checkpoint called Allenby Bridge, characterized by the implementation of a number of security techniques invented by Israel, as well as a millimeter wave scanner. This device is controversial because, in the interest of avoiding manual pat-downs, it compromises the privacy of the registered subject by exposing bodily details. This scanner also began to be used in all US airports and in some European airports a few years ago.

For their part, Gaza Strip citizens have no chance of leaving the Strip unless they have a permit from Israel and then only by crossing the border with Egypt.⁶⁴ Before the Second Intifada, Palestinians had relative freedom of movement, and many even had day jobs in Israel; after 2002, however, the Israeli government began to impede transit through the country and imported workers from the Philippines, Thailand, and Ethiopia to take the jobs for which Palestinians used to be employed.[65]

It is evident that the occupation affects the daily life and choices of Palestinians. Israel systematically expels them; for instance, for a student from Gaza to study abroad, Israel must grant them a permit, but upon accepting the permit, the Gazan must sign a paper giving up the right to come back to Gaza. Homes and crops are also routinely destroyed, private lands expropriated, and access to fields and workplaces systematically denied. For example, a small olive grove between Bethlehem and Ramallah comes to mind. It was destroyed, and only ten centimeters of each trunk remain. It's a desolating reminder of Israeli presence and power over the territory, the slow destruction of Palestine and its people.

The situation in Palestine has been variously described as genocide, ethnocide, and apartheid. In the West Bank and East Jerusalem, Israel discriminates against Palestinians in favor of half a million Israeli settlers. Movement restrictions for Palestinians, manifest in numerous checkpoints, are similar to the "pass laws" of South African apartheid that prohibited Black people from moving freely in their territory. The destruction of Palestinian homes and confiscation of Palestinian farms under the pretext of building the security wall are similar to the devastation of Black-owned homes under the South African Group Areas Act. In fact, having developed separate and unequal roads and highways across the West Bank, some for settlers and some for Palestinians, Israel has gone further than South African apartheid ever did. By confining Palestinians to designated spaces, PNA-controlled zones are like bantustans—areas set aside for Black people in South Africa and Central Africa.

The Israeli administration of the conflict is a paradigmatic and extreme case of neoliberalism. A massive process of accumulation is currently taking place through land expropriation, which has generated a worrisome mass of redundant people alienated from the productive economy, subject to a militarized state of exception and complex systems of control. In the case of Palestine, the land is "Israelized" as Palestinian culture, identity, and forms of life are silently and systematically obliterated. Dispossession is justified with an ideology of development and legitimated through a religious ideology coupled with security concerns. The denigration of Palestinians, as they are impoverished culturally and economically, is similar to systematic impoverishment in other parts of the planet in which wealthy bubbles coexist with enclaves of poverty inhabited by redundant populations (favelas in Brazil and elsewhere in Latin America, Skid Row in Los Angeles, Regent Park in Toronto, the Parisian banlieue, etc.).

Palestine is furthermore a laboratory for experimentation with war and security technologies. Taser guns, rubber bullets, and tear gas canisters previously tested on Palestinians have been used from Oklahoma to Cairo and Puebla to New York. Israel sells security and military training technology to the rest of the world. For instance, Kaibiles, a special military force in Guatemala, and the Brazilian military police were both trained and armed by Israeli security companies, and American soldiers drew on Israeli approaches to Arab culture to deal with Arabs in Iraq and Guantanamo, giving way to culturally specific interrogation and torture techniques.[66]

In sum, it could be said that Palestinians are governed as noncitizens by Israel through the occupation and apartheid using urbicide, annihilation through lawfare (the law as war instrument), and siege, in addition to martial law and collective psychological torture.[67] One of the reasons why there is no apparent solution for the conflict is that, underneath a varnish of "ethnic" or "religious" war, there is a war to gain control of resources. The water consumed in the Occupied Territories is managed by the Israeli company Mekorot: each Palestinian has access to a fifth of what an Israeli citizen is granted daily. Israel uses water as a tool of domination through blockages, cuts, and increasing prices. Water access was cut the first day of Ramadan in 2016 for twenty-four hours without warning.[68] In addition, Israel has developed technology to treat wastewater to which Palestinians have no access. In theory, Palestinians could build their own wells and develop infrastructure to access water, but Israel systematically denies them the permits. Israelis also control the infrastructure for gas and electricity, which they sell to Palestinians at exorbitant prices. Israeli hegemony is so extreme that if a woman in Gaza is given the option to get treatment in Hebron (a Palestinian city in the West Bank), the army controls the patient's time of departure and return to make sure she will not extend her time in the West Bank.

After decades of Israeli occupation and fifteen years of total siege in Gaza, which has been de facto transformed into the biggest open-air prison on earth, the situation is worsening. Beyond class struggle and repression, the hegemony of capitalist absolutism has executed structural changes in social relationships of which the Israeli-Palestinian conflict is an extreme case study. It is about managing inequality through the apartheid of redundant populations, developing new techniques of repression and separation based on racism, ultranationalism, sexism, xenophobia, and homophobia. In October

2015, a new wave of protests took place in Palestine linked to the increased restrictions imposed by Israeli authorities on access to the Al-Aqsa Mosque—the third most important religious site for Muslims—in occupied West Jerusalem. A series of attacks against Israeli citizens by *solitary wolves*, who attack without a network of support, followed. People began to talk about a "Knives Intifada," as many of the attackers used knives, but the attacks were by individuals rather than an organized group.[69] Israel's response is always disproportionate: when the attackers are killed, their families suffer administrative, economic, and psychological consequences as well. In July 2017, there was another wave of violence against Palestinians who were protesting daily against Israel's restrictions on access to the Al Aqsa mosque. Disturbances began when three Palestinian citizens of Israel shot two police officers in Jerusalem's Old City. In the shoot-out that ensued, Israeli forces killed the three men. In response to the attack, Israel installed metal detectors, cameras, and turnstiles at the entry of the mosque complex. Palestinians understood these security measures as an Israeli gesture to intensify control over them. In the two weeks of protests that followed, Israeli and settler forces killed five Palestinians. Under pressure, Israel took away the metal detectors, cameras, and turnstiles, but more than one hundred Palestinians who went to pray outside of the mosque as a form of civil disobedience were wounded by tear gas, grenades, and sound bombs launched by Israeli forces.[70] Clashes across the West Bank continue as I finish revising this manuscript.

Just prior to Donald Trump's ascent to power as president of the United States at the end of December 2016, Secretary of State John Kerry condemned the unbridled expansion of Jewish settlements in the Occupied West Bank; he declared that the expansion is a threat to Israeli democracy and that it represents the end of the possibility of a two-state solution for Palestinians.[71] Israel's systematic violation of international laws on the ground keep generating violence and terrorism. The expansion of settlements and the endless occupation have destroyed hopes for peace on both sides. As a response to Kerry's pronouncement, Palestinian president Mahmoud Abbas declared his willingness to go back to peace talks in return for a halt to the construction of settlements in the West Bank, which are illegal according to international law. After Kerry's statement, Donald Trump tweeted: "Stay strong Israel, January 20th is fast approaching!"[72] Three Republican senators immediately introduced a bill to move the US embassy from Tel Aviv to Jerusalem.[73] The status of Jerusalem remains a topic of negotiation; no country recognizes the city as Israel's capital because, according to UN Resolution 181 and the 1993 Oslo Accords, Jerusalem should be a shared international capital.[74] To recognize Jerusalem as the capital of Israel is a gesture that would end peace talks. Trump supported the legislation.

Although global anti-Semitism is very real and there are intermittent explosions across the world against Jews, the international community can impose sanctions against Israel. In 2006 Palestinians created the Boycott, Divestment, and Sanctions (BDS) campaign, a tool to fight for Palestine's inclusion in the United Nations, a halt to military financing of Israel, and the end to West Bank colonization and the siege of Gaza. Evidently Israel is not interested in the peace process, which is a diplomatic farce. Instead of continuing the ethnic cleansing of Palestine, the solution is to end the military occupation that is depriving Palestinians of basic liberties and to confer them a state, although by now, the reality on the ground created by the expansion of the settlements would relegate Palestinians to separate, uneven, segregated enclaves reminiscent of favelas or misery belts in Latin America, making a one-state solution the only one possible.

Mexico City, May 2017

# Brownie and *Brownie*

I HAD A SECOND ENCOUNTER with Brownie, the giraffe in Qalqilya. The zoo where she is housed is also home to three lions, four crocodiles, a sad and badly humidified hippopotamus, gazelles (apparently here there is a connection between love in Arabic and these animals—that the beloved one is called "gazeau" or "gazelle" is absolutely cryptic to me),[75] a kangaroo punching the air with left and right hooks in the corner of his pen, guinea pigs sharing their cage with turtles, many birds and snakes, a couple of camels, two panthers, a few of those monkeys with pink behinds—and more. I had an interesting exchange with one of the monkeys. He was visibly upset by my scrutinizing gaze that sought signs of recognition on his part. His eyes fleetingly and furiously encountered my gaze, which he probably perceived out of habit as objectifying, before going back to the task of getting the dirt off a piece of carrot. The zoo has a museum with a taxidermy collection that feels like a chilling cemetery of the unfortunate animals who found their death at the zoo. Now stiff, they have been dissected, stuffed, and sewn back together, then assembled in dioramas that emulate their natural habitat.

Perhaps it is not obvious that we can no longer speak about people taking political sympathy tours the old way, like the French in Moscow (1930s), the Italians in China (1960s and 1970s), or Germans in Cuba (1960s), all united under the sisterhood of humanity as Allan Sekula foresees it, of Marxist-Leninism fighting against imperialism.[76] In our contemporary globalized world, I think, we could posit these tours as prompted by global-scale cultural sympathy and humanitarian solidarity. For the past thirty years, ethics and solidarity have substituted for an anti-imperialist politics of struggle. The Austrian artist Peter Friedl, doing the now mandatory solidarity-cultural tour of the West Bank, was seduced by Brownie. He asked to borrow her to show as a readymade, "Zoo Story," in Dokumenta 12 in 2007 in Kassel.[77] Brownie was the larger of the two giraffes in the zoo's taxidermy collection. I wondered how the smaller one died. As the legend goes, Brownie was killed by a heart attack she suffered due to stress caused by the explosion of a nearby bomb during the IDF's Operation Defensive Shield in 2002. Circumnavigating complex bureaucratic paperwork, which is not foreign to the Kafkaesque hoops that Palestinians (those who can) jump through in order to travel outside the West Bank or Gaza, Friedl triangulated the German, Palestinian, and Israeli authorities. Paying thousands of dollars, he was able to borrow the giraffe with all the honors pertaining to her new branding as work of art. She arrived in Kassel to be shown in the newest pavilion of the cultural fairground. When I met Brownie for the first time in Kassel, I angrily lamented the futility of aestheticizing good intentions. When I mentioned I was just on my way home after my first trip to the Occupied Territories, Eric Alliez, a Deleuzean whom I ran into there, told me: "Là-bas, c'est pour de vrai."[78] What is the "true," the "authentic," the "real"? Experience itself or an image-object as the testimony of the experience? Is the real subjective or is it founded on an encounter with the other as something outside of myself?

Friedl declared that it was important for him to bring and to show the real, not an image of Palestine. The giraffe thus is neither a witness of Israeli annihilation nor does the giraffe carry information on herself about the Occupation—any photograph and caption could do that job. *Brownie* is a *piece of the real*: the reified proof, the incarnation of her own reality, of her fatal and tragic destiny. But what is *Brownie*'s "realness" or "reality" pointing toward? Perhaps it signals occupation and its ravages conjugated in the particular and in her pathetic, badly sewn snippets of skin. Maybe *Brownie* is the witness as a relic of her own tragic death. Or we could speculate that she is the index of the "Third World–like" qualities of the Qalqilya zoo, incarnated in her quirky frame and crooked mouth. In materialist terms, one could argue that she is the "real" of the reflection of a mirror showing a society devastated by occupation.

Friedl's intervention recalls Dario Fo's 1972 theatre piece, *Fedayn: La rivoluzione palestinese attraverso la sua cultura e i suoi canti*.[79] In Milan, Fo staged an extraordinary procession of nine PFLP fedayeen from Lebanon—they had been disbanded after Black September in Jordan, and they were in a critical stage of their struggle. The fedayeen told their story through traditional peasant and revolutionary songs in Arabic, translated at times by an actor and at other times accompanied by subtitles. In the play, the fedayeen presented not only their stories about the revolution but also their points of view on labor, world politics, and migration. For Fo, it was important to present and to listen to their story in the first person, while posing the moral question of whether doing so potentially made a "spectacle" out of the Palestinian revolution. Singularity was achieved through the presence of the actors' bodies and their speech. The materiality and historicity of the collective Palestinian struggle was rendered most concretely by way of the lament of the fedayeen, not only from their point of view of fighters but also from their perspective as peasants and workers. The piece operates within the aesthetic paradigm of political theater, grounded on *logos* and *poiesis*. The aesthetico-ethical task here is to bring to corporeal proximity the vanquished, embodying their lament. In this sense, what is at stake is not the self-presentation or the *real* presence of the fedayeen in a theater in Turin. Debatably, the play's inscription in the paradigm of theatrical representation does not overcome mimetical or identificatory enterprises; rather, the play purports an understanding of theatrical representation as a practice that calculates the place of things as they are observed. This is a geometrical task that reveals that what is far away (Palestinian struggle) is brought closer, catalyzed by storytelling, recitation, and singing and mediated by the stage, the translation, the subtitles, and the Italian actor.[80]

Back to Kassel. I wondered how the mandatory wall text explaining the giraffe's story affected the audience's habitual experience of the white box of the museum space. What kind of emotions did the viewer register when learning about Brownie's tragic death: sorrow, curiosity, rage, sympathy, or even pity? I also pondered the reception of the battered stitches on her skin and crooked teeth: perhaps they come across as signs of a situation that is hindered from progressing and developing—in the postcolonial cartographic mapping of the world the teleological model of progress has been replaced by "development," as the "unquestionable good" of the burden to civilize and develop those who are unable to define themselves politically and grow economically. Maybe *Brownie* served the function of propaganda and inspired some viewers to travel to Palestine to sign up for an NGO or a solidarity movement. Or it could be that *Brownie* made the European viewer feel disgusted with herself, reminding her of her own privileges and making her appreciate them through a neurotic sense of guilt or awakening a masochistic drive—because for sure German giraffes do not die of bomb-induced heart attacks, and in any case the taxidermy process in Germany is certainly more "developed." Perhaps she reminded a lucid spectator of the destruction of the Berliner Tiergarten during World War II, when many of its animals perished and its trees were cut down to be used as firewood. Repairs to the zoo did not begin until 1949.

It could be argued that the Mexican visual artist Teresa Margolles is closer to the real than Friedl, despite *Brownie*'s—or rather, Friedl's—"plea for the real." Margolles holds a degree in forensic medicine, and her studio is at the morgue in one of Mexico City's most violent neighborhoods. The parts from the dead bodies that she turns into partial objects, and thus relics, incarnate the real of "pure violence," as she makes artworks with bodies of people who have suffered violent deaths (with the consent of the deceaseds' families).⁸¹ In Margolles's work, it is not the body that testifies to violent death, but the artist herself: *autopsy* comes from the Greek *autoptes*, which means "witness" from *auto* (self) and *optes* (seen). Strangely enough, her artwork is rather successful in Germanic countries where it conjures up the specter of the Viennese Actionists (a pioneer group from the 1960s experimenting with performance, violent and sexually overt bodily gestures, and animal sacrifices). Should we think of Friedl's *Brownie* as a sublimated Teresa Margolles/Actionist piece sanitized of provocation and of fleshy, impure implications? "White-boxed"?

What does this desire for the "presence" of the real elsewhere—from Palestine—mean? What does it hope for, what is it a collective projection of? Meaning is bound to *Brownie*'s physical existence: once a living animal, she has been transformed into a specimen. She then becomes a survivor of the wrongs that man has done to her as a species; as a readymade, she conveys affective impact. Perhaps this drive to bring home foreign disaster "tries desperately to assimilate to experience what defies all experience."⁸² No wonder I got so obsessed with *Brownie*. I realized I was haunted by the image of a giraffe being slaughtered in Chris Marker's *Sunless* (1984). We hear: "as an exploration into the banality proper to the harshness of the mercenary hunter." We see the giraffe agonize and then be given the coup de grâce, right before the vultures start eating out her eyes. Is there an ethical difference in the life that is taken from necessity (as prey) or by (lawful or unlawful) violence? Are animals our others? Are Others our enemies? Are animals victims or prey? Are enemies prey or victims?

The fixation with conveying "the real" from the point of view of the ethics of human rights shadows Israel's policy of house demolitions and incursions, the network of three-dimensional borders such as the checkpoints, the apartheid wall, and the low-intensity war against besieged Gaza. I discussed the matter with a contemporary Palestinian artist, who vouched for *Brownie*, saying: "It's us. It is us dead, taxidermized with the stitches made visible." I wondered: "Do you mean that with the stitches the process is made visible so as not to cheat the viewer: it is a self-reflexive sculpture, and the bad taxidermy unveils the process of its own making?" He went on: "Brownie is us re-dead (dead again and again) of heart attacks prompted by the bombs. See? We don't even have the luxury of a proper, dignified death."

At this point I began to feel real pity for Brownie; this ethical, aesthetic, and political gesture, converted into a token of the relationships between the West and the East, the North and the South, the developed and the underdeveloped (the chosen coordinates do not matter), incarnating the victim as it is, appearing just as easily on CNN as in Kassel. I was so absorbed by the discussion with my friend that I did not have a chance to ask Brownie what her return to Qalqilya was like, how she was affected by the change in status from "European work of art" to "Palestinian taxidermied giraffe." I wanted to ask what she felt by having been dislocated from inciting pedagogic curiosity along with her peers at the diorama (the visitors to the zoo are mainly schoolchildren) to the position of inviting aesthetic judgment and then traveling back to the zoo. I also wanted to ask if she had come from Germany back to Qalqilya looking at things with Westernized, self-critical eyes.[83]

As a phenomenon, *Brownie* highlights a moment in which cultural producers and activists are caught between the unreliability of individual experience and the insufficiency of a scientific or cognitive model to account for such an experience, yet having the imperative to make a cognitive map of the world, making global processes accessible to the senses and to our own experience.[84] How can we understand the current global exchanges of gazes embedded in this discursive degree zero of mediation (a neutral aesthetic situated in response to and outside of cultural coding) due to the contemporary obsession with the real? *Brownie* is an allegory insofar as she is made to mean something of a supplementary and symbolic nature with moral import. As such, *Brownie* is an instance of the impulse to withdraw from the self-sufficiency of meaning and representation. Is this withdrawal marked by the insufficiency of the representation of catastrophe and victimhood? Or does Friedl's claim for Brownie's "realness" turn her into a relic with an apotropaic function, using the real (elsewhere) as a shield against the real (here)?

A comparison between Friedl and Fo highlights the demise of mediation expressed since the 1970s and the ethical interventionist mandate to bring forth victims' lament as a gesture of political solidarity. Both Friedl and Fo share a concern with the "real" or, rather, with the effort to bring real agents into presence by means of a decontextualization reframing them as aesthetic intervention. Mediated through the theatrical apparatus, Fo's intervention makes text, voice, and body prevail: the lament is embodied, brought forth in the flesh. In contrast, Friedl's indexical transfer is without mediation of the giraffe's direct self-presentation as a readymade. Moreover, lack of indistinction between visualization and embodiment embedded in *Brownie's* status as a proof reiterates the degree zero of discursivity embedded in ethical intervention. In Fo's intervention, presence is inextricable from voice, and political action (*praxis*) is manifested as *poiesis*. In Friedl's work, bringing to presence a piece of the real, *poiesis* is subsumed to *praxis* as an ethico-political imperative to attest to occupation in the West Bank. Both works highlight the differences of engagement elsewhere in two historical moments: Third-Worldism in the 1970s, at a time in which intellectuals and cultural producers from the West had a political relationship to the Third World (a kind of protoglobal cartography with Marxist-Leninism as the common code) and a geopolitical moment in which the ethics of human rights has become the grounds for intervention elsewhere. In aesthetic terms, interventionism is a practice that either functions as the aesthetic supplement of journalism, speaking truth to power, or seeks to implement more or less temporary site-specific "liberogenic" devices in public spaces or as social work *elsewhere*.[85] These tendencies have prevailed since the 1990s and at times are inextricable from the frame of ethnography and cultural analysis. Is it possible to disentangle the realms of culture, art, information, and neoliberalism to extricate aesthetic practice from the "nondiscourse" of rights and to repoliticize it?

# A Bohemia in Ariha (Jericho)

THIERRY AND I ENTERED PALESTINE in a car we had rented in Israel; I cannot deny that we were a bit afraid. We wanted to see what was there, what it was like, how the occupation actually felt. Miki Kratsman, the Israeli photographer who has been making portraits of Palestinians and documenting the conflict in its many manifestations for years, had given us the cell phone of his fixer in Jericho so he would help us find a place to stay for the night, to show us the way to the ruins of Hisham's Palace and to the cableway that goes up to the Orthodox Christian Monastery of the Temptation on the mount of the same name. Miki surely thought we would be interested in seeing the few cultural vestiges that the PNA has managed to maintain as tourist sites. Jericho is special because it is located at the same height as the Dead Sea: some four hundred meters under sea level. That makes it one of the most fertile places that border the Jordan River, surrounded by natural water sources. As it was our first time in the Occupied Territories, our sight had not been yet educated to read the landscape—that is to say, to distinguish the Palestinian from the Israeli areas and to see the evidence of which complex administrative regime operates in each portion of the territory. We were terrified by the first Israeli checkpoint we crossed; a Palestinian one followed. We wondered why there were simple greenhouses in ruins with torn plastic covers flapping in the wind. They were right next to what seemed to be state-of-the-art greenhouses. Is it that the Palestinians owned the first, and they were in tatters because of neglect? We would learn that the modest greenhouses were forcefully abandoned due to restrictions imposed on

Palestinians by the Israeli army that prevented them from accessing their lands. Forced abandonment is a way to manufacture misery through the administration of differential access to the means to make and sustain lives.

A flamboyant fountain sitting on a roundabout welcomed us to Jericho. The love story with Thierry was coming to an end. We scrutinized our relationship, contemplating the sunset, drinking Bohemias, and smoking on the terrace of the apartment Abu Salim had rented to us for the night. Stars had begun to appear, their dim light contrasted with the interior of the house, illuminated with fluorescent tubes. That light, which attacked our eyes and attracted mosquitoes, lingered on the pistachio green plastic curtains that served as doors.

The following morning we set out to discover the city in a fruitless search for Western coffee. Then, we tried to visit the impressive Monastery of the Temptation, carved in the mountains overlooking the Jordan Valley. To our disappointment, we were told that the cableway that could lead us there was broken. Instead, we visited Hisham's Palace, a Muslim archeological site located five kilometers away, which houses traces of a palace, baths, and an irrigation system from the eighth-century Umayyad dynasty. At the baths, we discovered a beautiful mosaic, "The Tree of Life," that depicts three deer congregated under a tree's shadow, one of them being devoured by a lion. The palace is one of the many "desert castles" from that era scattered throughout the Levant. The beauty of the ruins and the landscape, the feeling of the taste of home I got from the Bohemia on my tongue, the asphyxiating heat in Jericho and the sensation of floating in the Dead Sea did not quite fit the image I had constructed in my head of Palestine and the conflict. The discovery of a horizon that opened up before us was a beautiful epilogue for a farewell of that love that resisted, keeping me from exiting the West.

# To Get to Palestine You Must Pass through Israel

SINCE I ARRIVED TEN DAYS AGO in Ramallah, I haven't had a head to think or write. I experienced disorientation, couldn't remind myself why I had come. But soon I had the certitude that that which made me plan a prolonged stay in these lands was the atavistic need to settle accounts from a past life. Our idyll was literary from the start, and destined to fail in reality.

I spent the first few days arriving, landing, feeling disoriented and confused, overwhelmed by the intensity of the September dry heat. I kept getting lost in translation moving between languages, trying to invent a daily pattern of places, activities, and habits to shake off jetlag and the forty-eight sleepless hours, including a nine-hour layover in Budapest and then my entry into a schizophrenic highway.

When the plane landed in Budapest, my neighbor—a heavy man about thirty-five years old, who seemed to have quit lifting weights, exercising, and eating healthy to throw himself to being lazy and eating junk food—approached me to ask me where I was headed. Right then, I was trying to collect the mental and physical force to grab my bags and find out the best way to get to the center of the city.

"I'm on my way to Tel Aviv," I answered.

"Me too! Are you going to see the city a bit?"

In the three seconds I remained silent, eighty thoughts crossed my mind. Before I could shake him off, I realized that the guy had a map and knew which bus to take, so I decided to let him come with me. We arrived in Budapest, and I had my alibi: I am a curator and will be spending six weeks in

Israel doing research for an Israeli art exhibition in Mexico. He was from Haifa and had just spent three months in Canada looking for a job, as the previous summer he had fought in the Lebanon war. And in the horror he had seen in the eyes of his children and wife in the security bunker waiting for the Katyūshas to stop falling, he had decided to move his family out of Israel.[86] As he was telling me his story, I knew I could trust him. But I also enjoyed the feeling of being a "spy" with an actual alibi. So I did not reveal more. Of course, the doubt emerges any time.

He tells me: "One of the most beautiful synagogues in the world is in Budapest."

Trying to hide my ignorance, I answer: "Yeah? . . . You want us to go visit?"

Before that, we had come across a hydrating station for marathon runners who had not yet passed by. Entitled and without asking anyone, Oren approached the table, took two glasses of water and two more that contained a blue liquid of the kind with excess glucose. Throwing him a mistrustful look, one of the runners that was passing by to catch his breath and hydrate yelled angrily: "Hey! You should run for the water!" Oren's attitude, which I would see many times more in Israel, reminded me of Mexican prepotency; it reflects a way of being in the world that implies that one can take everything for granted without asking, only taking, with the feeling that one is entitled to break rules and the law.

My plan for the day was to go to the thermal baths on the other side of the river, but we were very far away. On the subway, I had asked for directions from a very drunk man accompanied by two adolescents, presumably his sons. There was a misunderstanding, and we got off four stations away from our stop! The boys spoke a bit of English, but the proud authoritarianism of the father figure hindered them from speaking for themselves and giving us the correct information. Oren and I walked for a long time, for about an hour, before we sat down to drink café au fuchs (coffee cut with some foamy milk); we finally found our way to the Gellert Baths, which date back to the thirteenth century, perhaps even earlier. I was amazed to see the socialist infrastructure still present in the dressing rooms and showers. Some three hundred changing cabins visibly dated from the 1950s and 1960s and reflected the look of ascetic massification of public spaces of socialist institutions from that time. The baths for and from the people. During the nine-hour layover, Oren and I exchanged more and more life data, and I began to feel guilty for not having told him the truth. I decided to do so as soon as we crossed the passport control at Ben Gurion. I made that decision because I had been carrying around all day a lot of anguish from being denied access to Israel, and I did not want him to have any responsibility in my crossing. Those thoughts haunted me all day, and my disquiet grew when we were back in downtown Budapest and ran into an Israeli couple eating a plate of goulash. When they found out that we were not a couple and that I was not Jewish, they expressed their disappointment. I felt their mistrust; a feeling that non-Jews sometimes provoke in Israelis who ask, "What the hell is a Christian doing in the Promised Land (outside of the Christian tourist sites anyway)?" I got the same feeling when I saw my friend M's grandmother's face when I entered her Dizengoff clothing store. Her gaze pierced my backpack, and I felt like a terrorist threatening her with a bomb.

This was my second time entering Israel, and I had no trouble going in. But I was afraid—as I always am, every time I enter—for the worst: being blacklisted, deported, taken to a detention center after long interrogations, or my computer being taken away. And mine is not unfounded paranoia as my Israeli friends think, but the reality of Arabs, Muslims, activists in solidarity with Palestinians, young single non-Jewish women traveling alone to Israel. We are the suspect profiles. As I stood next to the baggage claim to wait for my luggage, I decided it was the right moment to reveal the nature of my trip to Oren. But his cell phone rang. His family was waiting for him outside of the terminal. After an uncomfortable moment, I told him to go ahead, that I did not want to interrupt his being welcomed by his family. I came out a bit later and I found a small typical Israeli family. Too typical. I did not have the chance to tell Oren the purpose of my trip. I know I have five messages in my email inbox begging me to call him. The last one, "I miss you." Ugh.

By then, I already knew my way to Ramallah: I took the train at Ben Gurion to Tel Aviv, where I changed to Jerusalem (the trip across the mountains is very beautiful; you get a hint of the luscious forest surrounding Jerusalem). From the station, I took a cab to East Jerusalem. Every time I get a glimpse of Damascus Gate, the Palestinian bus station, and the Jerusalem Hotel I have the feeling of coming home. When I got to the place I had booked to stay in Ramallah—at the Evangelical School for Boys, where some of the classrooms are rented out as dorm rooms for foreigners—I felt exhausted and a little bit depressed. Although they had good internet, I had no privacy, the rates were super expensive, and during the day the building was full of children running around; something in the school reminded me of the Catholic school of my childhood and youth run by nuns, and after a few days, on the verge of exhaustion from the trip and frustration due to lack of comfort, I called my friend S. Luckily he was home. He sent a cab to collect me, and thanks to his hospitality, I installed myself in his bachelor pad for a week to recover from jet lag and acclimatize to Ramallah. Then I began to search for a place to live. S's home was like a bubble looking toward the West, full of high-tech gadgets and toys resting on Ikea furniture. He told me that he had gotten a special permit to go to Ikea in Herzlyia, in Israel, especially to buy his furniture. "What a luxury!" I told him, noting sadness settling in his eyes. This consumer manqué dreams of commodities offered by the first world, and he can very well afford them, although they are not always accessible to him. For example, the iPhone: he was dying to buy the newest model, and he found it in Amman for double the selling price in the US. Once back in Ramallah, he had the most unpleasant surprise realizing that his new iPhone only worked in the US, though an AT&T network would be available for iPhones in the Middle East a year later. He was very angry his gadget did not work in the West Bank. The ills of globalization are indeed shared.

Eventually, I rented a room in an apartment building in Al-Bireh, close to the Razy hospital, and some seven hundred meters in a straight line across the valley from an Israeli settlement. AH would later tell me that during the 2002 incursion he would see small stars, which were actually bullets that could kill anyone, coming from the settlement. An improvised real estate agent, whose phone number I had found on the Yahoo! group "Ramallah-Ramallah," took me to the home of Doctor Sultan, my new landlord for a few weeks. The agent wanted to charge me an outrageous commission. So I would not feel forced to pay him, Rana, the doctor's wife, advised me to tell him I had decided to take another apartment. Because I spoke no Arabic and was a stranger, everything got more expensive and complicated. The extra cost is the tax to be paid when visiting a war zone, having the privilege of leaving at any moment. For my Palestinian friends, it is hard to understand that people want to voluntarily gloat in that kind of privilege.

At first, the September heat and sun made me dizzy in Ramallah. I felt the pain of the war and the incertitude around me, expressed in the sweetness of Palestinians that in one way or another began to welcome me to their occupied no-country. After a couple of weeks I decided to answer Oren's emails. He thought that I was in Tel Aviv and insisted that I visit in Haifa. Sitting in the terrace of my new apartment, contemplating the only sight that I would capture in a photograph looking toward the P'sagot settlement, I finally called him; I told him where I was and what I was really doing. He remained silent and never contacted me again, although I knew that his trip to Canada was a response to the malaise taking part in the Lebanon war the previous summer had caused him. Something in the way he carried his heavy backpack walking alongside me through the streets of Budapest told me that Oren wanted to make sure that his small four children were not forced to do military service, to see and live the war, and eventually to torture and kill Palestinians.

FIG. 1. View from my terrace at Dr. Sultan's home, taken with my laptop's camera, 2007

**DEAR UNCLE JORGE EUGENIO,**

I received your last email exactly a month ago. For the first two weeks in December I was busy preparing two presentations, one for Qattan, the foundation in Ramallah, which is the home of the library where I go to write every day, and the other for Bezalel, the Tel Aviv branch of the prestigious Academy of Arts and Design. I decided to do a different thing for each presentation. I hesitated a lot to accept the Tel Aviv invitation, first considering the BDS campaign, which implies refusing to collaborate with Israeli cultural or academic institutions to avoid the normalization of the occupation, and then bearing in mind the experiences I have had talking with Israelis about my decision to live in the West Bank. Many of them seem to be ignorant of the fact that there are cities with life, entertainment, cultural activities, an active intellectual community, a society divided into classes including a privileged minority. I have noted that they feel deeply threatened by the fact that someone "like them"— who does not position herself as anarchist or activist, with a privileged education, global mobility, etc.—has decided to live in Ramallah. When they discuss Palestine with me, they get very uncomfortable; I would swear even their body language changes. Maybe it is because they unconsciously remember their military service in the territories, the prejudices they have against Palestinians (which they contemptuously call "Arabs"). In the end, my Palestinian friends encouraged me to do the talk in Bezalel. They told me it was important, so I didn't do it in their name, but for them. Fears that founded my reticence to take part, however, materialized. I remember I sent you a version of my script *random swerve in a downward motion of an atom*, a dialogue for two characters, SURFACE and REFLECTION, that discuss connectivity, love, activism, and creativity under late globalized capitalism. For the Bezalel presentation, I asked two good friends I have met here—Nora from England, with a Palestinian dad and Irish mom, and Nora from Jerusalem—to read the text out loud. For me, it was important that they were artists (British Nora is a sculptor, Jerusalem Nora is an architect) addressing artist colleagues. The reading caused a lot

[ 23 ]

of tension; the Israeli students immediately got defensive and unfortunately toned down the discussion to a very trivial level. Too quickly, they brought up the discourse of the Israeli Left, made up of a mix of guilt and paranoid terror. During the debate, the second question I was asked is whether I am Jewish. Apparently everyone believes all Palestinians are potential terrorists: total ignorance predominated. For instance, I was asked if there are banks, cabs, coffee shops, museums, or foreigners in the West Bank. One of the most salient comments was: "If they are the victims and we are the oppressors, then I am not interested in the problem!" An argument another Bezalel student gave was that Palestinians are dangerous for throwing stones and blowing themselves up in Israel, and that is why it is necessary to counterattack "eye for an eye." The student argued that Palestinians are to blame for the existence of the wall and the checkpoints. There was a lot of tension in the room, and we felt lynched by the audience. I spoke about my comings and goings between Israel and Palestine and admitted that it's impossible to be impartial, and that when I come and go I feel like I become a *Scapeghost* (a foreigner that becomes a sacrificial scapegoat carrying all the evils of the tribe), like the Egyptian man in Tijuana jailed for the massive femicides in the 1990s who becomes a character in Roberto Bolaño's novel *2666*.

When I told a Palestinian American friend that one of my best friends lives in Tel Aviv, he promised me that if I managed to convince an Israeli who was not an activist to visit Ramallah, he would throw him or her a party at Zan (the *Stammcafé* of intellectuals and foreigners). I extended the invitation to Bezalel's students; three Israelis said they would be interested, but they never came. After the talk, the event's sponsor, who had paid a $150 USD honorarium (which I split three ways with the Noras), invited us out to dinner. Mati, an American Israeli (I'm not sure what he does for a living), sat beside me. I was a bit intimidated by him, and yet I told him that what surprised me the most about Israel was the invisible theocratic substrata of the state, the links between religion, government, and army that become visible in places like the Wailing Wall in Jerusalem. In front of the Wall unfolds Tsahal Square (or Army Square), where initiation ceremonies for young soldiers are carried out. When I spoke a few words in Hebrew, Mati accused me of being a spy, and then he tediously and at great length mansplained how Israeli law is precisely designed not to be a theocracy in juridical terms but a democracy. He noted that Israel is not a racist state, as it includes a minority of Palestinians, Asians, and Arab, Ethiopian, Russian, and European Jews in addition to Catholic Russians who migrated in the 1990s because they had "Jewish grandmothers." And then, with an extremely condescending tone he gave me his card and told me: "Call me if you get in trouble at a border or something." I felt nauseous and went out to the street to smoke a cigarette (the law that forbids smoking in closed public spaces took effect a few weeks ago in Israel; *al-ḥamḍulillāh*, the PNA has not applied it yet to the West Bank).

My other talk in Ramallah was a discussion about Jean-Luc Godard's film *Ici et ailleurs*, which I analyze in the first half of my PhD thesis. In 1970, Godard was invited by Yasser Arafat to shoot a film about the Palestinian revolutionary movement. It was very interesting to project the movie for the audience members in my talk who were active back then, when Palestinians in the West Bank and Gaza had the hope that other Arab countries or the Palestinian guerrilla groups training in Lebanon, Syria, and Jordan (which Godard went to film) would come to save them from the Israeli occupation. My teacher Sonia had been arrested by the Israeli army for being a member of the Communist Party when she was a twenty-year-old student at Birzeit University. She was in prison for three years, and her case came to be so well-known that Noam Chomsky intervened on her behalf. Today she teaches cultural studies, philosophy, and religion at that university. I am doing an independent study with her, and when the projection of Godard's film ended, she said: "When I saw Godard's film I saw my own life marked by a series of events that begin with a gun pointing at me. The events are connected amongst themselves through Israel. While as Palestinian I don't exist for Israelis, the gun pointed at me was held by one of them."

I quoted Sonia at the Bezalel presentation, and the Israeli art students were shocked to learn that on this side, they exist only as soldiers carrying Uzis pointed at Palestinians.

# Dialogue in Bed

## Random Swerve in the Downward
## Motion of an Atom

*I wrote this dialogue thinking of Beckett's Hamm and Clov in* Waiting for Godot, *not as nihilistic subjects at the peak of European existentialism, but as hedonist globalized subjects with a foot in the Israeli-Palestinian conflict, pondering the relationship between culture, subjectivity, political action, and the new world order. At certain times, the characters stop addressing each other and only hear themselves talking because, in truth, they are not interested in having a discussion; they only want to hear themselves utter their own ideas. At some points in the dialogue there is an interplay of transparencies between Surface and Reflection: they express absolute individualism, projecting themselves onto each other, eliminating otherness. The dialogues are a parody of discussions in the academic, activist, and cultural realms across the globalized world.*

    *I lay out obsessions and questions that we were asking in Ramallah but that artists and intellectuals of my generation share across the planet. As the reading of this dialogue advanced at the Tel Aviv branch of the prestigious Bezalel Academy of Art and Design on Salameh Street, at the border between Tel Aviv and Jaffa (a neighborhood in the midst of gentrification or "betterment" achieved by expelling Palestinians), I felt paranoia and tension grow in the room. The Noras read, sitting on a pallet in the middle of a student art exhibition. Among other pieces, there was a cast of a hole made by a* qassām *rocket and a series of Jeff Wall–like photographs that reproduced scenes of the occupation. This particular background tinted the reading, as the works transmitted the point of view of the artists as soldiers, but with a typical vision of the Israeli army: soldiers do not think of themselves as people with the power to oppress, but as those who reluctantly follow orders; they are vulnerable rookies, feeling fear and guilt, acting because they must do so in the name of the future of their country and people, and also showing humane gestures toward the enemy. As they listened to the dialogue, the students were infuriated; my two Noras left in tears. I felt responsible for them, and for a long time a malaise still haunted me. On our way out, Maria, a Palestinian art student from Haifa doing her MFA there, came to greet us and discuss the text. "They do not understand and never will," she said, her dark eyes filled with anger and sadness. The cynicism and apathy palpable in Ramallah as in Tel Aviv and other cities across the globe preceded the indignation that was channeled through the Arab Spring, the Occupy movement, #YoSoy132, and other movements that followed a few years later. Curiously, these mobilizations did not originate as a means for emancipation and social justice but as expressions of indignation and discontent in the face of the financial crisis that derived from financial speculation and austerity measures. At the historical moment registered by* Random Swerve, *a frustrating and desperate search for new political models, new revolutionary subjects or figures of resistance, and new engaged positions took place, but there was also a great cynicism caused by the impotence of not knowing what to do, what to demand, soaked in the hedonism that characterized my generation.*

---

CHARACTERS:
SURFACE, the literal sign of an emotion, not a symbol.
REFLECTION, the attempt to symbolize the surface.

---

"Do you not see how horses, though eager to race, cannot move from their starting stalls when they are opened as quickly as their minds wish to? For the whole substance of the body has to be moved to follow the intention of the mind; so that you may see the beginning of motion is from the heart and that this then proceeds through the limbs of the body."

LUCRETIUS[87]

"The 'who' that you are as subject is nothing but the decision to become this subject."

ALAIN BADIOU[88]

SURFACE: I strongly believe in the revolutionary potential of favelas in Central America as the key social movement that will allow us to understand twenty-first-century subjectivity. You should be aware of the fact that the potential theoretical surplus value of the Israeli-Palestinian conflict is unfortunately hindered by the logic of nineteenth-century colonialism and twentieth-century fascism to which it is subject. It is not an instance of the production of the new. Forget it. I am not interested in succeeding. I've already tasted success—I was a star cook and owned my own vegetarian restaurant here in Washington. Ah! The bringing together of the hobbies of eating well and politics is a blissful mix—immanence and transcendence, right there. We were reviewed twice in the *New York Times*. My drive to open the restaurant was based on the wish to restore the art of eating with love, instead of with fear. We used the best ingredients, organically grown on small independent farms, the best imported European wines, earth-friendly animal protein, you name it. The finest dishes, prepared with the utmost care.

REFLECTION: Do you know Vatel? He was a valet at the service of Prince Louis Condé. Condé brought Vatel to his castle, Chantilly, where he served and organized legendary banquets with the purpose of flattering Louis XIV. Vatel fell in love with the woman that the king favored at the time, thus their encounters were secretive and contingent upon the king's nightly whims. Right before the famous Sea Banquet, for which Vatel had ordered a few hundred pounds of fresh seafood to be delivered from the North Sea, Vatel committed suicide. People thought it was because the seafood hadn't made it to Chantilly on time. It makes more sense to think that he killed himself because he realized that he was the master of neither his events nor his love. He was only a servant. He realized that he could never be the master-creator that he thought he was. What was worse, he could not have the woman he desired. During one of his famous events, the king asked to meet Vatel, but he refused on the grounds that he was too busy bring the event to perfect fruition. The servant could not bear to see himself in his mirror image as slave, having returned from the king. Is it because creators can never be masters, only slaves, that eighteenth-century romanticism invented the category of "genius" for them?

SURFACE: I got bored with having a five-star restaurant because it stopped being challenging. In my kitchen I mastered my team, once I figured out how to lead everyone to perfection, once I got the choreography down. It became a very special environment, stressful yet rewarding, we were all fucking each other. After September 11 my restaurant went down, people in the city were depressed, they stopped eating out, they were in shock. I had this urge to paint, so I decided to go to art school only to discover that painting had been invaded by theory. It was swimming in it and puking it out, you know, it, like, overcame itself, like Hegel said. So it didn't make any sense to paint. I got into theory and stuff through a friend (an ex-girlfriend, actually, now a curator at the Hirshhorn, at the time she was getting her master's at Columbia, so I was reading, like, stuff from her classes with Ben Buchloh). Forgive me sweetheart, I have stretch marks on my back, but I'm sure the sight of my torso makes up for them. I got so much into theory and philosophy that I decided to do my PhD in the only way possible—radically independently—so I enrolled in the only program that took me without a BA and with an MFA. Since then, I decided to live in between, you know, being a philosopher, like in the realm of transcendence, while striving toward pure immanence. That's why I hope to spend the rest of my life running away from my student loan growing vegetables near Cuautla, Mexico, (they play amazing music there in the main plaza on Sundays, man!). I felt the need to cultivate the immanent side because, you know, it is so hard to justify any kind of material or intellectual production. Inescapably I belong to Bartleby's army, it's got to be a syndrome. I haven't decided yet if the Bartleby syndrome is a curse bestowed upon me or some kind of temporary hideout from the guilt brought by the inability to engage conditioned by, you know, life under late capitalism.

REFLECTION: Liberty has become liberalism at the expense of equality and fraternity. Equality is a specter haunting the inexorable movement of capital becoming the American dream: *not everyone* is equally capable or endowed for success, we are not all equally gifted with the talent necessary for realizing the dream. Then, these days individualism is more important than fraternizing with the neighbors. This is likely due to the fact that the potential surplus value inherent to networks and connectedness is equated with bodily pleasure. I wonder how we can trace down the links between aleatory connectedness and the American dream. Apart from Hollywood movies starring Adam Sandler.

SURFACE: Sweetheart, you're so gorgeous to me . . . I can't believe how lucky I am to have found you. I know, I'm kind of exotic. I'm a becoming cook-artist-philosopher, a "pure philosopher" as my tutor calls me. What pisses me off is that they're trying to constantly frame me as the philosopher of immanence regarding eating, feeding, hedonism, taste, and nourishment. I'll show them. . . . Now I live in a studio with no kitchen—can you believe it? I never cook—I just eat almonds and milk and fruit—to keep myself fit, you know, slim; the older one gets, the less weight one should carry. I get my exercise walking everywhere, which saves me lots of money.

REFLECTION: Is sex an instance of the gift economy? Or is it a form of the economy of exchange? What's the best way to think about libidinal liberalism in order to extract surplus value from sex? Is sex an instance of random connectedness within a network of moving bodies? What attracts us to connectedness? Lucretius coined the neologism *clinamen* to describe atomic motion. This swerve privileges the spatio-temporal movements or relationships over static objects compelling us to move (or not). A will (voluntas) that is in the mind (animus) is purely physical, both at once. This motion is likely, but in some instances, the body will not move. The body is immanent in its *movement* toward motion and heteronomous in its being *attracted* toward motion. This motion is what we're exploring—the attraction to connectedness, having the Bartlebian syndrome "I would prefer not to . . ." as its condition.

SURFACE: If there is only movement between things, atoms, people, if there is only duration or change and *connectedness* immanent to bodies as opposed to connections, all within a network of random encounters, what is it that holds things, bodies, atoms together? What is the glue? What makes a link stronger or weaker? What makes a link last more or less time? Is it the intensity of the attraction? Is that measurable by the quantity of wetness or the quality of the hard-on? What is it that is produced by transient linkages? Is it surplus value, obscene excess, use value, or exchange value? Or nothingness? What would the logistical aspects of outsourcing connectedness look like?

REFLECTION: We need to work against consensus, to work against the desire to belong, to launch a crusade against the common, the collective, the social—because they tend to run out. That is why communism failed, you see? Celebrating the I is the only thing we've got left. You've got to ask yourself too, how do you account for antagonism in a world ruled by spectral appearances? In the narcissistic world, struggle takes place at the level of the other's desire for the object: the only instance of struggle relies in desiring the other's desire. It's a struggle that doesn't imply risking one's life, but a struggle for surplus ingestion. You are so perfect for me . . . yet, I would prefer not to. . . . You also have to watch out for exposing your raw desire—because that would utterly disgust the Other, provoking its rejection.

SURFACE: The need for informal networks undermines the moralizing aspect of condemning piracy and black markets. They are a mode of basic survival. It is sheer immanence, sheer improvisation—charged with liberatory potential. When women become active in the informal economy, eventually they get liberated from the constraints of gender difference and sexual oppression. Neoliberalism and feminine liberation are intrinsically linked, you know? It's all brought about by inflation. What are the links between this kind of liberation and fundamentalist populism? Is fundamentalist populism a seductive weapon to retrench back to a preliberal condition? We cannot underestimate the impact of global television. It has certainly created new modes of subjectivity, new modes of speech; it has given leeway to the invention of new desires, desires that cannot be fulfilled. Transcendence. Is fundamentalist populism a space for immanence reacting to those desires that cannot be fulfilled?

REFLECTION: I live in a world in which time has become a commodity. Is it possible to decommodify time? Can we uncover the dynamic moments filled with heterogeneity that come into tension with labor time? Can we relativize time instead of hyperexploiting productive time? Is there a kind of time between leisure time and labor time? Where can we locate the potential realm for the relativization of time? Is it in infra-mince instances in everyday life, is it activism or design, is it spending a week in a banana republic? An orgasm? To seek to be asynchronous with the social is the best guarantee of happiness. How and for how much longer will we struggle for the survival of the nuclear family in the era of late capitalism?

SURFACE: What about online dating? Would Match.com be love-as-Big Brother? Is online dating all about fulfilling our drive to enable ourselves to think without our bodies, folding up further into ourselves?

REFLECTION: Hedonism or stoicism, immanence or transcendence? Narcissism is not a symbol of the decadence of contemporary life, it is rather the abolition of suffering. Narcissism is a folding back to the private where we can simply be happy. There's so much chemistry between us . . . I'm so lucky. We fuck good. You know, we should enable everyone to substitute political intervention by making psychoanalysis democratically available. Confession gone scientific gone popular: isn't going to therapy, after all, to render a public service to one's neighbors? Well-being, wellness takes over the struggle for recognition. This is because there is no future. After all, we should get used to the idea that the past is irretrievable. Let's live in duration—within organic, creative time.

SURFACE: To make occasions special by dancing not because they were special, but because there was dancing: immanence over transcendence. An out-of- body experience. What has proved to be quite useful is to rely on queer theory to get laid—what I call "the pragmatics of the floating signifier" applied to gender difference. Using chocolate ChapStick—kisses taste definitely better—bear in mind that it is OK to cry (your mom never ceased to repeat that to you, remember?), use a soft voice, display your insecurities, pretend that deep inside you there's a superficial blond girl. Do away with the testosterone, dress it up in pheromones. Dwell in drama. After all, the phantasmic support of the main character in the most recent filmic version of *Hairspray*, the fat dancer, is John Travolta. What's behind the fat woman is a white male. Think about it. We must all be queer. Or is this all about pumping up our egos by feeling morally superior by being politically correct through coming to terms with the inequality propelled by gender difference—and exploiting that as a tool for conquest?

REFLECTION: If I had the choice, I would lead a hedonistic, globalite, crazy, and exotic lifestyle in a city that ends with i—like Shanghai, Mumbai, or Dubai. A mix of cosmopolitism and bohemian bourgeois-ism tinted by the curiosity to observe rampant capitalism in the Third World from the First, freed of good intentions and of any kind of self-serving crusade for justice. I agree with using free will to explain the aleatory relationships (love), doing away with what is transcendent to them: compromise, fidelity, jealousy. What takes place in the mind is merely physical, it is when the mind decides to focus in certain simulacra that free will leads to action. Whatever takes place in the mind (anima) is caused by a random swerve in a downward motion of an atom, causing an alteration in atomic motions, leading eventually to action. Is the external world ever consistent with the random swerve of the atom? Where does the clinamen fit in within the Lacanian trinity of the real, the symbolic, and the imaginary?

SURFACE: I have managed to transmit American liberal ideology washed over post-Puritan ethics to my offspring. I've taught them to eat "pure" organic healthy food. They are aware of the need to think about *everything* that goes into their mouths and how it is going to affect their bodies. Can you imagine what their brains would be like when they grow up, free of sugar, free of preservatives and of hormones? It's a new race. My children are also raised to be hyperaware of their genetic pool and its ethno-cultural implications. They know very well the stakes in carrying fragments of history in their bodies, and the potential surplus value inherent in carrying those fragments. Thriving in the myth of success, here everyone's hobby is politics, although I've got to admit that being into foreign policy is not that trendy these days.

REFLECTION: The crisis of the welfare state is based on the redefinition of the subject, making the link between individual action and collective transformation the fundamental social question. The individual becomes the visual expression of politics—where does that leave connectiveness? What is it that holds aleatory connections together, the condition for the political? On what does connectiveness rely, what is the strength or weakness of the link between random movements made of? Nice dreams, angel.

I MADE A TRIP TO Jordan with British Nora in December, accompanying her to visit her parents. There are three possibilities for crossing from Israel to Jordan: Allenby Bridge (right by Jericho), though the south at the Dead Sea (between Eilat and Aqaba), and Sheikh Hussein, which is very close to Nazareth. We decided to cross through the last one because Allenby, which is the nearest checkpoint to Ramallah and the only crossing possibility for Palestinians, is known to be a hell in which Palestinians are made to wait for hours to pass through while often being subject to eternal interrogations by the Israeli border agents. There, they always run the risk of being denied passage or being arrested. Also, Palestinians are customarily humiliated there, and that is why Allenby Bridge is avoided by tourists. In any case, when we went to Jordan by way of Sheikh Hussein, we also had problems. First, when we got there, two soldiers approached us and asked us aggressively: "Are you carrying any weapons?" To laugh a bit, I whispered to Nora: "Yes! Our eyes!" Nora comes from a prominent Gazan family. Her father is a writer, and she is related to a renowned Palestinian intellectual murdered in retaliation for the assassination of eleven athletes during a failed kidnapping by Palestinian terrorists at the 1972 Munich Olympics. One of the biggest hospitals in the Gaza Strip bears their last name, and that is perhaps why she was subject to an exhausting interrogation that lasted for two hours while her dad waited for us on the other side.

I spent ten days visiting them not as guest but as daughter. To say "Abuyee min Falastin, min Gaza" (My father is a Palestinian from Gaza) opens unimaginable doors. We traveled to Petra, to Jerash; we put our big toe in the Dead Sea on the Jordanian side (it was too cold to get in!). I rode the two kilometers of the main street in Petra at full gallop on a camel, allowing myself to live my politically incorrect childhood fantasy of being Indiana Jones. We went for a stroll on the beach in Aqaba, five hundred meters away from the Saudi Arabian border; we saw the Egyptian Sinai and Eilat, the Israeli Acapulco, and we even went for a jeep ride across the multicolored desert at Wadi Raa. I was surprised by a particularity of the Jordanian Hashemite monarchy: everywhere across the country, images of the king and his family are displayed in a variety of situations, like action figures. I saw a photograph of the king riding a motorcycle in full gear, snorkeling in Aqaba with his son, wearing the red Jordanian *kūfiyya*, dining at a family restaurant with his wife and children, standing at a gas station dressed as a general, standing by his father, both wearing traditional gear, outside a cultural center. A king of the people making himself present and accessible to the people through images disseminated across the country. This approach differs from that of European nobility, whose subjectivity, visible through paparazzi photos in magazines, is projected as above the people. The portraits of the king are the equivalent of *Hello!*, but for free and in businesses, restaurants, any public place.

With Nora's distant cousins, we celebrated 'Eid al-Adha, the Muslim holiday in which fasting is broken with the sacrifice of a lamb. In spite of the fact that the family followed the tradition that men and women mingle in separate rooms during the festivities and that women hurriedly cover themselves when a man enters the room, Jordan is a very modern place. For 99 dinars a lamb can be killed in the name of the family. The corresponding prayers are executed and the meat is delivered ready to be cooked; the patriarch no longer needs to get dirty at the slaughterhouse. During my visit, Nora's mom would not stop telling me family stories, about her life in Germany during the 1970s (that is when she met her husband, Nora's father, at the university), how she rebelled against her Protestant family in Ireland, how she hid her Palestinian friends in her attic during incursions by Israeli spies in German universities looking for accomplices of the Munich terrorists, how she crossed from Gaza to Egypt while being held at gunpoint by an Israeli soldier.

If a Mexican passport holder is conscious of anything, it is of the precarity of that document and their secondary status as world citizen when crossing borders. Nora flew back to London from Jordan by way of Amman uneventfully. I decided to cross back to Israel through Allenby on my way back to Ramallah, which was a terrible mistake. A woman alone, with a Mexican passport, entering Jordan with only a backpack, with a lot of passport stamps in and out of Israel and a visa to visit Morocco. The people making the decisions at the border are Israeli soldiers, twenty years old or younger, who are doing their military service as border agents. They asked me a few questions. One of them: "What are the names of your friends in Israel?" I got too nervous because I was carrying three books in Arabic, sweets, and pro-Palestinian paraphernalia (although all well-hidden) in my bag. Luckily, they did not take me to the interrogation room for questioning and a search, but they did stamp my passport with a tourist visa that would expire in two weeks. They said that if I wanted to stay longer in Israel, I had to sort out my situation at the Ministry of Interior. I was hoping to get at least a three-month tourist visa, and the thought of having to leave Israel in two weeks filled me with panic. A taste of the tyranny of incertitude. I phoned all my foreign friends in Ramallah to get their advice. They were surprised because, they said, *no one* gets two weeks at Allenby. To Arab, Muslim, and Palestinian travelers with foreign passports, the passage is made most difficult at that checkpoint, and restrictions there have been amplified since the time of my crossing.

No foreigner has the possibility of living in the West Bank legally unless he or she is employed by an NGO or a media company, or is part of a diplomatic mission; even in those cases, they don't have a guaranteed residency permit. My foreign friends advised me to create a credible alibi with contacts, letters, and documents that would justify my stay in Israel. I spent two days in Ramallah and one in Hebron; during the Israeli weekend (Friday and Saturday), there was nothing to be done. I called people at Bezalel and told them about my problem; they promised to help me by writing me a letter. My roommate, a volunteer for the International Solidarity Movement (ISM), advised me to bring an Israeli "boyfriend" with me to the Ministry of Interior when going to ask for a visa extension. She connected me to activist friends in Tel Aviv (they say the Ministry of Interior there is more merciful than the one in Jerusalem), and they promised they would find me a boyfriend. By Saturday night, I had a boyfriend and a letter and I went to Tel Aviv. My nonactivist Israeli friends were not very empathic. As a matter of fact, they did not believe that the PNA lacked the ability to confer a visa or that I could not declare residence in Ramallah due to risk of being deported.

I found out that in 2006 a policy was established designed to make life hard for foreigners married to Palestinians: they are given Palestinian papers but must renew their tourist visas every three months. If they only keep the Palestinian papers, they must get permission from Israel to travel anywhere forever, losing the rights granted by their country of origin.[89] Many of those foreigners began to get stamps with the legend "Last Renewal Permit" and had to either give up their foreign passports or leave the West Bank. I already have many friends who were forced to leave their lives and land from one day to the next. Before they were definitively expelled from Ramallah, my friends B and N (Palestinians who are also American and Danish) took turns going to Allenby to renew their visas every three months. They left separately, in case their visa was not renewed so that one of them was available back home to pack the house, pay the bills, say farewell to friends, disconnect the refrigerator. They managed to live in Ramallah for five years, with the "Last Renewal

Permit" scare every three months. Two of their daughters were born there, and Israeli authorities had the kind gesture of granting them a final one-year permit but with the condition that after it expired they could never go back to Ramallah. That was already five years ago, and since then they relocated to San Francisco. Another couple, Kiffah and Maria, got married and had a child. In one of their exits to renew Maria's visa, she was not authorized to come back with her Norwegian passport. They moved to Spain where they cultivate Mediterranean land similar to that in Palestine, but on the other side.

My problem, of course, was much lighter because I had the possibility of getting a visa extension. It is difficult to know if you fulfill the state's security risk profile, to know how much information they have on you, or to know whether you are already blacklisted. My situation was clearly much more privileged than that of Palestinians; they also need permits to leave Israel and visas to enter all countries except Iran and Venezuela. By Monday night, my boyfriend-alibi had backed out. On Tuesday I began making a bunch of desperate phone calls to put together another story until I got a letter from photographer Miki Kratsman, who said I was doing a project in Israel (which was not entirely untrue). I also got an activist, HM, to come with me on Wednesday, posing as my boyfriend to request the visa extension. I wrote a letter addressed to the ministry, establishing that I was a PhD student carrying out research in Israel for my thesis based on the premise of my dispossessed identity as *Bnei Anusim*—that is to say, as a descendant of Marranos from Seville, Spain. Is there a possibility for rebuilding secular Jewish identity through the landscape of the Promised Land?

HM had agreed to come with me as my boyfriend. He was willing to yell at the bureaucrat behind the desk if it came to that, so he would give me the visa extension. HM is a twenty-four-year-old refusenik who was in prison for two years as a conscientious objector of Israeli military service. I was deeply surprised when he appeared at the doorstep of the ministry bearing pro-Palestinian pins and an "Anarchists against the wall" button on his jacket. In 2001, HM decided to go public in his refusal to join the army on the basis of ethical and political principles. He did so not as an individual, but together with five other objectors. All five declared themselves to be against the occupation, the violations of Palestinian rights, the murdering of innocents, and so on. Most conscientious objectors refuse to join the army on medical, psychological, or religious grounds. With their declaration, HM and his friends collectively deserted the army. They stood in overt opposition to the policies of the State of Israel, appearing in the global mass media. The price for their action was high: in addition to spending two years in jail, they had difficulty being accepted by a university or finding a job afterward. As a curious coincidence, in 2006 Jean-Luc Godard dedicated two short videos, *Prière pour les refuseniks 1* and *2*, to this group of refuseniks. A friend had shown me the videos in London; at the time, they were not available online. I told HM about them and he was thrilled.

To my relief, before going into the ministry HM put away his anarchist paraphernalia; we were asked a lot of questions, and he helped as my Hebrew translator and Israeli lawyer. I kept thinking that, even with HM, I would be denied the visa, that I would be blacklisted or something like that. That is one of the inexplicable contradictions at the heart of Israeli "democracy." The process took three hours, during which HM, with a homemade cell phone the size of a brick, linked to a pirate cell phone network and kept making phone calls to find out the whereabouts of the identification papers of two young Palestinians who had been beaten up by Israeli settlers the previous night, in a village near Bil'in. That village is known because it is the site of weekly Friday protests against the construction of the wall that would separate its inhabitants from their arable lands and would isolate them from the rest of the West Bank, severing what is left of contiguous territory. The protests usually meet heavy repression, but they have persisted. And since 2001, activists from all over the world gather to reclaim a few square kilometers of Palestinian territory, which has been legally and physically confiscated by the imminent construction of the wall.

I was finally given a visa extension for three months. I breathed a sigh of relief as I started the New Year (which I spent sick with a cold in Tel Aviv, waiting for my application for the extension to be completed).

THE BORDER WITH RAFAH IS closed, Hamas loses control over the border with Egypt, Egyptians begin to expel the Palestinians who crossed illegally to get food, medicine, and fuel. Abbas refuses to negotiate with Haniyeh and demands that he give Abbas control over Gaza; the Lebanon war almost cost Olmert his post, but he remained in power to see if he could negotiate peace. Palestinians in Gaza are living through another exile, as they have again become refugees in Sinai, trying to find food and other basics. Popular Gazan resistance, in coalition with Hamas, broke a section of the wall. From the West Bank, the action is perceived almost as a hopeful signal. But was it necessary to push so hard (with the siege) that people would do something?

And Hamas took the credit, of course. Hamas expected to take advantage of the few moments of world attention to claim a symbolic victory by crossing the wall, at least for a few days. In truth, Palestinians were only able to advance some fifty kilometers inside Egypt. In Sinai, police began to check identity papers and forced Palestinians back into Gaza. There were attempts to protest this week in Ramallah: demonstrators carried posters or stamps on their clothes with the legend: *Gaza ʿala bāly* (Gaza in my thoughts, in my heart).

FIG. 2. Palestinian children playing on a destroyed section of the border wall separating the Gaza Strip from Egypt, Rafah, Gaza, 26 January 2008. Photo credits Victoria Hazou/IRIN. Egypt said that they would keep on allowing Palestinians to cross the toppled wall and that they would be furnished with basics. This is the fourth day of free access from the Gaza Strip

# Solidarity, Empathy

THIRD-WORLDISM IN THE 1960S GATHERED struggles of colonized peoples fighting for independence, self-determination, and socialism all over the world. A new figure of "the people" in the political sense had emerged: the Third World *guerrillero* or *campesino* fighting to topple colonial powers and institute socialist regimes. By the mid-1970s, Third World revolutions had become dictatorships—for instance, communist Vietnam or Chile's turn to the right. This is when the *guerrillero* or *campesino* was replaced by a new regime of representation with new figures of alterity. On the one hand, there is the figure of the victim subject of humanitarian aid; this figure is the wretched without political subjectivity reduced to pure otherness as helplessness. On the other hand, there is the figure of the terrorist (or criminal) who threatens my life and my lifestyle. Terrorism is the violent act of inscribing sheer presence by means of self-destruction. In the West, terrorism is a complex matter, especially after the attacks in New York, London, Madrid, and elsewhere in the past twenty years. When the Second Intifada began in 2002, Palestinians took up terrorism again as a weapon to liberate themselves against the asymmetry that characterizes Israeli occupation. For those inside, the only means to resist and attack the enemy was transforming the body into a lethal weapon of self-sacrifice. From the outside point of view, terrorism is not considered to be an ethical form of warfare because it violates human rights: the fact that it targets civilians and infrastructure makes this form of attack intolerable and illegal. When the Palestinians first resorted to terrorism in the 1970s, liberal sympathizers drew a line. A Sylvère Lotringer's statement sums it up: "In 1974 we were in the last gasp of

Marxism, and I knew that the terrorists were right, but I could not condone their actions. This is still the way I feel right now."[90]

I realized that for my Palestinian friends, discussing terrorism with foreigners was taboo. In March 2008 I was on my way to Zan (the fashionable bar in Ramallah back then) with N, a Hindu friend who worked for the Ramallah office of the International Monetary Fund. She received an urgent text message: "Palestinian terrorists murder eight students at the Mercaz Harav Yeshiva," a Torah school in Jerusalem. After she read the message out loud to me, we kept on walking toward the bar. As we entered, the tension was tangible. Palestinians were keen on not having their daily lives interrupted again by the conflict: the situation could be an excuse for the Israeli army to invade Ramallah any second. We would know for sure in a couple of hours if soldiers began to appear in al-Manara Square. Everyone was nervous, avoiding the topic but feeling, at the same time and in a certain way, vindicated by the attack.

When the Palestinian militia was vanquished and expelled from Jordan in 1970, the cadres and leaders of Palestinian Liberation Organization moved to Lebanon, establishing themselves mainly in Beirut. The relocation of the Palestinian resistance movement divided the Lebanese, some of whom were in favor and some opposed, and contributed to unleashing fifteen years of civil war in the host country. As a consequence, external support for the Palestinian struggle diminished even further. In 1982 after the First Lebanon War, when Israel invaded southern Lebanon to counter the PLO's attacks, the Palestinians negotiated the safe relocation of their headquarters again, this time to Tripoli. In the West, leftist modes of engagement with struggles elsewhere changed—or perhaps waned with the fall of Communism and leftist melancholia. Solidarity with Palestine during the 1980s and 1990s diminished and was further limited by restrictions on journalists during the First Intifada (1987–1993). When the Camp David Accords were signed, global attention was drawn again to the Israeli-Palestinian conflict, as it became one of the sites of the potential future utopia of global multicultural democracy. Because the Camp David Accords were not carried out as Palestinians expected, a Second Intifada was launched (2000–2005), coinciding with the new division of the world between "Islamic East" and "Modern/Capitalist West." The events of September 11, 2001, bestowed new stakes to the conflict. The Second Intifada is known as the "Media Intifada" because of the international visibility the struggle achieved in the mass media.

In 2000, Palestinian, international, and pro-Palestinian Israeli activists founded the International Solidarity Movement (ISM). The organization

gathers "human rights activists" from different parts of the world who travel
to Palestine to do solidarity work. The ISM marks a shift away from the 1970s
Marxist-Leninist solidarity with workers and peoples fighting decolonization
struggles toward a new kind of humanitarian work. In the shift, there is a
practical and a theoretical change. ISM activists work as "human shields" and
as witnesses to the horrors of the occupation, giving voice to the occupied
seeking political self-determination. Their work consists of peacefully resisting, and their concrete objectives are to dissuade military operations through
the "white face defense" (that is, hoping that the army won't attack in the
presence of the "white faces" of the activists); to accompany Palestinians as
they go to work or school to minimize harassment by settlers or soldiers; to
move blockages that hinder passage on the roads assigned to Palestinians;
to break the curfew; and to interfere with the construction of the wall and
settler-only roads. The ISM has repeatedly attempted to break through the
siege in Gaza by carrying out the Freedom Flotillas of 2010, 2011, and 2015
and the Women's Boat to Gaza" in 2016. In each case, the IDF intercepted
the ship, then arrested and deported the activists and crew from the Israeli
port of Ashdod.[91] ISM activists also served as human shields during the siege
of Yasser Arafat's military complex in Ramallah (2002–2004) and during the
siege of the Nativity Church in Bethlehem, which occurred during the Second Intifada.[92] The activists also served as human shields to accompany a
group of girls to school in Hebron, because they are generally troubled on
their way by Israeli settlers, and to help peasants harvest olives, because
they are sometimes attacked by settlers or the IDF. There is a pantheon
of martyred ISM members murdered by the IDF: Rachel Corrie, who was
killed trying to stop a bulldozer from destroying a family's house in Rafah,
Gaza, and Tom Hurndall, who also died on a solidarity mission in Gaza. In
addition to the innumerable Palestinian victims, there have also been Irish,
North American, Swedish, and Italian activists who were wounded, handi-
capped, or killed.[93]

   The passionate engagement I saw in Ramallah and other cities across
the West Bank, the activists' curiosity for war experiences, and their search
for meaning in their lives is related to what Kant describes as "enthusiasm."
For Kant, there is a "moral tendency" in humans that sometimes becomes
enthusiasm for the political processes of other people, in which external observers act on behalf of universal and uninterested empathy for one of the
groups.[94] Enthusiasm, and the search for justice, drives these activists to do
solidarity work.

The thing that concerns me about this form of solidarity, however, is that it falls extremely short, if we must consider it without the global Boycott, Divestment, Sanctions campaign to pressure Israel to end the occupation, because the goal of this form of "ethical solidarity" is to transmit "objective" information. As I mentioned, one of the ISM's tasks is to register, document, and bear witness to the ongoing catastrophe of daily Israeli abuses against Palestinians, based on the premise that "to inform" means "to act," presupposing a public that could be mobilized by outrage to change the situation. This form of solidarity operates in the "now" of urgency and thus lacks the possibility of establishing medium- and long-term goals to ally with political groups outside Palestine. Participation of foreign activists is also premised on the fact that "others need my help." In my view, this humanitarian ethic is far removed from a politics of self-determination, keeps Palestinians in a site of helplessness (from the point of view of westerners, denying them other forms of resistance), and belongs to the logic of colonization. It reminds me of how Spanish conquerors brought not only catastrophe to the Mesoamerican peoples but also a remedy: to save them from hell by converting them to Catholicism. During the early stages of colonization, their destruction and exploitation was parallel to their salvation. Just like the defense of human rights comes with the occupation.

Solidarity tourists, the secular missionaries of the twenty-first century preaching human rights who are clearly not aware of this history, inhabit a great contradiction: On the one hand, as citizens of rich and developed countries in a globalized world, they take responsibility for their racial and material privileges and for their status as citizens of a country that bestows them rights. On the other, many activists who come to the territories become intoxicated by the "good conscience" solidarity work gives them and by the adrenaline high provided by the state of exception under occupation. This mental state blinds them to the urgency of long-term political organization, action, and resistance. Without a doubt, minimal interventions can make great changes in the everyday lives of Palestinian civilians, and the actions of an absent-minded "solidarity tourist" are valid if they enable a young child to attend a day of school in Hebron rather than not being able to attend at all. And by no means am I underestimating what the incredible and necessary solidarity work done by activists has achieved, especially in the case of Neta Golan and Huwaida Arraf, whom I admire greatly and who have made the movement their life. In spite of this, anger, outrage, empathy, and mercy are not helpful as political emotions because they hinder the possibility for "others" to define themselves as autonomous, politically constituted communities. My teacher Sonia, for instance, complained often that well-intended foreigners visiting the West Bank would talk Palestinian young people into painting the wall instead of focusing on articulating a strategy to liberate the country.

Grounded on equal doses of empathic enthusiasm and heroic martyrdom, moreover, the ISM's model of pacific resistance and denunciation lies inside the green zones of "moral security" that have been created by liberal political ideology that advocates for counter-information, the defense of human rights, pacific coexistence, global peace, prosperity, and security for all. The problem is that we know by now that the cost of the privileges of the few (of those who bear rights and live as "citizens" across the world) is the dispossession of the forms of lives of others who live as "non-citizens" so that the "citizens" can have access to land, resources, services, goods, credits, and the global markets. This form of politicization, moreover, supports economic development and culture as solutions or means to "pacify" armed conflict. And this is how liberalism, in the name of universalization, democracy, rights, and perpetual peace has normalized war elsewhere, everywhere: because it is perceived that the ravages of war can be fixed by writing counter-histories and denouncing human rights violations or by enabling survivors to have access to cultural goods, de facto invisibilizing the ongoing dispossession of the redundant populations executed in the name of development and progress.

I am writing this as I take a deep breath and look up to contemplate the Sea of Marmara in Istanbul spread before me in 2011. I think about the Israeli attack on the Turkish ship *Mavi Marmara* carrying six hundred activists, journalists, doctors, nurses, politicians, artists, and so on at the end of May 2010. The *Mavi Marmara* was part of the Freedom Flotilla, a total of six ships carrying humanitarian help (such as construction materials and food) to Gaza to protest against the Israeli economic, cultural, and sanitary siege of the Strip that had been in place since 2007. Gaza has also been surrounded by a concrete wall since 2006, and is thus known as the "biggest open-air prison in the world." Israel attacked the boat, arguing that the members of the crew violently resisted the soldiers' invasion of the ship in international waters. Nine members of the boat were murdered and ten were wounded. The rest were taken to Israeli detention centers and then deported.

The Freedom Flotilla has a historical precedent in *Un Bateau pour le Vietnam*, which carried humanitarian help to Vietnam in 1976. The action was organized by Bernard Kouchner, former Maoist and cofounder of the NGO Doctors without Borders in 1971. The Boat to Vietnam marks the beginning of humanitarian work as the means through which world powers began to relate to their former colonies, by then independent countries. In addition to seriously harming Israel-Turkey relations, the attack against the *Mavi Marmara* inaugurated a radical change in international solidarity discourses. Israel argued that if the objective of the Freedom Flotilla was to bring humanitarian help to Gaza, activists could leave the goods in the port of Ashdod and Israeli authorities would bring the help to the Gazans. The movement behind the flotilla was thus obliged to change the purpose of their trip: from taking humanitarian help (and taking a political stand against the depoliticization of NGOs) to openly expressing solidarity and seeking the end of the siege in Gaza. Otherwise, the humanitarian excuse would not have been a direct act of defiance against the Israeli siege.

YOUSEF OFFERED TO BE MY NATIVE INFORMANT; or maybe Sonia, our teacher, asked him to look after me. My independent study with Sonia has consisted, until now, of visiting together the *ḥamām turky* (the Turkish bath), drinking coffee, and spending time at her home talking. She is an incredible woman who has lived the occupation from within. In the 1980s, she was given the option of being a Marxist or a Muslim; her choice cost her three years of her life in an Israeli jail. Yousef is a great and patient teacher: he makes a little bit too much of an effort (he corrects my spelling every time I text him in English with a few words in Arabic). He is a third-year biology student with an inclination toward political science and art. He showed me amazing sepias he had drawn. He is also a poet (as are many here, Sonia already told me). Together with Norwegian activists, Yousef set up an activist business. For thirty Euros, he and his friends will write a message of your choice on the wall, take a picture of it, and send it to whomever you like. They have been already commissioned to write 123 messages for Valentine's Day. Yousef belongs to the same generation as Abuljaz and Abed. They are between twenty-three and twenty-five, too young to have been involved in the First or Second Intifadas. During the 2002 invasion, they were too busy trying to get to school, being subject to Israeli checkpoints, sometimes unable to get to Birzeit University. I don't know this generation too well; they are the no-future herd, the Manu Chaos, the globalization to come, better be abroad. Abed and Abuljaz are from Gaza; they are passing through Ramallah waiting to hear back from the Israeli Ministry of Interior to get a permit to get to Jordan. Abuljaz hopes to leave from there to Germany, where he got a Konrad-Adenauer-Stiftung scholarship to pursue an MA in political science. Abed had luck, and a few days ago Israeli authorities gave him a twenty-four-hour permit to travel to Jordan where he took a flight to visit his girlfriend in Florida. She is a legend, a member of the salon of illustrious foreigners who have confronted Israeli soldiers in the name of Palestinians. She's also known by her peculiar deportation from Israel: she ran out of money and, as she could not find work in the West Bank, she couldn't buy a ticket to go back home. So, the legend goes, she planted herself in the middle of West Jerusalem waving a Palestinian flag; it was only a matter of hours before she was sent back to Florida for free.

These kids are the renegades from Birzeit University—renegades because they don't belong to any political party, they are not religious or snobs (there is a band of privileged kids who believe that the future of resistance is found in economic development and sustainability, although they really dream of having supermalls, Ikea, Virgin Megastores, and Starbucks throughout the West Bank). The renegades are regularly harassed by the secret police because they smoke hash, hang out with foreigners, have Westernizing secular habits, and enthusiastically participate in demonstrations. Before he travelled to Florida, Abed told me he had been detained for five hours at the police office in Ramallah for nothing. These soft radicals and underground nihilists are perceived as a threat by the establishment although they are minimally organized, don't make a lot of noise and have jobs at places like the Qattan Foundation, local newspapers, and the French-German Cultural Center.

Yousef has a brother and a sister who wears a veil, a mother who used to be beautiful, and an absent father (dead or in jail, I don't know yet). His family is from the village upon whose ruins is presently erected Ben Gurion Airport. During the First Intifada, Israeli soldiers destroyed his home, which contained his grandfather's oven, with tanks; after that, the family relocated to Ramallah. Nora—my British friend who has been back in Berlin for a month or so—spent a lot of time with Yousef when she was visiting Palestine. She became a kind of mentor to him. In his rebellion against Palestinian conservative ways, Nora convinced Yousef to move out of his family home until he eventually came back for lack of funds. He had a girlfriend; the secret police told her parents that he was a bad influence, a liberal smoker. The matter ended on New Year's Eve at Zan.

The first walk we took together was through Shar' Al-Quds toward Al-Bireh, going up by the art academy and passing by the Friends school and coming back to Zan, where I vented my spleen with my friend F. During our walk, we spoke about the core that keeps things together; if things are like a 3D polygon, when there is *fawḍa* (or chaos) is it because the center explodes or one of the sides explodes? We weren't sure. When chaos comes, it's necessary to look out for the remaining pieces of the polygon, build new ones, organize them once more. Yousef suggested taking a series of trips together to cities throughout the West Bank. We agreed to meet the following Sunday in al-Manara Square, the central plaza of Ramallah, at nine o'clock. Yousef showed up with his younger brother, and they took me to a *saḥlab* stand, a kind of white corn-flour drink with coconut, cacao, and peanuts that is really good for the winter cold. The best *sahlab* of the city is made at the Maq ḥa Ramallah (or Ramallah Coffee Shop). The locale is a traditional coffee shop that only allows male customers; they play backgammon there, smoke 'argyla, and drink coffee, tea, and *sahlab*. The customers discuss politics, the corruption of the Palestinian Authority, and Abbas's politics (they call him "the collaborator"). The owner, Abuljaz, speaks Spanish; he told me he had a Mexican girlfriend from the north who was not allowed to marry him because he is Palestinian. I regularly visit the coffee shop. A group of girlfriends and I are thinking of conquering some of that masculine space. We are curious to see how long they tolerate the presence of women. Yousef, his brother, and I waited some twenty-five minutes on the street, staring at our empty *sa hlab* cups. We were joined by a friend of his brother who gave fifty shekels to Yousef—that was our signal to leave for Nablus. We took the *servīs* (or collective taxi) all the way to *huwwara*, one of the most inflexible checkpoints in all of the West Bank. We got there without any problems, although there are three checkpoints before *huwwara*, and one never knows what can happen. We got off the *servīs* and walked through the mud up to a taxi that dropped us off near the kasbah, or old city.

Nablus is cradled between two mountains facing each other: the city spreads out in the valley and extends all the way up the hill on the eastern side (where the kasbah is); it ends at an Israeli surveillance tower that frames a military base on one side. On the western side, the castle owned by of one of the richest men in Palestine, Munib al-Masri, also known as the Duke of Nablus or the Palestinian Rothschild, has been erected. Al-Masri has been involved as patron of many progressive projects throughout the region, such as Al-Quds University; it is said that he amassed a fortune commercializing energy and mass media. He was a close friend and supporter of Yasser Arafat. Rumor has it that he visits his palace in Nablus once a year, always during the summer. The other side, at the top of the hill, is crowned by trees. Here and there can be seen a few cedars and pine trees that have survived the implacable razings of the IDF, which by deforesting Palestinian lands seeks to impede members of the militia from taking cover inside the thick woods.

At a first glance, the kasbah in Nablus is not very different from the old city in Jerusalem; it is also similar to the kasbah in Hebron. A special kind of tension, though, is felt in Nablus: people walk in a hurry, without stopping. For its part, the kasbah in Hebron is a ghost city, as 98 percent of it is empty. Its inhabitants are now Israeli settlers who are protected by the army. The Hebron kasbah is one of the places where the daily reality of the occupation is the toughest. In Nablus there are food stands, bakeries, convenience stores, barber shops, and stores that sell clothing, bags, and plastic Chinese objects (what my Belgian friend calls "signs of the Third World"). Going around, we try to find one of the famous olive oil soap factories that Nablus is known for, but with don't have any luck and figure that they shut down since the Second Intifada. Instead, we come across a bakery where the baker makes us delicious *dfiḥas*, a kind of bread pizza with *za'atter* (a mix of spices based on a mountain herb with sesame seeds, which is so good) and olive oil; we also had a kind of tart with egg and *za'atter*. We sat at the bakery for a really long time waiting for our food to be ready. The place was small; the baker was very young, around fourteen, and behaving like a boss and good host. He set a small table for us and offered us tea in glasses. The TV played an Egyptian movie on a local channel. On the wall behind us, there was a collage of newspaper clippings with photographs of the invasion in 2002. The images registered the traces of events that had taken place five years earlier just around the corner. In one of the photographs, three soldiers were seen forcing two Palestinians to push a broken jeep. There is another image in which a tank is standing in the middle of the city. Other clippings commemorate the resistance of the martyrs: they show funerals. In addition to bearing witness to the 2002 invasion and its destruction, it was as if the images arranged on the wall represented a way to endure the losses.

As we left the bakery, we looked for the shop that made *knāfa* (my most favorite desert: I forget what it is made of besides cheese and honey, but it is typical for Nablus). After we passed a home that appeared to have sunk down into the ground, along with everything around it, including a well. According to Yousef, that building was part of a subterranean layer: an old house that was underneath a modern one, unearthed by the Israeli bombings to kill combatants who were entrenched there. Nablus and Ariha (Jericho) are two of the world's oldest cities. We continued our fruitless search for the *knāfa* factory; instead, we found a shop that made delicious gummies by hand. The place, run by a man and his son, was small and dirty; it reminded me of a tortillería in a poor village. We bought boxes of the sweets for two shekels. As we continued our promenade, we played a guessing game: whether the building had been destroyed by a grenade, tank, or missile. The walls bordering a nearby street appeared completely covered with posters of martyrs. One second glance, we realized that they were not posters, but something more permanent, acrylic light boxes measuring 1 meter by 50 centimeters, reaffirming and commemorating the courage and pride family members who regularly come to leave flowers.

Nablus is home to one of the Palestinian militias, the Al-Aqsa Martyrs Brigade, which was the target of the IDF in 2002.[95] The guerrillas took refuge in the old city, and that is why the Israeli bombs nearly completely destroyed it. Palestinians are, however, resilient and stubborn, and quickly rebuilt the place by any means possible (they say that Palestinians rebuild with money from the rich Arab countries). In Nablus, life in the old city is back and yet it feels heavy, a vibe of horror mixed with pain and a ruin that reconstruction did not hide. In Ramallah, I have gotten used to living with the dark side of the city and its people, sensing the traces of the catastrophe and the sensation of accumulated losses. For those who live there, it is enough to talk about the horror from memory transformed into anecdotes or adventures, but that's all. After our stroll through the kasbah, we took a cab to Jāma' a An-Najaḥ, or An-Najah National University. We went in through the visitor's gate, and someone from the public relations office greeted us and gave us a short tour. The university has twenty thousand students enrolled in a very small campus. What surprised me the most was not that I saw only a few women without the veil, but that boys and girls existed in the patios across the campus in diverging dimensions, as if separated by crystal sheets. This form of coexistence without apparent mutual recognition reminded me of Manet's *Le Balcon* (1868-1869) exhibited at the Musée d'Orsay, in which the characters appear as encased in different visual perspectives within the pictorial plane, as if they were separated on their own individual spatio-temporal glass capsules. The university's patio also reminded me of *L'Année dernière à Marienbad* (1961), Alain Resnais's film in which all the characters exist in parallel worlds without being aware of each other. At least we saw three(!) brave couples in conversation. My yarn-like covered head floated through the smoke blown by the students smoking cigarettes and I felt hyperconscious of my status as zoo animal.

When we left, we took the road leading to the Martyrs' Cemetery, and as we passed by we noticed that a grave was being dug right on the path that crosses the cemetery. It reminded me a bit of Père Lachaise but in miniature. The tombs were beautiful: long and thin sarcophagi placed on the soil, with ridges on the ends used as pillars to hold two long palms that make a triangle above the crypts. In the middle, light boxes with photos commemorate the heroism and martyrdom of the deceased. We continued going down the hill toward the kasbah. We passed by the small shop of Jewish fortune tellers who read the *Qābala* upon request and for a price. Palestinian Jews make up a small community of three hundred members who have always been present in Nablus. They have resisted the occupation and live in solidarity with

Muslims and Christians. It is known that the State of Israel continuously tries to relocate them inside official Israeli territory to confer citizenship status, but they have never accepted. Seeing their small community diminish, they began bringing Jewish women from Russia to extend their families.

We watched while the fortune teller told a man about a girl he had asked about: he's apparently in a bad marriage. When it was my turn, I paid the same amount, then gave him my name and my mother's name, Nora. (Would the fortune have been different if I had told him Nora Maryamí or Luz María or Lucero?) He spoke very fast, and upon his request, Yousef began taking notes. He didn't say anything worthy that I could catch, and he also didn't give me a lot of information. We continued going down the road, playing our guessing game of what had destroyed the buildings we walked by: bomb, grenade, tank. Another place devastated by the IDF between 2002 and 2004, as much or more than Nablus, was the refugee camp in Jenin (also the home of Al-Aqsa Brigade militias). A UN agency rebuilt the camp, enlarging the streets so that, in the event of another invasion, Israeli tanks would be able to pass through without destroying buildings or sidewalks. In Ramallah, Nablus, and Jenin I felt how the dust from the debris had not yet finished settling: the smell of destruction is still present. The dust is tasteless and colorless, but it goes up your nose, seeps through shut windows, and forms a thin reddish layer that covers everything. We finally found the *knāfa* shop: tiny and filthy. We were served the fresh, sweet, and warm dessert on plastic plates. I had promised Sally, my librarian friend at the Qattan Foundation, that I would be back early so we could get a massage at the *ḥamām turky*, so we started back to Ramallah. It would normally take us some forty minutes to go from Nablus to Ramallah, but because there are three checkpoints on the way, one never knows if there will be problems or if the IDF will shut down *huwwara*, the most perverse checkpoint in all of the West Bank. We walked some more, passed by the *muqāṭaʿ* (the PLO's compound in Nablus), which had been completely destroyed by the IDF invasion. It has been rehabilitated, but quickly and badly, without removing the debris.

We passed more abandoned and partially destroyed homes: grenade, tank, missile? We took a cab to *huwwara* because it was almost three o'clock in the afternoon. We separated in lines by gender. I went through quickly, and I didn't know what to do with myself while I was waiting for Yousef. I tried to pass unnoticed while two subjects caught my attention. A woman, around thirty-five years old, small and disheveled, wearing glasses and a Hebrew-language badge, carried a camera; on her side, a guy around the same age was dressed very fashionably, like a cultural producer. He looked like a designer or architect from Berlin, Barcelona, Tel Aviv, or Los Angeles (I was not wrong: he was a designer from Tel Aviv). I stood by them while I waited for Yousef to cross the checkpoint. They addressed me in Hebrew. "Ani lo medaberet ivrit," I answered, to their surprise. I really don't speak Hebrew! We exchanged the corresponding banalities: "Where are you from?" "What are you doing here?" She was a member of an Israeli NGO dedicated to documenting abuses against Palestinians at checkpoints across the West Bank. Armed with a camera, she observed, together with another woman, as women exited the checkpoint. They communicated through hand signs. Amit, the designer, and Galit were childhood friends; they had grown up together in a kibbutz near the border with Lebanon.

"So you went to Shrejot?"

"No! I'm coming back from Nablus; I spent the day there visiting with my friend Yousef."

"Did you know that calling the city 'Nablus' and not by its Jewish name, 'Shrejot,' means taking a political position?"

"Oh yeah? I didn't know. Here everyone calls it Nablus, I'd never heard the word 'Shrejot' in my life."

The designer from Tel Aviv had spent five months traveling through Mexico from Tijuana, passing through San Cristóbal in Chiapas and through Puebla, then making his way over to the Caribbean. He told me he had liked it a lot.

"Corona beers are only a dollar! How is life in Ramallah?" they asked me.

"Yofi! (beautiful)," I answered, with a smile that came from my heart. "No one in the West Bank has ever has asked me my religion."

When I said that, Galit and Amit did not dare to ask me if I was Jewish. It was the first time in over fifteen years that Amit visited the West Bank (since his military service?). For Galit, it was a weekly routine, going from one checkpoint to another every time she could to document atrocities and abuses.

"How moving! How generous of her!" my friend J told me when I told him about my strange encounter with the two Israelis, the only I've seen in the West Bank without Uzis or wearing Crocs (the sort of hideous Canadian plastic shoes all settlers wear).

Amit had gone to ḥuwwara with his friend out of curiosity. His eyes were as wide open as a plate. He told me that on the way to ḥuwwara from Tel Aviv, there are check points, and on the way there he got dizzy and felt like vomiting. It seemed to me that his arrogance covered his vulnerability; calling Nablus Shrejot was a gesture of precarious assertiveness.

"How brave you are to live in Ramallah!," both told me.

"Not really!" I answered. "I feel very safe walking around the streets. You should come visit one day." They looked at me with a mix of fear and mistrust.

"That's crazy! They would realize I'm Israeli, then kidnap and lynch me."

"If Palestinians hosted you, you would have nothing to be afraid of; if you had Palestinian friends to trust, you wouldn't have any problems. You would be welcome and have a good time."

Later that day, at the *ḥamām*, I told Sally about the conversation I had with Amit in *huwwara* and she said: "But you know? He is right. A few years ago, a Palestinian girl seduced an Israeli guy on the Internet, and she made him come to Qalandya. There, he was kidnapped and killed; he had no idea."

Amit had told me: "I guess it's the same feeling I had in Mexico when I visited cities with political tension, like Tijuana and San Cristóbal. As a tourist, you don't know very well what is going on, you don't measure the danger."

That moment I thought of pointing out the difference between *political tension* and *occupation*, but I gave up because I began to feel very frustrated. Instead, I explained my purpose:

I came to the West Bank to understand the ongoing history of colonization in Mexico, the occupation of Texas and the rest of the north of my country, the Zapatista struggle, and the wall between Mexico and the US, which by the way, is being built with Israeli technology. There, like you here, I inherited the perspective of the oppressor. It is very difficult to establish, for example, a dialogue with an indigenous person from the point of view of colonization.

As a foreigner, I feel very privileged to be able to be in Ramallah, and more so because they have an educated elite from whom I can learn and with whom I can dialogue. Here the poor and rich, artists and merchants suffer from the occupation. In indigenous Chiapas there is no equivalent of the Palestinian elite; they are communities that have been culturally and materially impoverished for centuries. What do I say to a peasant whose land has been stolen, who has nothing to eat? Do I promise him land? A better future if he goes to school? Do I tell him to put himself in the hands of God?

I have no idea if my ideas caught Amit's interest. He asked me if I was a journalist; I think he didn't get anything of what I had tried to explain to him. At that moment, three Palestinian young men approached and addressed us:

"Hi! What is your name?"

I answered in Arabic: "I'm Gardi, this is Amit."

A few more teens approached, they had just passed through the checkpoint and began to ask us things in Hebrew and English. Amit's body language changed immediately.

"Do you have Messenger?"

Amit responded, "No, I have Gmail, and I use The Marker Café, an Israeli site where you can post blogs, your CV, communicate. Do you know it? (It is like the Israeli LinkedIn.)"

Amit spoke to the Palestinian young man with such arrogance that I only stayed in the conversation because I am curious and didn't want to be by myself surrounded by eight Palestinian teenage boys.

They were all students in Nablus; two studied at the university. They lived in refugee camps on the outskirts of the city and crossed through *huwwara* every day. Suddenly, one of their friends came through, disheveled, shoeless, and with his belt, cell phone and wallet in his hand, somewhere in there a half-torn *ḥawiya* ( Palestinian ID).

"Look what they've done to me! Take my photo!" he said, smiling, addressing Amit.

The rest of us laughed at his joke. Another kid invited Amit to visit him and his family at the refugee camp. A bolder kid asked me for my email address. Another one asked about my *kūfiyya*, which combined red and black embroidery over white. In general, the red *kūfiyya* is associated with George Habash's Palestinian Popular Liberation Front (PPLF), which was anti-imperialist and revolutionary, and the black is associated with Fateḥ or the PLO, Yasser Arafat's organization, which was revolutionary and Marxist.

"I don't believe in adhering to good old political organizations, that is why my *kūfiyya* mixes both colors. I also don't believe in God, so I'm not for Hamas. I am pro-Palestinian. With Habash's passing away yesterday, political organizations are a thing of the past." In response, the kid asked me to exchange *kūfiyyas*.

"Of course!"

Galit invited us to have a coffee further down the street, at a stand by the parking lot where taxis wait for passengers. We drank it surrounded by curious *huwwara* crossers. We were the animals in the zoo for a few minutes. After forty-five minutes had passed, Yousef finally came through, smiling. We took the *servīs* back to Ramallah. At the second checkpoint, we were detained. There was a trunk check, in spite of the fact that one of the passengers had told the soldier: "My son is ill! Please, I am in a hurry." The woman had to get as fast as possible to Bethlehem. The quickest way was to go to Ramallah and from there to Jerusalem—although in truth, the shortest way was to go directly to Bethlehem from Nablus. The problem is that the way from

FIG. 3. Photograph of the author, sent by a friend.

Ramallah to Bethlehem is three hours long, not only because of the check-points but because the *servīs* have to go *tora bora*—traveling the hidden, il-legal roads, crossing through villages and taking roundabout routes. There weren't any problems at the third checkpoint, so I got back in time to meet Sally to go to the *ḥamām*. The next day, Amit sent me the photographs he had taken in *huwwara*, along with a link to his blog, with no greeting, not even a "Hi! Nice running into you yesterday" or "Hey! Here are the photos, hope all is well," nothing. Days after, my friend M would forward me the same link:

"Motek! What are you up to? Where are you?"

# Chronicle of a Centrifugal Fearless Delirious-Becoming

Jardins où saigne abondement le laurier rose fleur guerrière

APOLLINAIRE, from "La Colombe poignardée et le jet d'eau"

THERE IS A SAYING IN ARABIC: when something breaks, it is because a *jin* has run away. Not because the *jin* is amusing herself making mischief, but because evil is trapped in that which holds things together. Carelessness and chance, the principles of chaos, enable the *jin* to escape by shattering the cohesion of things. Once the forces of the *jin* are unleashed, it is impossible to restore things to their previous state. This theory has nothing to do with the iconoclast Islamic position that supposes that evil gets inside man-made things and thus that human creation is a crime because only Allah can be at the origin of everything. Somehow, the explanation of the unleashing of chaos by the *jin*'s escape from things made me think about my own tragedy of desiring someone with whom I had, in essence, an aesthetic disagreement. Tolerance enables us to live with people with whom we have political differences. If one expands tolerance—as it can be infinitely stretchable—one can live, talk, even fall in love with someone with whom one has an ethical and political disagreement. But this only applies when tolerance is bilateral. When it is not, it's as if the *jin* had escaped, and something fundamental— that which lies between us: language, conventions, empathy, habits, spoken and unspoken agreements—irreparably breaks.

The day we visited Qalqilya, J, Omaya, and I ran hurriedly out from the zoo because our taxi driver had called to let us know that the only entry and exit point from the city—a checkpoint guarded by Israeli soldiers—had been shut down. We crossed by foot, passing by waving our passports and identity cards. When we got to the other end, we climbed into a different cab that drove us to Ramallah. The road back offered us a paradigmatic image of the West Bank: a Palestinian talking to an Israeli with two meters of distance between them. When we drove by the refugee camp next to Qalqilya, we saw another paradigmatic scene: about twenty Hamas militants being arrested by the IDF (J offered this information, but I had no way to know if they were in fact Hamas). A week later, eight students from the Jerusalem Yeshiva would be murdered. A handful of militia, including Hezbollah in Lebanon, would take responsibility for the massacre.[96]

My delirium, or becoming-fearless, began on that trip, as I suddenly entered a state of self-absorption that is difficult to describe and that is very different from spleen. A state that can neither be accounted for by the different kinds of war of the mind against itself that I have taxonomized, and against which the prophet has expressed strong disagreement: clinical depression, stress, panic attack, anxiety attack, shock. Picturing him as a fleeing horse, zigzagging away in a whisper I could hear inside the taxi that was smoothly crossing the hills of red earth. I felt as if a lobotomy was being performed on my brain and my chest cracked open. My whole body felt cauterized as I entered a kind of Zen limbo where my mind went blank and I had intermittent feelings of becoming-fearless. Then, something pressed the button that replayed in my memory the last conversation we had: hysteria times two leading nowhere. Lethargic, I felt the sadness tearing away along with my heart; I willed him to disappear from time and space. By then I had gotten really good at making him disappear. I mastered it the day when he had seen me sitting on the edge of the library's balcony while I was having a conversation on the phone with my friend in Tel Aviv. Azmi had come out to reproach my circus-like temerity, telling me that the library did not offer health insurance to its users. "Azmi, haven't I told you I'm like a cat so if I fall I will land standing up and keep on walking?" The words I had uttered had made him vanish from time and space. Afterward, I realized I was able to breathe differently, with another rhythm. Maybe Brownie's amnesia is contagious, I thought, on the taxi ride back to Ramallah. The driver was very kind and curious about me. He pointed out how I had the power to make the wall porous with my foreign passport. With a smile I said, *'akīd 'ustāz*, give me that belt. The day after the trip to Qalqilya I realized that I had forgotten about the blow, just like sobriety comes unnoticed after a cigarette hangover, as if desire had vanished like smoke itself. The crack in my chest was no longer painful. The channels through which desire used to flow felt clotted. I spent another day in this strange state of self-absorption. The following day I woke up exhausted but convinced that I had finally managed to write him away into a literary regime. Such achievement, I thought, came from an exceptional and exhausting mental effort of hyperrationalization. I was given the news, passing by Daur al Cinema that afternoon. From Thursday to Friday he had expelled me for good from his torment: He got married. Since then, Rami Khalifé's "Scene from Helleck" keeps on hammering my mind as I listen to it obsessively while I rock sitting on the floor at the library staring at my computer. That is why Sally's hair and face were made up beautifully that day. I went to get my *al-ṭayba* at 6:23 PM. I feel numb as the prophet tries to console me with words by Hussein Barghouti, while I hear his voice, reciting while "Scene from Helleck" plays, what the Gypsy had said: "I said: I came from a river bank in which I cannot distinguish between the ghosts that come out of the water that has been fermented by the moon and those that come out of the memory, like the frogs.

How can I distinguish?

She said: The ghosts of memory come from a different world, the world to which the spirit travels in dreams, and the gypsies know her. In her ears gold rings and it likes the ancient dance and writing a different kind of reality. So, make use of what you know, and then mysteriously she said: if the river Euphrates asks for this silver chain on my neck I would have given him a lot of wheat. And stretched my hand to her neck to shake the chain (necklace) to find it merely a tattoo over the flesh like a pale painting in the form of a silver chain. The ghosts are playing in me, again, how can I distinguish?"[97]

# War against the Night

'ALBY IS WARRING A NIGHTLY battle side by side the ghosts pullulating Ramallah. They roam about the city when they are not walled-in between the palimpsests of décollages that decorate the metal doors of shops and walls of homes of the buildings in the old city. The *affiches* trap and mute the ghosts, although they can sometimes be heard singing prayers at the hour of the first muezzin at daybreak. They are silenced because people forget to listen to their whispers shining through their papered gazes full of faith and courage. After 2002, the flesh inhabitants of the memoryless city erased the traces of the bullets, picked up all rubble, covered the scars with innumerable new buildings. The amnesiac city is pregnant with her story, but the story itself is trapped between those sheets of paper, like the nation that will never come. We will have to do in Ramallah with what there is, even with the smell of pain, which is difficult to recognize because it is trapped in another palimpsest: that of postponed mourning.

I had woken up dreaming that I was halfway to Beirut, passing through Haifa but inexplicably delayed in Tel Aviv. I no longer felt nausea or like crying. And right before being fully conscious, in my dream, I was arriving in Sarajevo as if it were home. The previous night, I was sleeping a sweet and resigned sleep, listening to the rainfall when the song of the first muezzin had woken me up.

Some other night, I remember feeling grateful to the rain because it had suddenly pulled me away from a deep alcoholic sleep as if an invisible fist had snatched my breath for a second, only so I could keep on raining and the mist could arrive. I realized I was wide awake, crying on a wet floor, just in time to hear the first prayer of the morning. I recall that other night, populated by ghosts that had given me the mandate to write and write until his name left the page for good. They also ordered me to get up from bed before he would come back to hide beneath the pillow again. When would I manage to expel him from my pages, I wondered? After a few insomniac nights, forgetting worked on me again.

I had grown tired of the tyranny of footnotes and exhausted by the occupation. One of the effects of this exhaustion is the internalization, the normalization, the becoming used to the occupation. Another effect of getting worn out by the occupation was the shattering of my virtual stereoscope—that apparatus of vision that had, until then, enabled me to see a double image from the Israeli and Palestinian perspectives, giving me the illusion of three dimensionality (or objectivity). Acknowledging the exhaustion and the shattering of the stereoscope gave me a new feeling of liberation. The other day, speaking with my friend M from Tel Aviv on her landline, I noticed some strange sounds between us, as if they were extraterrestrial beings letting us know that a third uninvited party had joined our conversation. I was sitting in Zyriab (a local coffee shop and restaurant), and I turned off the Wi-Fi connection because I feel paranoid someone would invite herself to read my emails and to look at the pages I was navigating on the Internet without asking for my permission.

After a long wait, a copy of Hussein Barghouti's book, translated to French, *Lumière bleue*, makes it to my hands. Barghouti was the most influential figure of the Palestinian "New Poets" movement in Ramallah in the 1990s. He died in 2002 of cancer, surrounded by friends and protégés, about ten of them. I was very much touched by his poem, "What the Gypsy Said," which the prophet translated for me the night in which solitude had fallen upon me. I find the book difficult to read, the language seems plain—is it the translation? I persist, scratching the lines, and I discover a hallucinating world in Seattle in the 1980s painted by Barghouti from the point of view of an observer who tries to survive individualistic decadence documenting the impossibility of living in a democracy of hedonistic people. The character never leaves his head and poses the big existential questions during an initiation trip guided by a Turkish Sufi; his trip is sometimes bathed with a bit of New Age and precolonial mysticism. A wonderful delirium. One passage from the book seized me in particular. In it, he talks about aesthetic disagreement. For Barghouti, the problem of bad poets is not so much that the poetry in itself is mediocre. The badness of the poet is more related to the kind of life writers have chosen to lead. Battles are not only waged on the page in black and white, but in every-day life, in the life one builds for oneself as a political and aesthetic position.

# United Hands
# and Feet of Benetton

IF WRITING IS THE DISSOLUTION of the voice through an expressive self performing a gesture of inscription, then the act of thinking and writing is feeling through the fingers. I was reminded of this when I saw at the movie theater a video of a Palestinian writer telling the story of discovering his big toe when an erotic tongue licked it for the first time. The video also shows an elder of an African tribe who refused to wear shoes and a Japanese dancer describing how he connects with the earth bearing the soul at his feet. United hands and feet of Benetton. Bodily and cultural specificity, the multicultural utopia of globalization, a French man that comes to show videos about people who talk about their hands, evoking those painted by Pablo Picasso, or those in Sliman Mansour's portraits, proud and working hands, loving the land and the nation.[98] Or Andrea Mantegna's feet, comparable only to Michelangelo's. Then the vision of your thin, long hands, bearing a golden band, toying with my gaze two rows behind me during the projection. Then, your hands accompanied with gestures, your unbearable and mansplaining monologue about a novel whose main character is a one-armed man who felt itching on the amputated limb. You asked the French man if he had thought about filming spoken self-portraits of an amputee; you expressed curiosity about the ways in which a limb can make itself manifest once it has been lost or amputated. Elucidating from a vulnerable ego how you yourself would tell the story of your hands and feet. The hand transformed into a partial object, disconnected from the body and the voice, in a pure gesture of inscription, not of expression, creating traces without origin that are pure language. Pure voice, pure voice without a hand, heartless? I departed from you, from the almond trees that did not bloom, from your hands that were so battered they could not hold me.

There are images of things that cannot be shown and that are like the skins or peels of something that is not on view because it is happening inside. After the winter, the almond tees spit out *rabī* (the spring) and bring comfort, and I find myself going uphill on the right side of the street where, on the left, I notice a shop with the neon sign "True Love." The shop and the sign shine as an instance of the embodiment of erotic desires in stuffed red teddy bears and other made-in-China bibelots that freeze reified oxytocin and enable courtship. Caetano sings: "Quema la casa, quema la casa azul, cuando la cama incendiada comience a escaparse en el horizonte, ven a ver los fuegos artificiales, quémate junto con la casa y con el cielo, quema al cielo con el frío de la mañana, envuelto en terciopelo rojo, desvanécete junto con mi soñarte." [Burn the house, burn the blue house, when the burnt bed begins to flee on the horizon, come see the fireworks, burn together with the house and the sky, burn the sky with the morning cold, enveloped in red velvet, vanish alongside with my dreaming you].

The devil is unleashed, and when staring at the unconceivable universe in its sheer opacity, without superposition, I feel vertigo. Did the Aleph show up in a vision?

I pass by your name when I am alone
like a Damascene passing through al-Andalus

MAHMOUD DARWISH


**YOUR NAME PASSES BEFORE ME,** we do not see each other, the lute is
heard breathing when every one of its chords is touched, the cat smells the
chemicals ignoring the pulse and the chemicals and I curse the stranger
and the pulse and I get you out of my space, you are back to torment me in
my sleep, I feel relief screaming at you with all the strength from my two
lungs before your empty name with x-ray vision the inquisitive cat neutral
mask neutral neutral neutral Oedipus Tiresias the cat is Tiresias in Ramallah
Antigone does not fold Antigone subject to patriarchal law leaves the feminine to burn alive in self-negation masculine world law space and law sub-
jection unidirectional pulse I keep telling myself the cat is concerned neutral neutral neutral evaporates thought certitude crossing between moon
moon unidirectional masochism femininity masochism becoming-woman
masochism Ramallah without eating, poetry, hungerless sloth, fury, avoiding eyes, oblique eyes, certitude, incredulity, knowledge, intuition, elusive
is better oblique the cat prefers not to stare at elusive eyes, Tiresias's mask,
Oedipus, Antigone.

THE WORD NFSI TO DESIGNATE "myself" is minimally different from the word "breath" in Arabic: *nafasi*, with a discrete *fatha* adorning the *f*. As if in Arabic breathing is almost the largest part of existing. The horizon displays at least four tones of blue, from pink passing through an intense gray all the way to unforgivable blue. Imperial nostalgia for the Arab world that is still current is like the Cuban nostalgia for prerevolutionary times in the 1950s. Things feel smooth in general, although the situation has never been worse for Palestinians. And it's not just me who says it: Salam Fayyad, the prime minister, is signing free trade agreements and economic cooperation treaties with Israel, Norway, Japan, USAID.[99] Neoliberal policy treaties in which Palestinians become cheap labor and captive consumers, or are subsumed under forms of contemporary enslavement, with a pocket tied to everything getting more expensive, cheap credit and currency always subject to inflation. Mexico is also not doing well, I tell them. We know this story by heart. In the West Bank, the feeling of defeat dissolves too quickly in the liquidity of conformism; the feeling that there is nothing to do prevails. From one day to the next, graphic demonstrations flooded the streets of Ramallah with the prevailing mood. The slogan *Gaza ʿala bāly* (Gaza in my mind, in my heart) becomes ubiquitous. At the end of the day, West Bank focus on the situation in Gaza, which is much worse than in the West Bank. Under the perception that "things are not so bad in Ramallah," a parody of a martyr poster appears covering the martyr posters disseminated across the city. It's surely the work of an artist. The posters represent a prototype, a graphic skeleton of a cartoon of a "martyr poster" that invites passersby to insert a face and to write the name of the martyr in English and in Arabic. The design, more or less sophisticated, contrasts with the folkloric traits of the martyr posters plastered through the streets of Palestinian cities. A parody? An invitation? Being tired of thinking of themselves as victims all the time? Under the occupation, we are all potential martyrs because we live a haphazard destiny of a potentially heroic death.

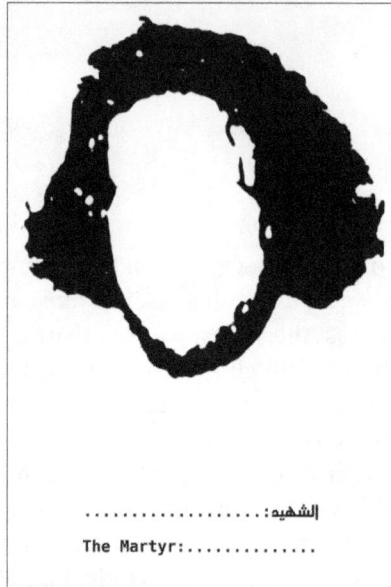

الشهيد: ....................

The Martyr: .............

FIG. 4. Bashar Alhroub, Martyr Project (2007)

The other day S, the Swedish gal who studies Arabic with me at Birzeit, came by. She came to tell me yet another one of her unfortunate love stories: The third since November! The first one unfolded with her neighbor, who left her because he felt pressured by his friends and the PNA's secret police to leave her. They threatened to let his family know that he was dishonoring them with a foreigner. Then, she hooked up with Nadim, my neighbor and Don Juan who goes up the stairs in my building with a different foreign girl every night. S and I agreed we'd put up some sort of sign on the stairs warning future visitors of Nadim's habits. Her last amorous fallout was with Ala, the son of a Syrian close to Arafat who grew up in Tunis and moved to Ramallah in the 1990s. It seems like they spent three or four days exchanging expressions of love and confidential life experiences. Among the secrets, he told her how his life had been in danger from the age of two. His father had always been under death threats, and he had to hide a lot. He also told her that he didn't learn his actual name or his fathers' until he was ten years old. These confidences made S feel extremely privileged because she realized how protected and insouciant her own childhood had been. In the end, Ala asked her just to be friends. To cheer her up, I told her to apply the middle rule: it takes half the time that one was with a person to forget him or her, so tomorrow by the latest she will have recovered from the affair. She smiled and said she was ready for the new. We went to get a shawarma for myself and a falafel for S (what is it with foreigners in Palestine that they are all vegetarian?). On the way there, a man stared at us and repeated many times: *rū-siyye, rūsiyye* (Russians, Russians). S was aware of what we were being called but not of the insult: I decided not to let her know. I didn't tell her about the implacable gaze of veiled women upon foreign women either. It can be more chilling than a man staring at us like he thinks we are whores (I know from a trustworthy source that the Ramallah whorehouse is full of Eastern European and Russian women). When we said goodbye, I advised S to keep herself safe from guys who might just want to take advantage of her.

# "Don't Think This Is the Next Chiapas"

EDWARD SAID POSITS COLONIALISM as a kind of *pharmakon* that contains two movements:[100] one of merciless conquest and one of decolonization: "Ich bin ein Teil von jener Kraft, die stets das Böse will und stets das Gute schafft" (I am part of a power that brings forth evil that has good intentions and puts them to work).[101] Especially in this place, inundated with the adrenaline of war, the sexiness of someone else's disgrace, and, if you look, victims' complaints. "Revolutionary tourism" or "international politics" has become war tourism. A sequence from *The Baader Meinhof Complex* (2008), a film about the German revolutionary cell, narrates the episode in which the group, after leaving Ulrike Meinhof's children behind in Sicily, goes to Jordan to get training in a PLO camp but manage to infuriate their Muslim hosts with their promiscuity, hedonism, and nakedness. Differences intensify in extreme situations, and revolutionary tourism from the last century was free of neither contradictions nor problems. Contemporary forms of humanitarian solidarity tourism differ from yesteryear's political tourism because before there was no distinction between political and aesthetic action, or perhaps there was just tension. Today, on the other hand, there is a division between activists and cultural producers. From the point of view of old school (Marxist-Leninist) militants, foreign activists have only imported pacific resistance methods from Europe and the United States, advising Palestinians to show their other cheek to Israeli aggressions. Where will these solidarity resistance tactics lead? Specifically, the ISM specializes in direct and nonviolent action in the Occupied Territories by directly confronting the IDF.

S was inspired by Rachel Corrie's parents to come to the West Bank. Rachel Corrie is the US activist who was murdered in March 2003 in Rafah, Gaza, at the border with Egypt, after being run over by a bulldozer while she acted as human shield in front of a Palestinian doctor's home that was about to be demolished by the IDF.[102] It comforted S to know that there are parents who get involved with their activist children. Hers, in contrast, insist, every time they call her, that she come back to Göteborg. Since their daughter's death, Rachel's parents have devoted themselves to traveling across the world giving presentations, sharing her story, and publicly reading passages from her diary and emails. They also seek international support in their struggle against US authorities and the Israeli government to solve a controversy related to Rachel's autopsy and the conditions in which her body was transported back to the US. They are also suing Caterpillar, the company that produces the specially designed bulldozers used to destroy Palestinian homes.[103] Rachel Corrie's martyrdom sheds light on the value of an American life—"grievable life" in Judith Butler's terms[104]—compared to nonmournable or naked Palestinian life. The mourning of a mournable life is translates to much greater global media coverage and presence in globalized information circuits compared to Palestinian lives. The image of a dead Rachel, run over by the Caterpillar, with a broken spine and exposed guts, generates the real shock of biopower, the solidarity theater of horror. Her story has been disseminated through *My Name Is Rachel Corrie*, a play staged in Arabic in Haifa and Ramallah but censored in New York and Toronto by the Israeli lobby. Her image and diaries have been widely disseminated around the world, and Simone Bitton, the French-Israeli filmmaker, released in 2008 a documentary in which she reviews, step by step and from many points of view, Rachel's case after her parents lost the lawsuit against Israel for unjust death.

Before I participated in one of their solidarity actions, I spent a night in October at the ISM apartment in Nablus. There I met two English women typical for their age (braless, divorced, vegetarian, committed old-school style), a guy from London, the Palestinian coordinator, two German girls, and S. We were divided into teams and were assigned to go to two villages to support the peasants' olive harvest. I was on S's team, and we were sent to Yanun; she was going back to the site where she had done solidarity work ten days earlier, when settlers attacked the peasants and activists with stones, rubber ammunition, and tear gas. During the attack, two men were badly wounded (the image of one with his head wide open and bleeding is available for viewing on the ISM's website). S was hit on the leg with a stone. In the same area, but on a different day, Nick, an Australian activist, came between a Palestinian and a settler, and he got hit pretty bad. The role of foreigners who come to work with the ISM is to bear witness, monitor, protect, denounce, absorb the shocks, and upload videos and photos. The night before the action, there were only a few activists at the Nablus apartment; the rest had gone out early in the morning to participate in an action and hadn't yet returned. The group managed to block an Israeli road in the West Bank for fifteen minutes, originating a very long traffic jam before the army and the police came to clear them out. Some of the activists were arrested and then quickly released. Others got a stamp on their passports limiting their movement across the West Bank. Nobody was deported and the action was done in conjunction with Anarchists Against the Wall, the organization my friend HM belongs to. They even got a note in the Israeli newspaper, *Ha'aretz* and this made the action a fully successful event of counter-information.

The next morning, we arrived in Yanun at 7:15. There, we bought fresh bread and began to eat it compulsively because we all had empty stomachs. After drinking tea and coffee generously offered by a local family, we got to the olive tree terraces. The olive grove is crowned by a settlement. Barely visible, the settlement includes an IDF surveillance tower that the Palestinians are forbidden to look at. Looking in that direction gives soldiers legal justification to shoot. That is usually where attacks against peasants come from. I was deeply moved by the olive trees' generosity: to collect the olives, you only have to pass your fingers softly through the branches and the olives fall lightly with an opaque sound on plastic tarps extended on the ground to receive them. At the end of the day, the peasants we helped bade grateful farewell to us. Free labor, human shields, and foreign solidarity observers are not a matter of privilege, but of survival. Sami, who had been with us since early in the morning, stayed until we finished; Chris had the idea of putting ourselves at the service of the family that lived on the other side of the valley without ISM support. None of us knew that Sami was actually a baker and that he had to go to bed soon because his day started at midnight. He must had been very tired, and more so because he had only one leg and had been jumping from olive tree to olive tree all day. In spite of his difficulties moving around and his baker schedule, he decided to accompany us and be our translator.

The family across the valley accepted our help. They prepared tea for us while we waited for a car, coming through from the Israeli road, to load up the harvest. Their home was much closer to the Israeli settlement and tower; we weren't sure whether we'd get into trouble being there. We stayed for a while, and they offered us bread. The family was large and at its center was a beautiful matriarch dressed in an olive oil green dress with a black *kūfiyya* as a veil on her head; five daughters and a son, teenagers and small children, were all around helping with the harvest. The harvest is a family festivity to be enjoyed, an excuse to spend the day together, talk, eat, relax, and play while the sacks are slowly filled up with olives. When the car finally arrived, the bags were taken uneventfully to the highway. Someone said we were there to watch and protect, not to help carry things around, especially the women. We started our way back, but Chris said he wanted to make sure everyone left the grove safely, that we needed to get ready for danger if it came. Chris sells Palestinian olive oil in London: half a liter for five pounds, turning all the profits back to the Palestinian producers.

Like specimens contemplating each other in a double zoo, we smiled at the children playing on the dirt road and practiced our Arabic a bit, intoxicated with good conscience. During the trip back, the highlight of the day showed itself to us: a beautiful huge full moon visible from the left behind the hill. It took exactly four minutes for it to go up while the sun went down at the same speed on the opposite side. Activism as a mirror for the self, bringing out one's "good" side, projecting it onto the face of the unfortunate. Empathy transformed into adrenaline to push forth the limits of courage until reaching trauma to prove oneself, saving or helping the other to remind oneself "I am alive." Activism and anonymity: subjectivity completely thrown to a struggle dissolved into a critical mass, mixing singularity within a multitude of white, sweaty, anguished faces. On the way back, my companions exchanged tactics to provoke soldiers at checkpoints; they were all vegetarian, globalized, and living in prestigious occupied houses in Europe or in third-rate university campuses across North America. They listened to Manu Chau, admired Marcos.

What does it mean to be radical today? What pushes someone to be radical? Who is more radical? Foreign activists, Palestinian guerrillas from the 1970s, Islamic militants? Grassroots activists operate under the logic of human rights defense; that is to say, they denounce their violation and demand restitution but without long-term solutions; they use information and the media as weapons. They fluctuate between human rights advocacy, momentary combat in occupations, and transitory tactics; they are archivists of radical evil. What are the ethicopolitical implications of this means of activism elsewhere? What are the lessons that were learned or not learned from activism from the end of the 1960s and 1970s? Forty years ago, political work had to do with training, literacy, workshops from within or outside. Today it is about advocacy, documentation, and solidarity. The mandate of the ISM, commanded by the sometimes skeptical, other times enthusiastic Palestinians, is *passive* resistance. Palestinians work at the limit of these interventions: activists, in passion-action. A legendary US activist—Jack, the only person in the West Bank covered in tattoos and piercings head to toe—was deported last week after an eternal and unnecessary trial for having having been at a protest, in which he was hit by plastic bullets and swallowed tear gas, and for having overstayed his visa.

# Scapeg(h)o(s)at

For him whose name sounds like sa-l-t
Coinciding swift appearance,
When and why
A murmur passes through a falling horse
Whose scars he is making me bleed
And to his brother who is a warrior,
Translated to crystal blue light—
words bleeding me

## 1
## Ramallah [Warm] Spleen

Holding back the rain to come
Suddenly chose not to move toward me as a man or as a poet,
Amiss to name me Ophelia,
Instead you took me for a scape-ghost.

> Scape-goat
> Scape-ghoat
> Scape-ghost
> Guest + host = ghost

Windows and doors wide open,
I wish to break out from your silting triple equations,
Exile myself from the spell of the red earth, from the endless
    shaven hills.
Walking away from your mixed signals of capitulation and
    resistance,
From the confusion between movement with action

At best translated as impassibility, mon poète maudit.
You forgot
That these lips know how other lips have cut after,
Our hushed eco-graphia
On the skin: "Dans le véritable amour c'est l'âme qui enveloppe
    le corps."
And how songs of other times sailed back into our ears
Unannounced, out of joint, in eternal recurrence.
Knowing from the beginning that the odds were against me
I spoke words that can only be written, hid beneath.
Below, the memory that is now forgotten,
Once I could laugh my own tears.
From now on,
Make sure that window is tightly shut,
My soul might become the wind in the dark,
Come in and brush your skin with my breath until you fall asleep,
Sneak inside your chest so you breathe me,
Or having stumbled upon you in one of your Oliveiran walks,
My soul will be the moon embracing you with my rays.


## 2

Nah ist und schwer zu fassen der Gott.
Wo aber Gefahr ist, wächst
Das Rettende auch.
FRIEDRICH HÖLDERLIN[105]


## 3
## Waiting

Now, I know, settling accounts from a past life, I found myself living
on this side, walled-

*For Godot* in, *Waiting*. It was so dark and uncertain that I couldn't breathe.
I stopped reading signs. Instead, I addressed you sketching out a
theory of love, trying to resist the invisible forces making me move
oscillating, hesitating, making me fidgety and wonder: Will I be
more precious nights? As an attempt to breathe, I folded myself

into Orpheus-Eurydice, transforming doubt into its opposite, which is faith. Getting away from waiting, the first time I walked, I went too fast.

The face-to-face encounter is ethics and responsibility and it implies

Lévinas — responding to the call of the other, turning one's gaze toward his/her face. Yet, the face-to-face encounter is traumatic because I can never know how the other sees me, opening a

Lacan — rift between how I see myself and what I project onto the other, and that gives me anxiety. Also, in the face-to-face my scope of vision narrows because it is focused on the other's face. Postponing the face-to-face and walking facing forward are acts of faith—a leap out of incertitude and the eschewal of hope. The eschewal of hope in favor of the leap of faith I am trying to describe here is not a suspension of ethics, but its degree zero. It is not that I cease to address or to answer the other, but that I give my faith to the

Žižek — wholly other. Here faith is absolute difference, an absolute break, pure potentiality and possibility. Faith gives me the certitude of the other's love in its potential. I turn you into the subject of my faith, accepting that my desire is not enough to invite you to respond to my faith. What I believe is wholly independent of your will. The suspension

Saint-
Exupéry — of the face-to-face is not: "Aimer, ce n'est pas se regarder l'un l'autre, c'est regarder ensemble dans la même direction," as such love cannot be possible at the time of

Arendt — rampant individualism, when the future is still a bomb that we hear ticking in the present. Facing the tyranny of incertitude, all that can be afforded here is faith, neither hope (a luxury), nor doubt (doom). I have faith that Orpheus knows that I'm walking behind him,

For Godot — I have faith that Eurydice is walking behind me. Walking away from Waiting—but where to? There are no safe passages, as the roads I see are plagued with three-dimensional unbreachable obstacles, breaches of promises.

4

## Literary Misunderstandings

Deleuze   We are made out of pure pasts. The other (*autrui*) is the expression of a possible world—that is, the other presents himself or herself as a world to me, opening up in my past blisters that contain and envelop a multiplicity of possible worlds. When I encounter the world that the *autrui* presents to me, I inscribe in that one a possibility from an "I was" that can either be frightening or reassuring. Unknowingly, the encounter with the *autrui* actualizes a past that does not coincide with the subject I desire, the object of the possible world. When the possible world embedded in the *autrui* becomes frighteningly unbearable, the degree zero of ethics is endangered because such fear may cause the obliteration of intrasubjectivity, creating transparent machines. Insofar as narcissism is the realm of transparency, seeing through each other, we ceased to own our own appearances and became each other's

Žižek   masturbatory phantasms of our own, vulnerable narcissistic subjectivities. In making each other transparent, we became foreign to one another, uncanny, embodying hidden secrets.

Derrida   Operating under hostile-pitality we added up guests and hosts, summ(on)ing ghosts. We will never know how and which traces were actualized in the stories we told each other. In front of and behind the invisible, the inscription of our stories onto each other's skin threatened to return as a haunting. Seeing through, we leashed out memories before death, deception, the memorial sentiment of futile surrender and sacrifice. I fought in the name of opacity, tried to unveil secrets, to slice open spaces in between transparent images by speaking out, *touchée* . . . it was too late. You wouldn't hear about double souls, just about twins—and we already have twins elsewhere. Then, you'd become insensible

Schiller   even to your own affects and sufferings, poète maudit, absorbed with your impassible search for the gold that you believe can disentangle your loom, unfasten your freedom.

Today I point a finger back at you. I carried the burden of both of our desires, forced to disown my appearance and my knowledge, you bearing my gaze, silently, desperately gazing at the unseen. Your transparent silence said: memory is the prison of

MAH   desire, I am, we are trapped.

We were hardly able to separate the bad past from the potentially redemptive one, fearing that we would compromise memory. Yesterday a cat died inside *Endgame* and one of my lives—the one flayed bleeding the other's wounds—left accompanying him. Today I realize that I am rewriting the *autrui* from the site of my own forgotten memories.

## 5
## Unearthing the Clay Pots

"They are butchers when it comes to hospitality"

FROM "TRIP IN THE RUINS OF AL-WALAJA, Rihla Fi Atlal Al-Walaja," by Mustafa Khalil al-Sayfi[106]

The radically, unassimilable different needed to be sacrificed for the sake of the status quo. It was a sacrifice with no ritual, a killing with loving tenderness for the sake of self-

MAH   redemption, obliterating the excess proper to the appearance that could not be *factored*

into your life. In my despondency and certitude, what is there to do with the strict refusal of contradictions embedded in the possible world that I actualized from your

Nietzsche   past? We have known for a long time that, like in war, what is done out of love always takes place beyond good and evil, and that is why no end can ever correspond to the destructive potential of the weapon of choice: It was a deadly mortar. I am affected, not because I cannot believe in you any longer, but because you deceived us. That is why I amastonished, with Darwish—how can a ghost bleed?

Tuning out his cynicism, which is barely masking our bitterness, I started laughing. Glacial reason besieged him with her tentacles disguised as the last trench he could hold onto under the tyranny of incertitude, fighting the rule of temporariness with what seems to point toward normalization. What is a social legal pact for if not for the sake of preservation and permanence? Depositing his faith in his responsibility, amalgamating self-interest with common interests, he chose to be faithful to his responsibility, demanding what he believes he is entitled to receive from his community—if it comes, unearthed from hidden clay pots.

## 6
## What Remains

I am beginning to understand that it was not that revolutions failed but that the revolutionaries were poisoned with an illusory victory. Fake, because it disguised itself as such at a time in which other battles needed to be fought. And the revolutionaries couldn't see them. Slowly, I glimpse traces of safe passages, underneath. As you know, most of the time the road is lonely and we walk it under the tortuous illusion of desolation. This trip took me to a road inhabited by other loners, poet-warriors, waving

Arendt from afar and unveiling the illusion of the desolation of solitude to each other. We get together every now and then to confabulate new genealogies, seeking those lineages that

KF bind us together as the blue men tribe.

We are measuring the magnitude and the effect of misaffect and carelessness. It is the immeasurable mourning of the friend and the lover that had wings too heavy to accompany us. Desperate, he left to join Bartleby's army without warning while I

*State of* was reading the baskets of purple flowers in Darwish's poem. Sting-
*siege* ing scorpion blue, I am writing at dawn, haunted by the ghosts that begin to tell me their names, speaking their letters, intoxicated with the red of the earth. At night, I write intoxicatedwith nebulous arak shimmering nana. In the afternoons, I seek refuge in the fog, intoxicated by the crystal-clear light leaving bedlam with its dis-equation between the inside and the outside. The crystalline light is hard to bear here, and I am writing as a guest from the prophet's cave, inside Beckett's Endgame, a place beyond Sittlichkeit, which was blown away by the state of exception. Here the analogue of love is war, its opposite is pain instead of hate. We are sitting on the bare conditions of possibility for unconditional care, trying to assess the incommensurable consequences of disinterest and carelessness, figuring out how to practice radical ethics and hospitality, wondering where to aim our faith. The prophet is already pointing toward ethics without morality, suddenly lending me an eye to cry.

THE FIRST TIME I READ "Casa tomada," the short story by Julio Cortázar, I was puzzled because the takeover takes place in a "simple manner and without perfunctory circumstances." Cortázar wrote the story back in 1946; when I told it to the prophet he just smiled, as there are many parallels with his story, except for the simplicity of the takeover and how little resistance its inhabitants displayed as they were gradually expelled. The house in Cortázar's story is old and spacious, inhabited by a sort of marriage of siblings who receive money from their *fincas* and who are devoted to keeping up their home. The takeover begins one day, suddenly, at eight o'clock at night, with a deafening and imprecise sound. The first area to be occupied was one end of the hallway, so the siblings had to stay on the other side. The problem was that they had left many things that they were attached to in the occupied section. They started to live without thinking about their possessions or about the occupation, remaining silent in the kitchen and never raising their voices. Another day, at eleven o'clock at night, also unexpectedly, the house was completely taken over. The siblings had no choice but to lock up and leave. They felt sorry, the narrator tells us, when they threw the key down a nearby sewer to keep strangers from entering the now-abandoned house. The siblings' mix of resignation and silence reminds me of the impossibility of speaking out loud about the banal but real aspects of the occupation. Every day, Palestinians lose a bit of their territory, and it is impossible to measure the loss, speak about it, or imagine the invaders aside from their executors: the IDF.

I LET MEMORIES FLOURISH and begin flirting with fiction. Captivity is the Real; the experience of limits and falling in love delineate the extreme in which the *I* loses itself completely. When the heart's accounts don't add up, then the *I* begins to look for itself, reconstituting itself by being immersed in writing. In turn, writing becomes a thread that gets lost when it begins to outline a vertiginous labyrinth full of repetitions, turns, ellipses, a multiplicity of points of view, telling the same story over and over again as if I were filming a film scene with at least eight cameras. All to the rhythm of pirated Sufi techno and chain-smoking. Captivity and love are perceived as becoming Palestinian. Slowly, Palestine seeps under my skin, and I begin to stop fearing and hating the enemy. Beyond my prolonged visit, I start to feel at home, and although I don't share Palestinians' collective memory, the place has shown its scars to me, covered with a thin layer of dust that momentarily impedes bleeding but also prevents a scab from forming. "Stop speaking 'Muslim,'" Thierry told me the other day. I answered: "Are you upset because I said *In shā'allāh*? Oh, come on! It's the equivalent of 'Ojalá,' the title of Silvio Rodríguez's song (he is a Cuban protest singer). What about *yanni* (or whatever)?" "*Yanni* is a joker of a word, it is the exact equivalent of what Americans mean when they keep repeating *like*, *like*, *like*, which is the same as people in the Mexican north saying *tipo*, *tipo*, *tipo*." First of all, becoming is a linguistic operation soaking in pain and then pride, insolence and the impervious need to resist. The *I*'s complete fusion with writing for the cause feels futile, as is getting lost in the real of reportage recording the song of the victims so that the spectator enjoys the shame and indignation of the horror. Vulnerable narcissistic confession is for mediocre writers. I'd like to write against myself, to betray myself in writing, like Jean Genet.

I'm definitely not going to make it unscathed from my prolonged visit to the hell of the Palestinian tragedy, quoting Goytisolo in Sarajevo: as I bore witness to the tragedy, it entered into all of my body; it became a bomb that is ready to explode in the moral security zones, where those who enjoy luxuries after 1968, like the masturbathon for peace, and hippie organic food with yoga, techno, and MDMA; there, close to those celebrating differences, unaware that such celebration is a dispositive part of surveillance society that decided it is more effective to localize difference than to eradicate it. There, where those who enjoy globe-hopping and transnational connectivity, for whom borders are porous and who dare to condemn terrorist suicide attacks, without perceiving the crises propagated by the mass media like a virus, and without understanding the symbolism of desperate suicide. Art before life, why not?

"WHAT SORTS OF EXOTIC THINGS have you come across in Palestine?" Abul Jaz asked me the other day. I began to think and think and think . . . "Foreign activists!" I resist labeling or looking for the exotic, seeing the situation as ethnographer or anthropologist, like someone observing goldfish in a spherical crystal bowl, a sphere that has been created by my limited experience and knowledge. Instead of analyzing Palestinian resistance and the tragedy of the occupied, I do everything I can to make myself feel at home.

I try to live inside the tragedy, touching the keys that were not thrown into the sewer yet and that are inherited generation to generation, listening to talk about what has been stolen and expropriated, retouched by orality and memory. To observe the growth of religion neither as something unmodern nor as a sign of inverted development, but as a solution to the obscenity of an immoral situation, a simulacra of morality parallel to the simulacrum of the National Authority. What is better, Cuban or Soviet brutality in its last stages or at the beginning of market liberalization, sunken in amorality close to animal survival, or Saudi-style, Islamized capitalism? It seems that Islam (like all religions, as a matter of fact) accommodates itself well to the contradictions of "human rights" in late capitalism, which are the rights to happiness and success. Individual interests oppose the collective will of Islam and the interests of multinational corporations within capitalism. On March 20, key dates in the Christian and Islamic calendars coincided: the Messiah's crucifixion and the birth of the Prophet.

# Meanwhile, I Avoid Looking for Your Voice in Soundwaves

LAST NIGHT I GOT BACK FROM HAIFA where I spent the weekend with my new friends Maria and Dirar, and Dirar's roommate, Dabdoub. I met Maria the day of my talk at Bezalel, and I saw her again during her visit to Ramallah. To get to Haifa, I first took a bus on Friday to East Jerusalem. Maria came to fetch me at the station. She has a job at the mall just next door, in a discount clothing store. Her work uniform is black, and she told me that when Jewish clients come to her shop on Friday afternoons, they move quickly and nervously because they are in a hurry to go back home for Sabbath, and, she says, they are ruder to her than usual. While we were waiting for a bus that would take us to her home, a woman came up to Maria and began to talk to her in Arabic. Only 15 percent of the population in Haifa is Palestinian, and most of them come from elsewhere.[107] The glorious Haifa of their ancestors is gone: the buildings of Hadar are about to be gentrified, its filthy children keep running around, and the ghetto feeling overshadows the light of its past glory. What was yesteryear the city of lawyers and doctors, of educated, well-off Palestinians today exudes Northamericanizing vulgarity and bad architecture.

Dirar is a musician: he plays at least five instruments and is also a designer, filmmaker, and computer geek. Dabdoub is an actor and just moved to Dirar's house because he could no longer afford rent on his own; he also moved there because he noticed his friend was too isolated and depressed so he decided to keep him company and push him a bit to do things. They live in a big apartment in Hadar where I stayed for the first night. After having dinner we went to the German Colony, and we passed a place that I thought was very exotic: a twenty-four-hour dancing salon for Russian immigrants, full of middle-aged men and women, dancing and drinking, dressed in a very particular way. The ladies had high hairdos, leather ankle boots with heels, tight (mostly leather) skirts, a lot of makeup, and coats bordered with fake fur. We walked toward Ben Gurion Avenue, the long street that connects the esoteric Bahai Gardens with the Haifa port; in one of the many international Arab restaurants, we drank a *saḥlab* sitting among middle- and upper middle-class Israelis and Palestinians. Maybe because of the diversity of the people attending these gastronomic spaces, animosity and tension are felt everywhere; I felt my red *kūfiyya* attracting weird looks. After the *saḥlab* we enjoyed a chocolate cake, which for some reason inspired Dirar to go on a diatribe against what he calls the *calzones* (the term he uses for pretentious people) who hang around the place. For him, the people, the place, they were all *calzonic*.

Later at home, two friends of the trio showed up, students from Haifa University and members of the Palestinian Student Council. They gave me an issue of the journal the association publishes, and Samar told me about the camp she, along with her dad, uncle, and siblings, organizes every summer for children from her village, in the northeast, close to Lebanon. They told me that Palestinian students in Israeli universities suffer racism from both peers and professors. Something in the gaze of my new friends, "Palestinians from '48" reveals to me traces of racial and cultural alienation, that they have a thick skin, that they are tired from living like that. The Hadar is not only the Arab neighborhood in Haifa, but its poor zone, where the municipality recently did a project to fill the streets with what turned out to be quite mediocre in situ art installations, accompanied by guided visits to the neighborhood for those seeking culture and interested in liberal practices like visiting marginal urban dwellings. "We feel like we are the zoo!" exclaims Maria. When we toured the neighborhood, we passed her uncle's home where, in the summer of 2006, a missile from Hezbollah had fallen. Her uncle was badly injured and the neighbors, an elderly couple, died. The Israeli government gave them money to rebuild the house, and it is almost ready. It is possible that Maria's parents will move there because the uncle preferred staying in the temporary apartment the authorities offered him. The family's disgrace of having their home destroyed in this case is doubled: a bomb from Arabs that harmed Arabs in a war of ethnic factions fighting for territorial control.

The next day I took another walk with Dirar and Dabdoub around the Hadar (we had more light then). They showed me splendid houses, buildings from the British mandate, many in ruins, some inhabited. We were headed to the flea market when at the corner we came across someone else's memories, scattered in a pile of boxes full of books, vinyl records, toys, bibelots, photographs, letters, decorative objects, etc. It was sad to think that the person charged with emptying the apartment was probably not close to the person who had lived there. Otherwise her things wouldn't be in the trash. The memories seemed untouched, so we figured no one had been interested in them, expecting that the trash would take them away. We got very curious and began to explore the contents of the boxes without any passersby stopping to look at us suspiciously (the streets were empty, as it was Sabbath). How is it possible nobody cared about the memories of a dead old lady? Where were her granddaughters, who we assumed were the young ladies who appeared in the photographs dressed as soldiers? Her neighbors, friends, relatives? And the smiling Ethiopian women in the decades-old photographs? The boxes kept records from her whole life: letters in German, Romanian, English, and Hebrew that dated from the 1930s to the present. Portraits of the woman we presumed dead—the wife of Andrei Engel or Frau Engel, we deduced from the clues we found—in tourist sites and other unknown places in Europe, photographs of her husband at a bar called Mitzbah, the portrait of the 1950 *Clase pai* (or "dad's class") in Romania, snapshots of her granddaughters' birthdays.

We began to thread the stories together and decided that the woman had been of German origin and married to a Romanian photographer, and that they migrated to Haifa in 1948. We supposed that Mr. Engel was the owner of a photography studio because some of the photographs (taken in a studio or outside) bore the seal "A. Engel," with different addresses in Romania and Haifa. We inspected the content of the boxes for over an hour; we then felt responsible for giving life back to the memories, to extend the expiration date of those abandoned traces of a life. The inspection became a kind of ritual in which we exchanged hypotheses: "Are these her daughter and granddaughter?" "Around what time does she begin to appear by herself in the images? Perhaps she became a widow in the eighties." "Perhaps she did volunteer work with Ethiopian immigrants?" To complete the ritual, Dabdoub and I chose a bunch of images. I still have my part in a plastic bag, hidden in a book that has survived almost fifteen years of moving around. Postcards addressed to a Herr und Frau Andrei Engel; photographs of the couple surrounded by young black women; the couple standing before one of the doors of Old Jerusalem; images of her standing in front of a country house or a home in a European suburb (it looks like Germany); Frau Engel, very elegantly dressed, including gloves, in front of another suburban house in Europe; an image with, I assume, her daughters and granddaughters: one

FIG. 5. Archive intervention by Silvia Gruner (2017)

of the granddaughters is wearing her military uniform, as her Uzi rests verti-cally on the ground, held by her left hand. She has her grandmother's smile. Mr. Engel, sitting on fragments of roman capitals; his wife, floating on a pool aided by a plastic goose; a truck gone upside down on an Israeli highway from the 1950s; Frau Engel, holding a friend's hand, standing in front of many palm trees (Tel Aviv's Rothschild Avenue, perhaps?); a young woman pushing a baby stroller in a European city. In our minds, we drew a map of a life crossed by shared historical events in the twentieth century. Comfortable, prosperous lives, apparently easy and happy, and from the standpoint of my Palestinian friends, at the cost of the suffering of their people.

We continued our stroll all the way to the flea market, an impersonal ex-tension of Frau Engel's boxes—shoes, old *ḍūba* (heaters), clothes, bibelots—and we went back home. That evening I moved to Maria's house; she lives far away from the center of the Hadar, at the Hayam Bahar (the sea's eye). When I got there, Maria, her boyfriend, and a friend of theirs were drinking whiskey and smoking hash. And that's how an epic evening began in which we imagined absurd solutions to the conflict, played around with Mexican or Palestinian stereotypes, and kept laughing.

*insīt 'ini insīt* (I don't remember forgetting, I forgot forgetting, I lost my memory)

Maria's family is Christian and she is the second of three sisters. The next day I met one of them, an MA in Hebraic and Arabic letters. She accompa-nied me to the post office to send Nora—who was already back in Berlin—a CD and a book of Palestinian women artists. While I waited for my turn, a man cut in line in front of us. My new friend complained to him in Hebrew, and he responded furiously. I couldn't help meddle: "Excuse me, sir, you are being really impolite. Why are you screaming at my friend like this?" My comment only made him more angry. "How would you feel if a strange man yelled like this at your wife and daughter?" (He probably yells at them like that regularly.) The woman behind the counter gave us a sympathetic look and took care of us with kindness. From there, we went to have coffee on Mass Street, at the Hadara, and then went to see Dirar and Dabdoub so I could bid farewell to them.

I started my way back to Ramallah with a feeling of urgency; I felt a lot of nostalgia for the city, but I wasn't sure why. When I got there, I got together with J at Zan, we had a juice in al-Manara Square (I always get pomegranate, it is now my coming-back to the city ritual), and we came across a *Gaza ʿala bāly* protest. There were more soldiers and police officers (from the PNA) than protesters; Maha and Natasha, my activist pals from the ISM, were handing out candles to the participants, including the soldiers. The slogans were: "Gaza on my mind" and "*Fish Gaza fish baladi*" (Without Gaza I do not have a country). Around that time, the UN had finally declared the Gaza Strip a zone under humanitarian emergency because of the lack of electricity, gas, food, and medicine. *Qassām* missiles keep on falling around the Strip, and Israelis keep on imprisoning and killing people. J told me that a friend of his from school lost his life the day before yesterday, in a car accident, driving under the influence of alcohol.

I laugh at crying
Crying of laughter
I don't remember having forgotten
I had forgotten I didn't remember
Memory less
I laugh at crying


THE CURRENT MOMENT IS SERIOUS and very complicated. The three components of so-called globalization, which have been at work since the 1970s—the globalization of capitalism; neoliberalism as privatizing plunder of the commons; and, finally, the financialization of the economy—have failed to bring development and prosperity to the majority of the world population. To this we should add at least the energy crisis—the exhaustion of the fossil fuels that have been the basis of the world economy in the past two centuries—as well as the ecological crisis deriving from the destruction of global ecosystems that manifests in the catastrophic and ongoing climate crisis. The three crises of the economy, energy, and ecology were already on the horizon in the 1970s. In the war of the last fifty years, reactionary forces, obscurantism, and irresponsibility have triumphed over democratic and popular forces on a planetary scale. This has also meant losing decades in the resolution of very serious and urgent problems that were already laid forth at that time. In Peru, Nigeria, and Colombia, transnational lawsuits have been filed against extractive corporations that have damaged populations and their environments.[108] In Bil'in, the struggle is for decolonization through human rights and moral restitution through economic compensation.[109] I read in the news that Lula has given back land to the MST in Brazil.

AFTER A TORTUOUS WEEK IN TEL AVIV, preparing an alibi and putting together a dossier to justify my *séjour* in Israel, I once again manage to make it back to Ramallah. A thousand suns shine above the roofs of Ramallah in its dry winter. The rain simply did not come. Suddenly, a three-day storm, accompanied by strong winds, paralyzed the city with snow. The snow siege coincided with your visit, coming to tell me in person that you had gotten engaged. We had already said goodbye three times. *'Ana mrashḥa ktir* (I am very sick with a cold). Desperation and detachment go together. It's been a hundred days in Ramallah. The Sapphic honeymoon with Ramallah, indulgent love, attentive to my needs. She asks me if her streets are too slippery, if the convenience stores sell me what I need; she prods me to add another layer of clothing because of the cold. I spend a delicious morning in which sodomite ghosts visit me and take some of your space. Warm spleen. I give myself the task to write until I expel your name from the page. Normalization of relations, dialogue, cooperation, double bind, nullification of the possibility of resistance. . . . What maintains the normalization of everyday life is religion, the social tissue. Where is the space for subversion?

THE CITY IS BEAUTIFULLY COVERED with a thick layer of fog. A man came to fix the heating and we finally have hot water, *Al-ḥamḍulillāh!* Maria travelled from Haifa with her boyfriend, and we spent eight hours straight talking at Zan. Moheeb joined us and we discussed the cultural and political crisis; we also had a productive debate about the problematics of NGOs. Hanan, a gorgeous actress from Haifa, was also there because she had come to Ramallah to stage a feminist play that will open at Al-Kasaba in two months. Dirar and I decided we were going to found the Ramallah underground (with a branch, of course, in Haifa). I have been reading Emile Habiby's *The Secret Life of Saeed: The Pessoptimist* (1974). In the Arabic title, *mutashā'il* is composed from the words *mutashā'im* (pessimist) and *mutafā'il* (optimist).[110]

The novel mixes a lot of humor, the fantastic, the mystic, the tragic, and the true with the survival of a Palestinian from Haifa in Israel. After he is promised that if he cooperates with Israelis, he will receive help getting the woman he loves to return, the character becomes an informant. The pessoptimist cannot be judged; he is a comic fool, a human being who desires a simple and pleasurable life. His son is horrified by his father's attitude and dies fighting as a fedayeen; his death equals freedom, against the pessoptimist's pseudo-liberty, as lives immersed in contradictions trying to survive the situation of the occupation in differing ways. Habiby puts together disconnected fragments from the surface of reality to account for events and a catastrophe that seems contingent, even inexplicable; he accentuates a sense of suffering that derives from chaotic and senseless forces. In a way, he liberates the perpetrators of guilt and responsibility; he laments the situation instead of blaming the Israelis.

Against the grain of Habiby's strategy, when documenting histories of violence and suffering in marginalized communities, are we facilitating real change in people's lives? Or we are only appeasing our consciousness with what Luc Boltanski calls "a politics of piety"?[111] The use of testimony as a tool to mobilize solidarity has created a disquieting situation through which painful intimate memories are validated, manifesting their interiority, as if experiences were merchandise in ads. The theaters of witnessing have become a way to validate certain moments of historical memory, which acquire more weight than others and a greater intensity of loss and suffering.

Bush is visiting the city, that is why the streets were shut down yesterday and a curfew was imposed in certain areas. Along with him came about four hundred snipers who took posts on strategic rooftops across Ramallah. People are visibly annoyed, undone, sad; the mood is like the fog covering the hills today. In truth, the excessive security measures are lived like an insult, considering recent incursions and cleansing undertaken by the PNA and the IDF in the West Bank. The visit is perceived as a useless interruption of everyday life to remind us that we live under the tyranny of incertitude. Abdel came to celebrate with me the news that there will be a protest (which hasn't been officially cancelled) against Bush's visit. My first protest, I admit with a lot of shame. I admire what Nora from Berlin says: "I know that protesting is useless; I still do it, though, with the hopes that I am wrong."

I spent the afternoon—from one o'clock until eight thirty!—at Sonia's, talking and talking. I enjoy our discussions very much, though they sometimes take uncomfortable turns, especially when I feel inadequate or fear being insensitive, or when she prefers not to point at the obvious. Samar, her friend and neighbor, came down for a while; we had carrot cake and we discussed love, men, sex, and the possibility of opening a clandestine sex shop in Ramallah. My idea of a motel did not please them; Hamas would never allow it. Samar's daughter married someone important to rebel against her mother. Later on, Emad, her daughter Bisan, and Sonia's brother joined us. We had lamb head with rice and *labni* peasant style, digging with our fingers in between the skin and bone, opening up the skull and extracting pieces of brain. That form of eating was familiar to me, intimate, informal. Each dug inside their preferred parts of the head from the communal dish at the center. Sonia's brother told me that in old Arabic there were up to ninety-nine words to designate *sword*, each pointing at a situation or a characteristic of the bearer of the weapon. We discussed politics and Bush's visit; we noted that Bush came to discuss Iran and saw an incursion into Gaza as more or less a solution for peace, that *Al Jazeera* sides with Hamas and Mossad (is there an option?). According to Samar, a day before the famous visit, flyers were distributed in the city announcing the curfew and the four hundred American snipers.

That afternoon, I walked around Ramallah Tahta looking for the shop where you can find goat's cheese, but I couldn't find it;[112] I went up Rukab all the way to Jerusalem Street, and from there I came down Tireh and took a turn on your street. I could swear you were calling. I felt the disaster coming. The city was quiet and cold, there were a few cars going around, not a lot of movement. I hoped that the calmness outside would help me be calm from within. Eventually, I felt the anguish pass, I came home, had a bit to eat, and continued reading Žižek.

What is the logic of disaster? Disaster is a failure in the sustainable consideration of relationships among the given, when the relationship between one thing or another goes wrong. In economics, disaster occurs when commodities cannot be linked to markets, when capital stops flowing and cannot relate to work. AIDS and cancer are disasters because there is an overproduction of cells that stop relating to the body's logic. In philosophy, disaster implies the separation of thought from history. Psychological disaster is an instance in which individuals become incapable of relating to the world, and political disaster is when the relationship between those who wish to be represented and those authorized to guarantee representation is broken.

When I respond to the infinite call that emanates from the vulnerable face: Here I am! A free ego not only integrates perturbations but creates them, exploits all form or *stasis* (internal conflict). This is the degree zero of the elemental called by Freud *death pulsion*. The definitive traumatic thing is the encounter of the I with myself. The dialectic between homeostasis (normalcy) and shocks (traumatic effects) is not enough. The definitive shock is that of the violent imposition of a proper homeostatic order, it is the tracing of the limit between the internal and the external.[113]

Disaster is the imposition of an oppressing and denigrating normality.

# Second Version

*Budros*, *Hajar* = Peter (stone, rock). Hajar is an Islamic figure devoted to interpreting the Qur'an and also the character in the Bible who keeps the keys to heaven's gate. The keeper of the key to the gate of the Palestinian heaven seems to be remembrance.

I read Derrida on memory, trauma, and mourning: "Although we remember the worst in the name of respect for memory, of truth, for the victims, the worst always threatens to come back. Both memories (commemorative and traumatic), fuel, aggravate and conjure one another." And: "Mourning and haunting were unleashed at that moment, just before the mere possibility of death, that is to say, the trace is reborn as immediate survival as if were being 'televised.'"[114]

Resistance to mourning what was lost in the Nakba is part of the agenda of Palestinian resistance. How can the memory of the lost land be separated from mourning the damages of war and exile? How can the "useful" past and memories be kept beyond pathological melancholy but without normalizing dispossession and occupation? I am thinking of Cicero who refuses to bury his dead; his is a postponed mourning, out of sync with melancholic duration. In Freud, memory is the root of trauma, but it is also the source of its resolution: pain is relieved by mourning the events that caused the trauma, and thus mourning can be the key to a gradual return to normality.

One of the forms of resistance against Israeli occupation is refusing to mourn what has been lost. How can any kind of future be habilitated?

Your silences tell me all these things: that you are unable to mourn your losses and that resistance—or your inability to resist—became the prison of your desire. Your inability to mourn made you lose the horizon of the future and fall into melancholy. Melancholy is the incapacity of letting go of what has been lost: a destiny that is fulfilled before death.

Today I learned the most beautiful word in Arabic:

الكان (**kan**)

It is a verb that is conjugated in the present but that only acquires meaning as a "being" in the future or as "having been" in the past. In other words, it denotes a state of being only in the past but with a future possibility that can never be in the present (as an it will/was).

KHADIJEH WAS WAITING FOR ME beautifully and elegantly dressed. I tell her I want to know everything about you, your story. How is the personal not the political? Is it? She is from Jordan; her father was a politician who encouraged her to study and did not allow her to marry at fourteen. People were surprised that she had been reading Simone de Beauvoir. She moved to Cairo to study psychology at the Vienna School, which had the first university psychoanalysis department in the Arab world. She also studied Lacan, especially the mirror stage: the mirror is everywhere, and I can only see myself in the other or through the other. This concept marked a whole generation of women—how do we relate to it today in the era of mass hedonism?

What was her political awakening like? During the Nasser years, she tells me, she gravitated toward the Nationalist Student Party and the Palestinian Student Union. She was able to work for the latter, but she was engaged with the Nationalist party although she disagreed with their slogans such as "blood, land," which she found fascist. It is a pity that I can only get to know her story in English translation. I would very much like to listen to her tell it to me in her language, to be able to see her gestures describing in Arabic what it meant for a woman to be politicized in 1960s Cairo. She did a lot of theater, she was involved in the vanguardist scene, there were up to five plays a day plus opera and a lot of underground political energy. Back then, she did not know about the PLO, only later did she learn about it. This is when she met her Palestinian husband; for her it was natural to fight at his side for liberation. They moved to Jordan where she began to work as a psychologist for the PLO's soldiers. On the side, she began to work at a women's refugee camp. Mustapha, her husband, produced content for radio and television. Everything changed for them after Black September ("the worst battle I had ever seen," she said). I am still trying to understand the complexity of Black September and its consequences for the relationship between Jordanians and Palestinians ("We are the same people, 80 percent of us are bound to them by marriage ties") and the resistance movement there. She organized workshops for women. She tells me it was difficult to get to know the women, which is why she worked with them individually, visiting them in their homes, help-ing them with practical and everyday things, teaching literacy, and teaching them how they could be active in the revolution. The Hashemite kingdom sympathized with the Palestinian cause (Jordan's army fought spontaneously alongside the fedayeen in Karameh) until the Palestinians acquired too much power in Jordan and were expelled.

In 1969 the leadership of the resistance moved to Beirut where Nasser allowed the militia to live and organize. In Beirut she did the same work to help women better their everyday living conditions, taught them how to cook and adapt. She also taught refugee women to read; they were mostly workers in shoes and food factories. Then, she began to make films with her husband and to compile an audiovisual archive for the PLO. "It is all history now, we lost the revolution, we are in the worst situation possible, the PLO made many mistakes, Israelis are stronger." Khadijeh talked about the sol-idarity delegations, about when she was invited to Western Europe, to the Maghreb and other Arab countries, to Russia and China, to share her expe-rience in the struggle.

Foreign filmmakers came and went. In 1976 she began her first film about Palestinian children, *Children without Childhood*. She had two sons. In 1982 they had to flee from Beirut back to Jordan. We did not talk a lot about the 1980s but rather about the Intifada, about the resistance networks that were woven from the inside and from the outside; the Palestinians from the Oc-cupied Territories that came to Beirut on scholarships were politically and militarily trained, and became the leaders of the Intifada. At that moment, an Intifada seemed the only possibility for resistance because the fight from the outside seemed to have already been lost. The film archive she and Mus-tapha compiled was kept in a warehouse, guarded by two young women, for which they paid rent for thirty years. When the war began in 1982, the French Embassy protected the archive by placing the French flag outside the build-ing. After 1986, the archive disappeared without a trace. Only six movies re-mained, and in 2007 a book about the PLO's Film Archive was published. The book is more than a list of films: it is the partial reconstruction of the archive.

What were the films about? Life in refugee camps, the challenges of every-day life, resistance, political discussions. Sometimes the subsidy to make the movies conditioned the content (they had asked her to make a movie about the environment, they rarely funded fiction films because they thought they were useless). "When you think about it, the Palestinian Revolution was the only one that came with its own filmmaking: Russian movies were produced in the 1920s, Cuban in the 1960s, and none in the Algerian Revolution." For

Khadijeh, making a film means a lot of responsibility, "You have to find the right language, you need more than studying film to become a filmmaker. I spent many sleepless nights trying to find the connection between two shots—we have to make people see what you are trying to see and show." In 1989 she moved to the West Bank, and she talked about the contrast between Palestinians who were returning (who had a different vision of the world, training, education) and Palestinians from "here." The differences opened up breaches in the society between liberals and conservatives. For her, the current situation is a disaster. Khadijeh worked for the elections council for three years, again with women, and they managed to increase the quota of women participating in the elections.

What is the connection between psychoanalytical and political work? Political practice is a form of women's empowerment. I promised to give her copies of Godard's movies. She told me that she would like to find a way to subsidize a Palestinian film association but that she does not have the funds yet. She insists on something that can have continuity, like educating people to make high-quality movies: "A hundred years ago films were mute and today they are blind." Film is important because it is the most popular art form and therefore the most powerful. She discussed the problem of fragmentation in the Palestinian experience: those in exile in other Arab countries, Europe, or North America; Palestinians in Israel; those in Gaza; those from the Occupied Territories who came back after Oslo; those with privileges and education and the less fortunate. There is a huge gap also between the generation active in the 1960s to 1980s and the children of the Second Intifada; they hardly have discussions among themselves, and there are many pending difficult questions to be asked. The old generation talks about the errors they committed and blame each other. The old generation sees the young as attempting to solve the conflict by hugging the Israelis. J told me he was recently at a bar in Tel Aviv (he got a permit to cross over from Ramallah to attend an art exhibition), and when two Israelis heard he was Palestinian, they came to embrace him.

# 'Um Al Burjayn (The Mother of Two Towers)

KIFFAYAH FLOATED IN THE SWING while Aude was absorbed digging a hole in the earth. The voice of their grandmother reached them sweetly resounding in the space between them, calling them for '*asha*'. Their days passed by leisurely and quietly. Mornings, they helped the rest of the family work the land. They began a couple of hours after the sun had risen, the hour when the sky paints itself in clear blue and one invariably begins to feel trapped inside an oven. This atmospheric combination does not allow measuring distances according to degrees of clarity. Visibility is completely transparent, and that is why distance is measured at scale: according to the size of what is seen in the distance as opposed to its clarity on the visual horizon. Kiffayah squatted beneath the shadow of a generous olive tree. Thinking about the upcoming fall harvest she remembered the feeling of brushing her hands through the easy branches of the olive trees, the sound of the fruit falling on the plastic tarps, the smell of tea being prepared on the fire. After a while, the infinite red earth began to bore her, she felt tired and dislike for the task of fertilizing the earth with goats' manure; the shovel weighed on her and she was thirsty as dust harassed her throat. She looked at Aude from the corner of her eye; he had been given more difficult chores than his sister, but different ones, and he fooled around, postponing work without feeling bad. Cursing her summer vacation, her mind went back to the cool streets in the old city of Nablus where she lived with her parents, to the wooden balcony where she would drink tea sitting in a small chair attentively listening to conversations with the visitors. She evoked the scenes she saw on the street from the balcony, the comings and goings of people doing their shopping and gossiping, the offkeyness of the muezzin: Was it the voice or the genre? With her chin on her knee, her semilazy hand mixed the earth with the fertilizer, poc poc poc. She picked up weeds here and there. Her wild curls domesticated by a headscarf framed her face and, right then, Kiffayah wished her eyebrows and eyelashes were already thicker so the sun would not hurt her eyes so much. Her thoughts then wandered to the mixed flavor of cheese and sugar in her favorite desert, the *knāfa*. She stood up to collect another pail of shit and let Aude help her. In Sabbarin (Sebastia) there is nothing between the *jabal* (hill) and the sea. With undulating terraces, a continuous valley draws a platform that, when contemplated, creates vertigo. Nablus is very different: it is a deep valley surrounded by extremely high mountains, and this is why she feels protected there, at home. The wind comes with the curfew in the afternoons, without interrupting her internal peace, tucking the city in, her merchants, her nightmares and ideals from yesterday. Drops of sweat evaporated quickly leaving traces of salt in her hair and on her neck. The land extended immensely before her as her imagination revived the noisy streets in Nablus, the busy movement of people in the mosque at the end of the street, the community bakery, fresh young men out from the *ḥamām*, the guilt of skipping the mid-afternoon prayer transitorily expiated, with their ears full of politics, religion, and morality. She dreamt of fresh stones and wide open windows, marbles and soccer games, with secret ghost-haunting escapes to the old cemetery. At the end of the day, halfway between the house and the orchard, she ran into Abu Alhafiz, passing by in his car carrying olive oil bottles. If it were meant to be exported, the label would boast its properties and multiple uses: "To be consumed with food, to cover the body, for the hair, scalp, dry or normal skin, to lubricate passions and family fallouts, to intensify textures and smells, to celebrate community and the generosity of the land." Without hesitating, Kiffayah asked Abu Alhafiz to give her a ride back home. She set the bucket aside, announced her father's name, and got in the car. The trip was smooth, considering the usual inspections and hostility of the roadblocks and checkpoints, the internal reaffirmation, invariably and without hesitation: "I am from here." They made it home before sunset, her mother greeted her with love, she sat at the table for dinner and then went to bed and fell into a deep sleep. She began to dream with images of the place where the *jabal* and the sea become one. The commotion she heard downstairs hours later woke her up with a jolt. It was her grandmother and a dozen people from the village who had come to tell Kiffayah's father that the worst had happened: the woman's grandchild had been kidnapped by settlers from the neighboring settlement. Before giving up and coming to Nablus to give the news to the family, they had searched for her everywhere; they now wanted to call the national police, the United Nations. The enemy persists, fearing the others' memories, and since then Kiffayah is known in Sabbarin (Sebastia) and Nablus as *'um Al Burjayn*.

"FREEDOM HAS A SPACE, AND whoever is admitted into that space is free; whoever is excluded is not free."[115] Some confuse freedom with the loss of direction or the absence of goals. When I feel my spirit is dislocated, it seems to me painful to have to bear the crystalline beauty of the Palestinian sky. The sky exudes freedom. But not everyone have access to the space underneath it.

I spent the afternoon at Zan with J, who told me about the time of the invasion and of the Second Intifada, when he was thirteen or fourteen, and he would go up to the front to throw stones and Molotov cocktails. The vanguard was trapped between the Israelis and the stone throwers behind them, that is why the most common wound is having a stone hit you in the back of the head. Once, he and his friends made a huge slingshot to launch a gas tank. The tank did not get very far, but it exploded a couple hundred meters from an Israeli outpost. They would only invade the city partially. During the incursions, his parents had no clue where he was, and it was impossible to forbid him to throw stones against the invaders. Most of the men between eighteen and forty were in prison. A friend of his (a schoolmate from the prestigious Ramallah Friends School) is serving three life sentences for having taken part in a kidnapping and murder of an Israeli.

The psyche gets used to oppression: eventually, people stop complaining about the checkpoints as long as they're not detained there for too long. Yesterday, twenty Palestinians were killed in Gaza in a battle that lasted for almost a whole day. Among the dead there was the son of a Hamas leader and an Ecuadorian worker living in a nearby kibbutz.[116] Yesterday afternoon, a protest against the killings was repressed, and today Abbas called for a general strike in solidarity with Gaza.[117] But from here, Gaza feels like a different planet. A few weeks ago, J began to regularly teach chess to children from a refugee camp in Jenin.

Once the oppression is normalized, war gets embedded, constantly making the following mental states alternate: melancholia (warm spleen), furious anger, panic attacks, clinical depression—all underscored by divine madness and wild delirium.

FIG. 6. Cliché of Palestine as intractable (Edward Said). Photo during the shooting of the Schmesh short film taken by Rami Alarda and used as the cover for the journal *This Week in Palestine*, January 2008

DEAR M, Azmi was giving me a ride to al-Manara Square, just when you rang me. I lost the call, I returned it, you lost it, called me back. When I was crossing *Shar‘* Rukab by foot, on my way back home, I tried to describe to you the mood of the city, which is completely new to me. An *’iḍrāb* (or general strike) had been declared by the PNA in solidarity and in protest of the murdered in Gaza. The city was paralyzed all day; only a few people were walking on the streets at four o'clock in the afternoon when we were on the phone. All felt quiet; when I told you about the *’iḍrāb*, you whispered: "It feels like war." I stopped on my tracks. "What?!" I exclaimed, while I looked at the car coming toward me at medium speed. "It feels like the war is about to begin," you repeated, a bit louder this time. I stood paralyzed while the vehicle turned right to avoid me, and when I tried to squeeze words out from my brain, the neurons tried to direct my body away from the danger and toward the sidewalk, on the other side of the street. After the scare I thought: "You do know what war feels like and I don't. Maybe I will one day." I got safely to the other side of Birzeit Street, and at that moment the immanent cracks of the state of permanent crisis widened a breach between us. Here everything is in crisis. Capitalism itself is a crisis, so maybe we shouldn't worry when things don't work; rather, we should be concerned when things actually work. It is hard not to internalize the particular state of crisis from this place. As I began to feel the signs of low blood sugar in my body, you blamed me for always bringing my crises to you: for instance, when I visited you in Tel Aviv. And for not paying enough attention to your needs. But, as I said, the crisis is immanent, both here and there. Life is permanent stress—being in a hurry, like in French, *je suis (op)pressée* by the passage of time—always at the verge of something, with the mandate to be hyperproductive. As a solitary hedonist individual, I find it difficult to find airy recharging pauses in between your illness (permanent headaches and sleeplessness), sociopathic moments, the territoriality that is proper to your time and space, and my attempts to understand the possible ways in which we could negotiate our territories. You were yelling at me on the phone that you have no time to explain to me why you're yelling at me. You complain that I don't behave enough like your friend or like a guest when I visit you, that we don't spend enough time together. You know my misanthropic side and you know I'd rather stay home to read a book or watch a movie than go to the beach with a bunch of your friends. And I haven't told you, but yoga gives me panic because of the capacity it has to render me numb to certain stimuli, allowing me to fold myself within myself breathing and bringing mind and body in sync, when nothing outside feels in sync.

When I visit you, something weird happens: an asymmetry is developed between my Sartrean nausea and your strange illness derived from disquieting revelations regarding your conditions of existence that are triggered by my mere presence. Freedom for you is a given; to me, it is the culmination of a relationship that we establish with our own lives. That is why I become Magdalene. I know it is tough for you to know I live here, although I hadn't realized how much until now. But it's not personal! I wondered if our friendship would survive my prolonged visit to Ramallah. Remember I told you we should consider each other family, to avoid having our political differences distance us? The last two times I went to Tel Aviv I was experiencing bigger crises than usual. The first was when I had to fill out an express application at Foreign Relations to apply for a scholarship (because my faculty had refused to give me one to finish my PhD). I had to solve the problem of the application via Mexico City, Puebla, Lyon, Toronto, and Chicago, then somewhere in Texas. I was lucky enough I could be at your place where I had access to a phone, email, and Skype until I solved the situation. During the crisis you never asked me once if I needed anything (I had everything from you, I suppose), you asked me to spare you the details. The second crisis was the one I underwent at the border, which felt like a life crisis at the time. Thanks to your hospitality, I could stay at your home until I managed to get the necessary documentation to go to the Ministry of Interior to extend my visa. When I told you that to get my visa extended I needed to find an Israeli to accompany me to the ministry and vouch for me in Hebrew, you left me the keys to your apartment and went away on vacation. I don't blame you for not helping me out in this way; I suppose you think there is a lot at stake if you get in trouble because of me. I suppose there is a lot more at stake for you in your life than for HM, the refusenik who generously ended up accompanying me. I suppose, finally, I could say I am sorry for coming to you with unexpected crises linked to our attempts to contain our own territories (like when the police places those hollow semispherical containers on top of abandoned packages or luggage in public spaces to absorb the shock in case of a detonating bomb).

Am I your *scapeg(host)* too? I feel like you push the borders further and further away, and I'm hoping nothing gets destroyed in the process. It has become unbearable for you to have someone you care about living in the Occupied Territories, so blame me, because I never gave you the option. Your people are annihilating those I call my friends. In my naive impulse to mediate, I failed, of course, and became schizophrenic in the process. Every time I make an effort to come to Tel Aviv I try to put my Palestinian life behind so I can breathe in the streets of your city. Does something similar happen to you? This situation reminds me somehow of a passage from Sonia's book (Sonia is one of my teachers here) in which she tells the anecdote of an Israeli anthropology student who would visit her regularly in her cell during the thirty-six months that she remained in prison in her early twenties, in the late 1960s, incarcerated for belonging to the Communist Party. They were the same age, had similar interests, and became friends, until one day the Israeli woman asked Sonia: "If one day we would meet at a battlefront, would you shoot me or throw a stone at me?" Now I see what is at stake and what changed in the past thirty years; today, an Israeli would never be allowed to regularly visit a Palestinian in an Israeli jail. I worry that when you ask me not to visit you again during a crisis—and when you reproach me for not being sensitive enough to your needs—it's the same as the question that the Israeli anthropologist asked Sonia. Are you already? When did we become enemies? After all, at a given moment, individuals are always called to order by their community.

AT DAWN, THE WIND BEGAN screaming in Ramallah; I heard it from the bottom of the valley where my apartment building sits. The wind bounces right at the corners of my bedroom and comes back in a curved line, drawing an uneven pattern. When this happens, Ramallah forgets a little more, just as it has the names of streets and places from the 1960s, just as buildings demolished by tanks or bombs are erased and then rebuilt. Like memories exit my body through my hair and pores, Ramallah becomes memoryless, as its inhabitants are in perpetual movement, with each incursion, as change speeds up, under the tyranny of incertitude. Ghosts remain wallpapered among successive layers of martyr posters, transformed into *décollages*, decorating the doors of shops and the walls of homes across the city. Martyrs hide behind the freshest poster, the most recent hero. The memoryless city is not like Mahmoud Darwish's Beirut, nor like the city filmed and documented by Akram Zaatari, Walid Raad, or Waël Noureddine.[118] There are no traces of bullets, debris is scant, new buildings have been erected. All in Ramallah is impermanent, like Arafat's tomb, which is designed to be transferred to Jerusalem at any moment, like the refugees in exile waiting any other opportunity to go back to Palestine. Everyone passes through with the wind bouncing on the hill, and in each curve that the current draws as it whistles through the valley, people lose a bit of their strength, of their memory, and, when possible, they migrate elsewhere to wait, not to remember.

> Depression floats like suspended thinking
> Flying over the wall
> One is a clown

Sally came to greet me with a kiss and was truly happy when I told her I had a very productive day at the library. Sally is the most amazing woman I have ever met. She works at the library at Qattan, but she has another job at the Palestinian writers' association. Later on, she would move on to work at the municipality. She has two gorgeous daughters and a cat. When I visit her, she multitasks like no one I've ever seen before. Even more than me! "*Bisura'a!*" She tells her daughters. Hurry up with the homework! While she loads the washing machine, she tells me about her parents in Jenin, then she swiftly moves to the kitchen to heat up some delicious chicken and rice. She sends her daughters off to sleep, opens a bottle of wine, we each have a glass. Her husband arrives, says hello, goes upstairs. Sally is one of the people I admire the most, here and elsewhere. I can't overstate how generous she was to me during my stay in Ramallah and afterward.

I think about my discussions with the prophet about letting the universe devour us instead of trying to swallow the universe. Thirty is the age of physical plenitude. Forty, the age of prophecy. To overcome oneself or to live a different existence than the one that was predestined to us—that is the definition of prophecy.

I resist becoming foam. I put on my American Apparel boy's briefs and feel a little like Carrie B., and remember suddenly the strange conversation I had with AH about the book that won the foundation's award this year. The text tells the story of a guy who cannot forget the vision of a tattoo on his girlfriend's back as he fucks her from behind, but neither can he forget the sound of the exploding bomb that killed her, right when they were fucking. I spend my days in autistic ecstasy working on a text and feeding myself tahini with honey, bread, and coffee. From the ivory tower to the trench. In Palestine, no one has ever asked me my religion, ever. Sometimes I can't stand listening to Rami Khalifé's song "Scene from Helleck," but I can't stop listening to it either. The accursed poet is the one who cannot produce effeminate literature or poetry and thus avoids wasting his artistic sensibility on having sex. The artist rejects all kinds of passion that could chain him to emotional or physical reality. Embittered, he becomes insensitive to a life that he could imagine desiring, and he displaces his feelings on an unrealistic pathos, on the creation of a fictive heart. In this way, he can claim the most refined affects, the deepest suffering, while he remains impassible, both reclamation and impassiveness, simultaneous demands from his art. There is indeed a Mexican version of this pathology of the male genius poet. Clowns.

> *'ana zah'āna*: I'm bored
> *sa'dūny*: Help me
> *mishwār*: I'm taking a walk

In my country, journalists are murdered and silenced. Sally hugs the *ṣūba* and absorbs so much heat through the skin of her thighs that they are intensely red, almost burnt. The cold numbs her thighs and she can't feel the burning or the dryness.

COME MY WAY. Standing outside of Zan, two good friends, without being really sure what to do, make a decision. The couple who are my neighbors offer to give me a ride home. That's how F came to join me in the trench. He was so drunk that when two kittens approached him on the sidewalk and he petted them, he fell over and ended up landing on one of them. We shared the cold of the night, he took me in his arms and he touched me a little. The next morning, he hid his balding head under a hat, washed the dishes, and made coffee. We talked about Salman Rushdie, Shakespeare, and *Les Bienveillantes* by Jonathan Littell. He asked me if I found myself trapped between two visions of the conflict.

YOUSEF: Why did you leave with the last drunk at the bar? To try to wake him up?
ME: His arms would bring me consolation because his drunken eyes can look straight at my soul.

Later that day, at the library, a young woman came to do her afternoon prayer in the room where I was writing. It happens regularly. I feel very un-comfortable, and when they come, I always leave the room. The librarian gets mad at me and asks me to stay at my table: "Don't help them go to heaven!" she always tells me. That day, between 9:18 and 9:25 AM, I felt an intense pain in the middle of my chest.

I LIVE HALF AN HOUR of absolute happiness riding a horse a family we visited in Qalandya lent me. I had experienced a similar joy when I ran sinking in the snow, feeling temerarious and carefree, crossing back and forth across the small soccer field near the art academy from which you can see P'sagot, the Israeli settlement.

The remedy that finally worked to counter sadness consisted of rinsing my throat with heavily sweetened Nescafé. I think about the *qassām* missiles as a form of temporary relief of the asphyxia created by the siege. A desperate act, emptied of a political goal, even of destructive power. There was a suicide attack at a mall in Dimona, a city in the south of Israel, very close to Be'er Sheva, forty kilometers away from Ramallah. There were many wounded, among them a woman. The security guards killed one of the suiciders before he could blow up his belt. Responsibility for the attack was claimed by the Al-Aqsa Martyr Brigade and by the Popular Front for the Liberation of Palestine.[119] It is unknown if the attackers were from Hebron or Gaza.

Unlike anarchy, which means breaking the law in the name of collective freedom, corruption means breaking norms in the name of self-profit. A corrupt person monopolizes power for his or her own benefit, while anarchist power resides in its potential destruction in the name of a collective higher purpose.

Gilles Deleuze called the phenomenon "Oedipus in the Colonies," which happens when a person travels to an exotic or dangerous place without being able to leave behind a personal agenda or, even less so, a Western frame of reference.[120] For instance, you leave home because of a failed love story, looking for a new love or searching for a lost father figure. The result is a sum of activities, experiences, intentions, and finalities that happen *elsewhere*, that are inscribed in a text, film, photographs, or any other kind of artistic or journalistic expression as an allegedly objective state of affairs, told through a hidden personal drama.

The sunlight begins functioning again, and now warms everything up. My heart is no longer mine, and I submerge compulsively in "Scene from

Helleck," seven minutes and forty-five seconds, seven minutes and forty-five seconds, seven minutes and forty-five seconds, seven minutes and forty-five seconds. I visit *al-qanḍul al-maksīky* (the Mexican representative in the Palestinian Occupied Territories) and help him edit a report about the situation in the Middle East. I learn how he "says without saying" things, through diplomatic language. He tells me, condescendingly: "Don't you get into trouble like the Scandinavians or Canadians, I'm not coming to rescue you if you end up in an Israeli jail." Later on that day, I go up to the Stars & Bucks Café, on the third floor of one of the buildings overlooking al-Manara, to pay my rent. A huge protest was taking place, which I observed from one of the big windows looking down on Sharʿ Rukab. As I was served my filtered coffee, a white pickup truck, decorated with PNA paraphernalia, drove up to al-Manara carrying a little girl, around eight years old, in the back. She was reciting a poem with a small, angry voice magnified by the speakers also transported by the truck.

I let myself go, I flow with the current and it doesn't matter if I go up or down. I opt for remaining still until things begin to run their own course.

FOR AN INTERVIEW for *El País*, Ayaan Hirsi Ali stated:

> Islam as an ensemble of principles is very consistent, very coherent, very sim-
> ple and is not compatible with Western democracy. The principles of liberal
> democracy take human life as an end in itself, and Islam says that you will have
> a satisfactory life only if you subject yourself to God's wishes. Democratic prin-
> ciples establish that men and women are equal before the law, while Islamic
> principles declare that woman is subordinated to man and that practitioners
> of homosexuality must die. . . . The true debate is about the sexual morality
> represented by the veil, which is nothing other than making women respon-
> sible for male sexuality. We must cover our bodies so as not to excite him; we
> must remain locked up at home so as not to excite him. This morality, putting
> all responsibility on women, is what needs to be discussed.[121]

I agree with the second part: Hirsi Ali's argument about the sexual morality
behind the obligation of wearing the veil. But I do not agree with Hirsi Ali's
condemnation of Islam as that which reveals itself to the point of terrorism
against liberal democracy, when she is unable to see that the danger is pre-
cisely located in that form of government. Not as a principle, but as democracy
has been subordinated to the neoliberal political economy, whose ultimate
goal is to generate as much surplus value as possible, disseminating further
the myths of personal self-fulfillment and extreme individualism. How can
there be democracy if everything is focused on individual, personal realiza-
tion and the "collective" has dissolved into social media?

It is raining and I am infinitely grateful there is thick fog above the city. I
plan an escape to my new refuge at the prophet-friend-cat's cave. In the end,
I change my mind and decide to pay a visit to Sonia; I feel a lot better after my
*rauia* (storyteller) reads me her new novel for young people. She convinced
me it was not a good idea to flee to the cat's cave, or to Jenin, Beirut, or Akko:

I have things to do here and I better wrap them up.

# A Lesson to Be Learned from Palestinian Icons of Resistance?

ACCORDING TO SERGE DANEY, Jean-Luc Godard's work is a painful meditation on the topic of restitution or, more specifically, of reparation.[122] For Daney, repairing means giving back images and sounds to those from whom they have been stolen. Restitution-reparation takes place, at least ideally, in *Ici et ailleurs* (Here and Elsewhere), the film Godard made, together with Jean-Pierre Gorin and Anne-Marie Miéville, about the Palestinian revolutionary movement at the end of the 1960s. But, to whom is the restitution paid if some of the Palestinians Godard filmed in the refugee camp in Baqa'a, Jordan, were exterminated by King Hussein's troops during the operation known as Black September?

In the film, mourning the failure of the French and Palestinian revolutions becomes a kind of elegy. "We did not listen to them," we hear Godard bitterly lamenting in the film's voiceover, referring to Palestinian combatants. "And we wanted to yell 'Victory!' in their place." In *Ici et ailleurs*, Godard self-reflexively analyzes the theater of death of the revolution and allows images to speak in the name of the failure of the Palestinian revolt. Their cause, however, is as alive now as it was in 1974, when Godard finishing editing the film. But in a way, the instant in which Godard transforms his cause to the epitome of revolutionary failure, here and elsewhere, the image of Palestinians is obliterated.

Obliteration begins in the self-critical part of *Ici et ailleurs*, when Godard and Miéville analyze the relationship between revolutionary image, history, and discourse, and focus on the photogram that shows a little girl from

Fateḥ standing before the ruins of Karameh, a Palestinian village, where she recites, "I Will Resist," a poem by Mahmoud Darwish. Karameh is located at the border with Jordan and is known because it's the site of a crucial legendary battle fought on March 21, 1968, between Fateḥ and the Israeli army. The fedayeen's actions and achievements in Karameh were exaggerated on radio reports and press communiqués with the goal of getting support for the revolution from Jordan, Lebanon, Syria, and the rest of the Palestinian population in the diaspora.[123]

The battle of Karameh had a deep psychological impact on the consciousness of Palestinians. It consolidated the resistance, enabling Fateḥ to recruit a hundred combatants for the cause. In *Ici et ailleurs*, Karameh appears like the ruins of building threatening to crush the little girl, who is courageously standing amid the debris. In spite of her apparent fragility, her words and gestures give her power, which increases with the lines she borrows from Darwish's poem. In the voiceover, Miéville's voice pedagogically deconstructs the image; she highlights the theatrical aspects in relation to the history of political theater, comparing the girl with the Conventionistes during the French Revolution. The Conventionistes, or the National Convention, were legislators, mainly from the middle class, who became administrators or functionaries under Napoleon during postrevolutionary France.[124] It is said that they wanted to be active in public life and were horrified by anarchy. In the film, Miéville problematizes the grand rhetorical gestures drawn by the girl by situating them in the context of the genre of poetic declamation in the tradition of the Conventionistes who gave speeches making exaggerated gestures. Miéville describes this form of discourse as "political theater." We should also consider that the image of the girl is also inscribed in the tradition of teaching children, in both Palestine and the diaspora, to recite resistance poems.

Another cinematic example of the Palestinian icon of a girl reciting revolutionary or nationalistic poetry is the last scene of *Driving to Zigzigland*, by Palestinian director Bashar Da'as (2006). Marie-José Mondzain's paradigmatic inquiry into the icon is relevant here: How can a cause be made visible? Does it imply making the person's voice audible? Or incarnating an essence? Or personifying it? Does it mean restituting the verb to the flesh or giving body to a discourse? Who or what is in fact made visible by an image? The small Palestinian girl from Fateḥ? Darwish through his words? The failure of political theater? The Palestinian cause? Godard has attributed more and more iconic power to this image by repeating it in his films, notably in *Histoire(s) du cinema* (1978–1988) and in *Vrai Faux Passeport* (2006). In a certain way, the small girl is the icon of revolutionary failure who, in spite of defeat,

FIG. 6. Cliché of Palestine as intractable (Edward Said). Photo during the shooting of the Schmesh short film taken by Rami Alarda and used as the cover for the journal *This Week in Palestine, January 2008*

still resists, standing on top of the ruins. By contemplating and listening to that "ghost," a lament, tied to the Arabic tradition of lament poetry, is also evoked not for the lost revolution but for the loss of land. In such a tradition, Andalusia symbolizes a dramatic call to the past, to lament collectively about the lost paradise. In that tradition, the song must begin with a lament on the site that was lost. Then, the poet moves forward to lament that Layla passed by, Lubna too, and that his beloved is no longer there. Then, the horse and the camel are described, and, afterward, the poem addresses metaphysical questions. In the modernized version of this genre, Palestine was transformed into Andalusia, the originally lost place.[125]

In Godard's image of the Palestinian girl reciting the poem in Karameh, Palestinians and their cause remain absent. Insofar as Godard and Miéville depict the history behind the Palestinian images, those in the images, when viewed in the Palestinian "present," appear as historical agents rather than as political subjects. They disappear from their image as they are sucked up by the objective movement of their own history, becoming its anonymous machinery. Here, identification is replaced by the sociopolitical struggle of a failed armed group transformed into a terrorist cell: after the Black September massacre in 1971, Fateḥ created a terrorist wing that adopted the same name as the events.

In spite of having filmed the Palestinian guerrillas, Godard's film was very far removed from the political reality of the people. The filmmaker is aware of that, and that is why, also in the movie, he portrays his limitations by

FIG. 7. Still from Jean-Luc Godard, the little girl in Karameh, in Ici et ailleurs (1974)

emphasizing that the point of view of the state of affairs he is presenting from "here" (France) is obviously conditioned by a Eurocentric vision. The option Godard gives himself to illuminate the situation *from here* implies using the Palestinian images to criticize French Maoism (and its failure) through self-criticism.

In *Vrai Faux Passeport*, Godard juxtaposes the scene of a small girl in Karameh with another resisting Palestinian: this second image was gleaned from Elia Suleiman's *Divine Intervention* (2002). The scene from Suleiman's film begins with members from the IDF training with targets shaped like a fedayee. Placed in the middle of the training field, the target remains indestructible, then suddenly assumes a defensive crouch and counterattacks the soldiers, against whom she fights like a ninja, employing weapons that become Palestinian nationalist symbols: darts shaped like a half-crescent moon, a slingshot, grenades that obliterate their targets and leave behind a Palestinian flag, and a shield from the geography of historical Palestine that becomes a boomerang to destroy a helicopter hovering above her. The super fedayee transforms the bullets being shot at her by the soldiers into a saintly nimbus reminiscent of the iconography of the crucifixion. In the only shot in which she appears with the IDF's soldiers, the combatant is crucified, evoking Palestinian martyrdom. Afterward, and before the general's stunned gaze, she disappears behind one of the training targets, a reproduction of her own image. In *Vrai Faux*, Godard dialogues with Suleiman's response to his little girl in Karameh, almost forty years later. Suleiman resuscitates the cause through the symbolic image of an adult woman taking defensive action against the oppressors.

No political goal can justify the means and neither does it correspond to the destructive potential nor to the use of weapons in conflicts.

HANNAH ARENDT[126]

IN 1969, ARENDT WROTE A TREATY on student violence in which she critiques destructive resistance and the influence of Frantz Fanon's *The Damned of the Earth* on the generation of students she was teaching at the time. Arendt did not believe in revolutions. She rejected violence and war, whatever the end was. For the students of that generation, power had demonstrated that it was only possible to maintain itself at gun point, and that is why violence had to be dealt with as a phenomenon in its own right on the political field. For Arendt, in contrast to the students, power and violence are not the same thing, as they reflect different phenomena. Violence may destroy power but is incapable of producing it; in turn, power produces violence. And incorrectly exercised power cannot deliver justice but only hypocrisy, which becomes despotism and the reign of terror.

Unlike in the 1960s, contemporary forms of power now reside in the differentiation of populations and the creation of inequality. We live in securitized societies that produce and instigate freedom; circles of control are created and conduct is governed. The passage from a disciplinary society to a security society implies offering differentiated freedoms. In the case of Israel-Palestine, the major differentiation resides in freedom of movement, as the flux of people—but also of commodities and finances—is limited by Israeli authorities.

In Jacques Rancière's definition of the aesthetic regime, art is a specific activity that suspends spatio-temporal connections and sensorial experience.[127] In such a regimen, the active and passive dualisms, sensibility and understanding, distribute the sensible, and they are political because they hierarchize or divide society. This regimen supposes that intellectual work gives autonomy and that manual labor is subordinating. Art as a *specific* and heterogeneous sensorium is opposed to work as a form of domination insofar as it promises the abolition of the separation between play and work, which are two extremes. However, it is less and less separated under semiocapitalism.[128] Under semiocapitalism, the difference between the work of art and merchandise is empty. It is a field of forces, of principles that constitute values geared to the production of subjectivity and forms of life. How, then, can we rethink power, forms of resistance, ways to change the state of things in this context?

In the morning I leave for Be'er Sheva to visit Alice and Michel, my friends from Toronto; they are living there now because Michel is a medical student at the prestigious Medical School for International Health. On the bus ride there I get very dizzy; the uneasiness persists even hours after I arrive. The bus was more than full: 70 percent of the passengers were soldiers on leave. The driver let me find a place to sit on the floor. I spent the journey observing a young solider carrying one of the most sophisticated guns I've seen so far around here. A purple beret hung from his shoulder, next to insignias and distinctions, which are also uncommon. The soldier standing next to him wouldn't stop admiring the decorated officer's gun either, so the officer ended up showing it off and handing it to him. The oscillation of the bellicose instrument as it went back and forth between the young men made me very nervous because there were moments in which it felt it was pointing at me. I know that the guns are never loaded and that they weren't aiming at me on purpose, but I still felt uncomfortable.

In Be'er Sheva, Alice and I cooked lasagna and meringues that turned out a bit crushed, but were regardless tasty. Michi came home late, so after we caught up quickly, we collapsed on a couch to watch Olivier Assayas's film in which Maggie Cheung plays a drug addict traveling from Toronto to Paris. That's what I got out of the film because I was exhausted and fell immediately asleep.

"Life-affirming energy is good for me," Alice tells me. She looks gorgeous pregnant. I feel hope when I talk about children, I enjoy imagining together with her what her life will be like with the two children they're planning on having. Alice is very lonely and does not stop talking! The next day we cook a delicious meal, and the house feels very warm. Fidel Castro just ceded power to his brother and has allowed Cuba to open up its markets to the international financial scene. I am missing Ramallah, my jealous, dangerous, and possessive lover who claims my return. On the way back I thought I wanted to go by the American Colony Hotel bookstore in Jerusalem to look for something to read. I realize that the longer I'm in Palestine, the harder it is to discuss politics in Israel, especially with people who are superficially critical of Israeli state politics. Everyone seems to be aware of the situation of the checkpoints, the sieges, the violence, the jails, the Gaza siege. In spite of being against the occupation, liberal Israelis won't see the justification behind terrorist attacks, and, for them, every Palestinian is potentially a terrorist. Many believe in the appropriateness of the wall and, deep inside, they feel that they deserve that kind of security from their enemies. How can people shake off their manufactured consciousness? How can they shake off liberal Israeli doxa? They are so easily and comfortably misinformed, without wanting to really see. All this feels very painful to me. And as Michel said, Hamas is a tragedy: they are obsessed with power, which they disguise as the utopia of the Islamic republic, but Hamas is a product of the first Intifada. Israel deescalated it, and it is now very easy for Hamas to let things implode, that's how they look better in the eyes of international opinion: "We freed the Gaza Strip in 2005 and look what happened."

On the north side of Be'er Sheva, a small city in the Negev desert, Israel's aspiration to be a "modern" civilization has materialized in the past few years. The new neighborhood is reminiscent of a US suburb, with streets built exclusively for cars, designed around massive shopping centers and corporate businesses, restaurants, and national chain coffee shops. On the edges of the neighborhood I saw buildings from 1950s functionalist Israeli architecture still inhabited or in ruins, similar to elevated shoeboxes on thin pillars, with small windows very close to each other, like dove's nests, with the blinds down all the time to protect the inside from the heat. These buildings were built to lodge the thousands of new immigrants and that is why they symbolize the Israeli utopia that seduced Arab Jews across the Maghreb to migrate to the promised land. These homes are now inhabited by Ethiopian and Russian Jews. Across from the buildings there are Bedouins living in semidetached buildings. Bedouins are nomadic Palestinians who were forced by the occupation to settle. Some tribes had to leave their nomadic lives due to Israeli state policies. There remain a few nomadic tribes in the Negev, where they live in precarious tin homes that are systemically demolished by the Israelis and rebuilt by the Bedouins in different places, depending on the season. The police, or rather the "Battle for the Negev," has the objective of uprooting the Bedouins from the desert.[129] For instance, in 2002, at al-'Araqib, four years after a family of Bedouins came back to settle in the places from which they had been forcefully expelled fifty years earlier, began to be demolished.

*Irmgard Emmelhainz* [ 119 ]

The Bedouins have filed legal petitions in Israeli courts with the hopes that the law will help them protect their homes.[130]

The Prawer Plan, however, is a policy designed to offer permanent homes and jobs in factories to the Bedouins.[131] As their nomadic lives have already been modified and they have been culturally and materially impoverished, many of them have accepted this change of lifestyle, in spite of the fact that relocation is considered to be ethnic cleansing.[132] Only a few Bedouins can keep hanging onto their traditional life forms, and they are always subject to being managed, contained, and oppressed by the state. This is because they are unwanted people on desirable lands, and that makes them a redundant population. In January 2017, when doing a Google search about the correct way of writing *Negev* in Spanish, I came across the news that Palestinians had declared a general strike and that demonstrations across the West Bank, Haifa, Akko, Nazareth, and Jerusalem exploded after an Israeli incursion into the Bedouin village of Um Al Hiran to demolish homes caused the death of a Palestinian man from the village, Jacoub Mussa Abu al-Qiyan; an Israeli official, Erez Levi, and a Palestinian politician, Aymen Odeh, were wounded in the confrontation.[133] According to the news report, Israel plans to demolish Um Al Hiran and replace it with a Jewish village called Hiran. Um Al Hiran is one of the forty Bedouin populations in the Negev that are not recognized by Israel, waiting to be demolished. Due to its "nonrecognized" status, its thousands of inhabitants lack access to electricity, water, and other municipal services.

In a key book, Eyal Weizman explains how the Negev desert is a mobile frontier that advances and pulls back in response to colonization, displacement, urbanization, agriculture, and climate change, all intrinsically linked to dispossession. Using a very useful and radical hypothesis to explain today's conflicts, Weizman connects colonialism and climate change. He lays forth the "Battle for the Negev" as a state-sponsored campaign geared, on the one hand, to uproot the Bedouins and, on the other, to expand the line of forests.[134] In general, climate change is understood as an unintentional effect of modernity. For Weizman, from the point of view of colonization, climate change has never been collateral damage, but a declared goal. In the case of the Negev, to make the desert bloom is, in effect, changing the climate. A similar history linking colonization and environmental devastation on Lake Chalco in Mexico City could be written. Iñigo Noriega Laso sought to expand arable lands by drying up Lake Xico (adjacent to Chalco and Xochimilco) and transforming its inhabitants into peons, or hacienda laborers, during Porfirio Díaz's regime; similarly, Israeli governments have sought to move the desert's frontier to expand the limits of agricultural land and to place the nomads under the control of the state. In the Negev as in Chalco, climate change and the displacement of originary populations go hand in hand. This has generated invisible forms of environmental violence, like land degradation, the destruction of fields and forests, pollution, and water rerouting. For Weizman, conflict interacts reciprocally with environmental transformation, and that relationship unfolds from the constant moving of the desert frontier toward the south, to make it green, expanding the forest line.[135]

I hadn't measured the amount of energy I required to spend time with Alice and Michi. But I realize that I need to spend it to get out from my own life sorrow under the occupation and under what I've seen so far. Maybe, looking at my friends pregnantly gazing at the future filled me with hope again. What is the difference between solidarity you show toward a stranger and toward a friend? I let go of my own incapacity to write everything I see and I shut my laptop down. Not without writing, first, that in Be'er Sheva, the hills are not razed but covered with pine trees. I wonder if Israeli soldiers have left some of those trees anywhere in the West Bank, because I haven't seen them.

RAMALLAH WELCOMES ME with a blue sky, the smell of rain and of buds about to bloom. And yet, I don't feel welcome, it's the jealousy of my city lover who can hardly forgive my absence. I spend the afternoon with Khadijeh at Zyriab; that's where I give her the DVDs with Godard's films I had promised her. I tell her about the work I have been doing with Sonia and explain that with both of them, I enjoy the privilege of being able to begin to understand the last forty years of Palestinian history through their extraordinary lives, through the eyes of such exceptional women. They know each other well. Khadijeh tells me that Mustapha was the love of her life; they met when they were sixteen years old and lived together for two decades. But they have been separated for three. Both ended up in Ramallah. One of their sons lives in San Francisco, and the other one with her. She tells me she carried out a campaign to get women on the board of the PNA's parliament. It took her two and a half years, but they managed to establish a quota of 30 percent female participation, although at the end only seventeen women could occupy a parliamentary seat (out of 131 seats available).[136] It's an impressive achievement.

"How did you manage?" I asked her.

"I approached women's organizations, I wrote letters, I organized press conferences; forty-nine women and I went to see Yasser Arafat two times."

She also told me about her work with women in refugee camps: "What matters the most is for them to create a consciousness of their own knowledge so that they use it to become aware of their strengths—it's about empowering them." I showed her still images from my Japanese copy of *Ici et ailleurs*, and she recognized Mustapha's sister in one of the images. When she was young, she received training in one of the camps in Amman. I asked Khadijeh what the world was like before 1989, when, it seemed to me, connections were interwoven between people of different nationalities and throughout the communist bloc: Moscow-Beirut-Berlin-Havana-Santiago-Beijing. Today, English is spoken, as all global exchanges are mediated by the West. She also tells me about when she met a cosmonaut during her visit to Moscow as a member of a delegation seeking support for the Palestinian cause.

Khadijeh wrote a dissertation about the different ways in which men and women communicate.

"Where are the battles today, K?"

She tells me: "People have to realize the magnitude of the mistake they made by having voted for Hamas. Their slogan is 'No to resistance,' and they absolutely reject the State of Israel."

According to her analysis, Israel has always eliminated radicals in the hope that moderates would be ready to negotiate. That is the current situation in Gaza. What do people do in the Gaza Strip? What can they do? They can try to convince their leaders to negotiate; last week there was a demonstration in which they asked Hamas to protest against their situation. Khadijeh also tells me that in the 1960s, political work led everyone to become a Marxist revolutionary. Hamas is the product of the First Intifada and of the Iranian Islamic Republic. Currently, imams are the ones who carry out the political work, as they propagate a new form of politicized religion centered on identity. The bomb at the YMCA in Jerusalem was a really stupid operation; the Israelis denied all responsibility, but for Khadijeh it seems like it was an act of internal cleansing. She thinks it's convenient for Israelis to let Gaza collapse.

"Where are the battles, Khadijeh?"

"Information. People produce and consume information, they become anesthetized, they are being dispossessed of their humanity, we are becoming more instinctual and animal. To shoot *qassām* rockets is a means to be relieved of the weight of the occupation as symbolic act; it's the same when one delivers one's children to martyrdom for the cause."

"How can we restitute humanity to people living at an absolutely instinctive level, trying to survive?"

"Young women bearing the veil are simply wrong. God did not order them to wear it, it is a false reading of the Quran; they must begin to accept that they wear it because they feel pressured to do so, not convinced."

"Where else are the battles, Khadijeh?"

She looks at me for a long moment with her sad and elegant eyes.

After Zyriab, Khadijeh invites me over to have a bite at her home before the storm begins, which apparently will not be as bad as had been predicted. It will only be very cold and rainy, maybe a bit of wet snow will fall. But who knows? "It's something coming in from Athens," she tells me. She tells me more about the stupidity of Hamas's operations, but what surprises me the most is not her knowledge or experience of resistance, but her son, who is my age, and completely lost and depressed. We turn the television on and we see a fragment of the speech by Hasan Nasrallah, the Hezbollah leader and representative of the Shi'ite community in Lebanon, financed by Iran, talking about the resistance and the occupation and the destruction of Israel (for Khadijeh, the political stand of wanting to destroy Israel attracts people to the cause; it sells well). Although she knows that there is no perfect regime, she believes in democracy, and that there will be always something to fight for, discuss; there will always be occasions to organize and resist. Something resonates with me a lot: the idea Khadijeh has of making a movie that would reflect the situation in the West Bank, but without showing it to a lot of people, only to a few that could understand it. I asked her if it is very difficult to talk about Palestine with Western liberals who are against the occupation; she said that this occupation should be called ethnic cleansing and terrorism. She tells me that something that is difficult to describe has been broken, something has changed to prevent the transmission of political knowledge from one generation to the other (and I wonder, who is speaking here? The mother or the militant? The woman or the activist?) I began a pseudotheological conversation with Ali, her son, who tried to convince me that we need to believe in something, in a creator. Beyond religious fanaticism, belief unites people, it originates communities ruled by religion. For Khadijeh, religion used to be something private but now is an excuse for segregation among Jews, Muslims, and Christians, between Muslim, Jewish, and Christian sects.

The women I have met here—Hanadi, the secretary at the office of the Palestinian National Authority (PNA); Zainab, my tutor in Birzeit; Yousef's sister; Nuha, my Arabic teacher; Rohilia, the girl at the library who insists on becoming my friend after asking me advice about a marriage offer she got by email from a guy who courts her through the internet and who lives in Egypt; Maisa! with her anorexia and demands—all have in common that they are very strict and hard on themselves, also perfectionists. They are eager and have energy to work, to do many things, and to perform at the top level. I suspect, however, that the fact that they are too hard on themselves has to do with the occupation, linked to the belief that one can better one's life. Sally is a bit different, more temperate, sweet, and warm, but she also expects too much of herself and will not stop working.

Hannah Arendt equates walls with law and order. The political realm, according to her, is guaranteed by two kinds of walls (or laws that function as walls): the wall that surrounds the city, which used to define the zone of the political, and the walls that separate private from public space, which assures autonomy for the domestic realm. The interdependence between the wall and the law is equal to the legal factory and to built space. The *unwilling* of the wall supposes undoing, dismounting the law. The Israeli military practice of traversing walls when they have invaded Palestinian homes interlinks the physical properties of the construction with the syntaxis of the architectural, social, and political orders. The refugee camps, as they are subject to Israeli war tactics, the city, and the home become interchangeable. When breaking through the physical, conceptual, and visual walls, they are exposing a new domain of political power and delineating a clearer physical diagram of the state of exception.[137] This results in Palestinian women being hard and hyperdemanding on themselves as a means to protect themselves from the internal *unwilling* by the Israeli occupation.

My neighbor Shadi gives me a lift home in one of the three Vespas in the city. The wind on my face felt incredible, I felt alive.

# Of Marbles and Almonds

DURING THE GESTATION PERIOD OF the protuberance, she began to endearingly call him "unicorn." It achieved its definite size while the love was battling against obstacles that seemed to be unbridgeable. Differences exacerbated, there was a small death, jealousy gradually managed to make cracks in the eagerness of being together, and disquiet and doubt channeled energies toward separate roads. Once the marble took comfortably root on the right side, very close to the brow, the unicorn found himself on his own, and he let the garden wither, the cats tyrannize the everyday, entropy invade the heart. Outside there was invasion and defeat; fleeting loves came and went, painful deaths and sudden losses added up. Within, the excess of encapsulated cells seemed to be like a lazy almond who wanted to take ten, no, eleven years to leave its shell whole. No one knows if it was because it had been persistently massaged with alcohol or because a love that came to an end could open up a new beginning. The marble suddenly erupted like a volcano for a whole week. With immense joy, she observed and contributed to the ejaculation, watching him become something other than a unicorn.

WE DISCUSSED LOVE AND MARRIAGE; we talked about the different kinds of love in pre-Islamic poetry, and he told me that the ten best poems begin with crying on the ruins of the tribe because matters of love required them to leave it and begin a new life. In Arabic, *hub* designates love, *ashiq* transcendental love, the kind of love in which one cannot exist without the other; there are also words to designate having a crush on someone, lost love, uncertain love, mad love, sick love, passionate love. I have the impression that here people make an effort to make life easier for the other because it's very hard for them.

Gaza is undergoing a slow death; all the money is invested in rebuilding everything that has been devastated, ruined, and destroyed by the Israeli army. Ruined reconstruction. Everyone around is at war, even with themselves.

I spoke with the administrator of my department in Toronto, who informed me that there are no available funds for me to finish my PhD. She suggested that I take a year or a semester off from the university to finish my thesis. This would create a lot of problems for me, not only financially but in terms of compromising my student status in Canada. Taking a semester or a year off is not an option. But neither should I have to work to pay for my tuition. I don't have access to loans or scholarships because I am not Canadian, and my project, to my disgrace, does not fit into current diplomatic interests between Canada and Mexico. That's why I'm not getting support right now. What am I going to do?

And, I have to pay if they force me to take a year off. I will be obliged to outsource my work, which means going somewhere where I can live for free—that is to say, with family and not in Canada (because I would have visa problems if I tried to stay in Canada). But if I'm not in Canada I will be deprived of the university's resources. Any kind of academic activity I pursue would be as an independent scholar, not as part of my faculty or *that* university. I did not become a legal resident of Canada, a country where allegedly difference is encouraged and supported, for the sole reason that residency requirements would have hindered international mobility and thus affected my research. Maybe I am going to have to sell my eggs. I am willing to work as a teacher or as a teaching assistant in order to support myself, but not in order to pay for tuition (which would double my workload and affect the outcome of my dissertation). I am also being forced to pay full international fees. Requiring me to take a leave of absence would push me toward labor exploitation (Canadian citizens, for instance, could apply for loans or do less intellectually demanding jobs than teaching). Is the university a tomato farm? Hiring cheap Mexican labor like farms across Ontario? In addition, I would not be able to finish the thesis in a year if I were obliged to work full time. Why would I lower the expectations for the quality of my own project? My January scholarship money hasn't come through the bank. Ugh.

But things seem a bit better with the warm sun and almond trees in full bloom. I completely recover my combative energy and focus on my writing. Yousef told me today about the coercion and blackmail strategies used by the Israelis to enroll collaborators: they offer them money, alcohol, drugs, and Russian prostitutes. Once they accept the favors, Israelis take their photographs and compromise them—then they're in as informants for life. The Israelis have information that, if known, would cut them off from their families and friends; in some cases they would have to pay with death. Thousands of Palestinian teenagers are also coerced by spending a portion of their adolescence rotting in Israeli jails, so they get broken young. This creates anger and desire for vengeance. Are they victims or survivors?

My Arabic lessons with Nuha are going well; we're reading a children's book together, and I am learning many new words. She also makes me write a lot—she's a little dictator: "Let's see, say *aaaaa* or *aaeaa*, write *tha*." If she weren't so charming or pretty she wouldn't get much out of me with her dictatorial methods. She just graduated from Damascus University in English literature and is looking for a job. She's so hard on herself! During our lesson she never accepts any drinks I offer her so she doesn't have to waste time in the bathroom. For an hour and a half, she glues herself to the table to teach me, and she has so much patience. She asks for fifty shekels an hour, half of what I paid to *ustaz* Mohamed, the teacher who has a small school in the rusty half-built building across from the taxi stop to Birzeit University. I stopped taking classes from him because, too often, he visibly touched his sex during the lesson, which obviously made me very uncomfortable and grossed me out.

I was thinking that perhaps the West Bank could be thought of as a simulated semiautonomous police state, as violence and control predominate. It is a despotic society administered by Palestinians allied with neoliberal globalizing forces and Israel. Today, after Arafat, there's no figure with whom people could identify; there is no leader capable of unifying generations that have lived the occupation, responded to it in different ways, and now blame one another for their failures and mistakes. Also, it is easy to identify with religion while the nationalist project withers away.

In another image-world, thousands of kilometers away, Marcelo Ebrard, left-wing head of government of Mexico City, announced that by 2011 he plans to install ten thousand security cameras across the city.[138] The oppression of surveillance is set as the background of everyday life and establishes the paradox of being able to make things visible only from an oblique perspective, where the visible relies in between the background and the foreground.

Israeli prime minister Benjamin Netanyahu threatened to create a Holocaust in Gaza.[139] About a month ago, Israel destroyed its Ministry of Interior; launched a foray in a refugee camp, murdered citizens and children.[140] All the West Bank has declared a 'iḍrāb (strike), that is why it was difficult to find a shawarma restaurant open; I have at home two cucumbers, two eggs, bread, *labna*, and hummus, but I didn't feel like eating any of that. My brain was demanding carbs and sugar, and felt too tired to attend the Gaza protest. It takes two days for Ban Ki-Moon to denounce the disproportionate violence in Gaza. It's not hatred, but a toxic mix of apathy and condescension that creates an environment where an unbearable wall separates an *us* from a *them*. What inflames such a conduct—according to a soldier in testimony shown in one of the videos of the *Bare Life* exhibition in Jerusalem, and in which said soldier poses next to the photograph of a young Palestinian man hunching on a chair, with his eyes with the typical IDF band—is the idea that a Palestinian "is not a dog, or an animal; don't think about him as an inferior being, he simply *does not exist*."[141]

After the First Intifada, the situation brought about the Oslo Accords: the return of the PNA and thus the institutionalization of an interim Palestinian government and the normalization of pending negotiations. What kind of normalization? After the Oslo Accords, were Palestinians reborn from the ashes, having healed broken arms and legs? Did they mean a sort of renaissance, having a country after the PNA was transplanted to the Occupied Territories? In truth, the PNA became a simulated state subject to the demands of the US and Israel. How did this simulated state affect subjective and collective voices resisting the occupation? They are repressed ceaselessly while Palestinians in the West Bank try to lead normal lives and people in Gaza just try to survive. It's an existential issue. *Gaza 'ala bāly*: there are demonstrations at one, four, and six o'clock. Shots are heard on the streets. I walk home and

I stop to get a *sfiha* in the only open bakery I find. I didn't know that Abul Jaz's family lived in Jabalya, the biggest refugee camp in Gaza, in the north. His family confirmed everyone was OK. The IDF is blaming Hamas for the deaths because they direct their missiles to inhabited areas and the militia members hide themselves among civilians.

We are navigating in an implacable and invisible ocean of persuasion called *capitalism*, an accomplice to the normalization of the occupation in the West Bank, international indifference regarding the siege, and ongoing destruction of the Gaza Strip.

I'M SUPPOSED TO MEET M later today in Jerusalem. She's bringing with her the *Scapeghost* book, fresh off the press, which includes my contribution (after the insistence of my Palestinian friends again, who advised me to overlook BDS and publish my text in Hebrew). We said we would go check out the *Bare Life* exhibition, but I want to be back to Ramallah by six to see the movie at Qattan. I had a tough crossing to Jerusalem. I cried, and I don't know if it was because I saw three boys being taken to prison by the PNA or because of the vibe on the streets in Ramallah or because it is upsetting now for me to cross to Israel period. I met M and Avi, a friend of hers, and we sat down for a long, fun lunch. I told them Palestinian stories, and they were shocked by the one AH told me about people sneaking in illegally through the sewer to pray at Al-Aqsa in Jerusalem. AH compares this form of crossing to the metaphor of traversing an "impure road" to reach the purity of prayer. But more than the metaphor of having to navigate through shit to pray, what shocked my friends the most was that they are often caught and sent home right back through the sewer, even though there is a door right next to it.

They weren't amused by the anecdote I told them about the day I spent as an assistant crew member at a film production, trying to make a donkey run in one of the scenes. As a joke, I asked my peers if we could perhaps bring settlers to come scare him away.

When I go back to Ramallah, I have the chance to observe my roommate hanging around the Ramallah art world. I perceive a sharp contrast between her activism and worldview of the Palestinian privileged elite, with their relative global mobility, foreign passports, perfect English, and an education better than hers. Samar asks her in a skeptical tone: "What have been the long-term results of ISM activism?" Without hesitating, she listed the changes they achieved in Tal Rumeida and gave a few examples when they had made a difference. I did not want to take part in the discussion; to me, what's important in this form of activism is the *here and now*: to take *this* kid to school *today*. To help *this* family cross this checkpoint and fast, *now*.

The horizon of the Mediterranean, framed by the Tel Aviv lights, can be seen from my Swedish friend's apartment. Once, I am told, Ariel Sharon declared that he would place Israeli lights five hundred meters away from Palestinians, where they could almost touch them but would not have access to them. I said this out loud around Omaya, Samar, and Khaled, and they looked at me with surprise. Sharon's declaration came true. I attest that Palestinians do not know a lot about their enemy. They only know the enemy as their oppressor, fanatic settler, violent or intransigent soldier, someone whom they search for traces of humanity. They don't see their enemy as a strategist, ideologist, a person with a complex history inevitably linked to theirs. Invariably, the stories I hear about Palestinians' encounters with soldiers have in common that soldiers show themselves as comprehensive and humanized. They don't tell me (or maybe they don't tell foreigners in general?) stories in which soldiers were assholes to them. Palestinian finesse.

From terrified Alishka, in Be'er Sheva:

hi irmgard, i have some sad news, unfortunately we won't be able to come to ramallah this weekend. i've thought abt it and thought abt it and i just feel uncomfortable travelling to another country at this stage of the pregnancy. i'm 8ms now and although i feel pretty good i do feel dizzy and tired and misjudge distances etc and generally don't feel all that stable and if i were to fall i'd be quite worried abt what wd happen.

i'm sure there is a good hospital in ramallah but the thought just makes me too anxious.

i'm sorry. i wish i cd visit again, especially as it must be quite beautiful right now with everything in bloom. i feel ok to travel to jerusalem or tel aviv and if you are there just let me know and i'll hop on the bus and meet you, have lunch or coffee. i wd love that. maybe next week? i'm free all day on Tuesday. it's not so much the travelling, it's the uncertainty and crossing borders/check points that worries me—i know it's not a "real" border, but it also is. it doesn't seem like the best thing to do right now.

i can meet you in east jerusalem if you don't want to go to the west side, i totally understand.

that's tragic what you had to witness, and it must be very traumatic for you. this situation is getting worse and worse and i am afraid that it'll get horrible. there are days when i am really worried and there are days when i don't think abt it. i don't know if there is more tension here or just the same tension—it just always feels tense all the time, though there have been more planes and "commotion." i have been having a lot of nightmares. i think too giving birth to a child is changing things for me. and giving birth at a hospital where there was a bomb threat a month ago is not the way i imagined it.

again, ''m sorry. i wish i cd and i hope you understand. love, alice

Alice was smart not to come. I was with a friend when she got the news through an SMS on her phone. I went to the Stammcafé and people were speculating who'd done it and who would claim it. Then, someone else said that the brigades from Al-Jihad had claimed it, that the attacker was from Bethlehem and that is why the IDF had already invaded the city. Later on, I got a lift back home and they were surprised not to see tanks on the main roundabout, al-Manara. The heading in *Ha'aretz*: "Hundreds of mourners of the attacks against the Yeshiva in Jerusalem."[142] All the next day I felt like crying, my eyes felt watery a lot. At night, I had dinner with the Swedish journalist, and he told me that during the 2002 incursion, bullets coming in from P'sagot appeared like shooting stars and that the attacks were transmitted live on television. For some strange reason that can only be explained by physics, electrons make sound travel faster on TV and that is why the bullets would be heard first through the TV monitor and only after in reality.

dave,

hope these lines find you well. I had to write you to tell you that the image that you described to me once, of how you finished your thesis, came to my mind today! (The Doritos, head up, typing away. . .) I'm struggling with chapter 3, stuck in the seventies, which are so far removed from my "here and now." Can't wait to get to 2004 and 2008. I'm also running out of funding, outsourcing in the West Bank and trying to do everything possible as not to have to join the ranks of academic proletariat (again) next year. . . I've been using the library of the Qattan Foundation, here in Ramallah, an amazing place for creative production. A month ago I moved in to the "Audiovisual House" of Qattan. . . It is a metal structure (very much like those that Israeli settlers use to start their settlements) where I write with my laptop on my stomach, feet up, chain-smoking and listening to techno-suff with my friends—who are keeping me going! WHATEVER IT TAKES, I can't wait to finish! Let me know if you have any advice!

bests,
i.

Care, expectations, deceit, and deception. Development and progress. To internalize the occupation. The obscenity and the amorality of the situation call for a simulacrum of morality (religion), and it's not like Cuba, where all is completely amoral.

FOUR STUDENTS FROM THE PHILOSOPHY and Letters Faculty at the Universidad Nacional Autónoma de México (UNAM) were killed during an attack by the Colombian Army against one of the camps of the Revolutionary Armed Forces of Colombia (FARC). The Mexican students had traveled to Colombia to interview Raúl Reyes (number two of that organization). In 2002, President Vicente Fox shut down the FARC offices in Mexico.[143] Were the students recruited by the FARC and how? How did they get there in the first place?

The other day, when I ran into Neta on the Jerusalem-Ramallah bus, she told me the story of when she tied herself to a tree and explained that since then, she's been on probation with the Israeli police, which means she needs to see a social worker in Jerusalem once a week. She considers it state-subsidized therapy. Neta is an amazing, strong woman; I admire how she focuses all her energy into the cause. She's a founding member of the ISM, and she's been living in Ramallah for almost ten years, where she married a Palestinian with whom she bore three daughters. They live the utopia of a mixed couple, which represents a real threat to the Israeli status quo.

On a Skype call, I discussed with Stephen, my old undergrad professor from Texas in Mexico, the negative critique of my article published in Arabic. "It shouldn't surprise you," he told me, "they're all a bunch of reactionaries serving bureaucratic and pseudonationalist interests, and they're far from being interested in true dialogue." While this might be in part true, what bothered me is that he insisted that I was seeing Palestinians as if they were inside a fish bowl, with the bowl as my ethnographic laboratory. And what about you? I thought. I'd always suspected he was a CIA agent, stationed in Mexico posing as a colonial art specialist in the 1970s spying on communists and Vietnam veterans in Cholula. After we hung up, I had to escape from Zyriab to the library because, out of all people, Moheeb and Maisa had shown up and I didn't feel like seeing them, maybe because of my petty soul (I preferred being an asshole of a friend rather than a well-behaved guest). Honestly, my last encounter with Moheeb was very uncomfortable. He made a pass at me and got so insistent that I had to be rude to turn him down. And Maisa is just too crazy. I heard she was having an affair with a married Christian man, father of two gorgeous twins. We try to be normal, but, like everyone else, we are all fucked up, and the consequences of the bad decisions we make don't really matter—I don't judge them. Here, the normal thing seems to be to do irrational things. What other kinds of choices do people make in this shattered society? While we are propelled to make efforts to normalize life and relationships, the whole of society is forced to deal with memories of pain and to resist normalizing the occupation. I think this leads in women to neurosis and perfectionism and in men to attempts to forget humiliations imposed by the enemy: insolence as a means to expel the weight of shame. How can people work through the pain and trauma of the humiliation while the occupation is still in place? Shamelessness in the enemy is *so* different. In the meantime, everyone lives asking themselves about how to hang on to values while cynicism poisons hope. Years later, I would come to understand that when a community or society is subject to violence and oppression, its people come to internalize it, exuding it like poison toward each other, causing epidemics of addiction, codependence, and self-destruction. This phenomenon is not exclusive to Palestine but inherent to the heteropatriarchal capitalist modern colonial complex across the world.

Later today I went to visit Sonia. We talked for hours about Palestinian dresses. She told me that the most elegant ones take up to three years to embroider. When girls turn twelve, they begin to prepare their trousseau and their potential mother-in-law comes to check their stitches; the stitches reflect her personality—whether they are too tight or loose, whether she is a hard worker or lazy, difficult or has a good temperament. The amount of red in a dress indicates her age: the redder the dress, the more fertile. The dress also indicates if the girl is married or single, her story, her political affiliation, the number of children (if any) she has, etc. Then she told me that weddings begin with a horse procession, during which the bride leaves her home to go to her future husband's, and all the wedding dances and songs are charged with symbolism. Then she told me about mourning traditions: they have laments, and women let their hair loose and tear their *Fusṭān* to express through action the extent of their pain, represented materially by the many years they had worked embroidering their dresses.

*Mental note*: Ask Nithya about the project of establishing export processing zones (EPZs) in the West Bank with Turkish, Japanese, Israeli, and USAID money. The PNA supports a form of "economic peace" (seen by others as a form of normalizing the occupation) through establishing economic ties with

Israel.[144] The fact that those links would be asymmetrical (as the Israeli position will be more advantageous in the deal) is a sign of neocolonialism. Fifty of the most important Palestinian businessmen were invited to buy land that had been confiscated by the Israelis to develop IZs (Industrial Zones).[145] Negotiations are laid forth as collaborative peace projects. Colonial projects end when profit by other means is greater than profits made through colonization.

I BREATHE IN. My visa was renewed yesterday for the second time at the Ministry of International Relations. They made it tough for me because I was suspected of working under the table in Israel. The Mexican passport did not help, of course. For three days, I remained frozen with diarrhea. I decided not to let M know I was coming and instead only let her know once I managed to renew it. While I was waiting for my hosts to get home from work for the night, I went to a place on the street parallel to Rehov Shalama, near Bezalel, where I had a beer with Nora and Thierry back in December. I sat down with the moon over my head—actually, I was craving to see it from Ramallah, I was missing the city and F so much. I felt miserable and lonely and was silently cursing Israelis. Sipping a glass of wine, I wrote notes for the short story I am planning to write: I want it to be some sort of Elena Garro–like rendering of a fictive account of working at Qattan after AH's wedding, but the subject overwhelms me. Matan and his roommate live in an apartment on Yerushalaim Street, close to Yaffa. I spent the evening talking with them about Ramallah and other things. The two men, together with HM, were refuseniks (or conscientious army dissidents) in 2002; their case got a lot of visibility because the father of one of them is a well-known journalist in Israel. These refuseniks remain engaged with activism although they are quite pessimistic. This week's emergency was Darfur refugees, as they were overcrowded in tents near Tel Aviv's central bus station. They mobilized to stop the police from arresting and deporting them.

The next morning, HM accompanied me again to the ministry. We met outside at 7:30. I am so grateful to this guy, who came prepared with a book, for easing my nerves, for keeping me focused on *making them let me stay!* My alibi was flimsy, to say the least: I was armed with an unsigned letter from one of my university professors, one from the editor of the book that includes my Scapeghost essay, a generous letter from an Israeli artist dated in January vouching for me as an international cultural producer, M's address, a new letter stating that I need more time to complete my research on Israeli contemporary art. They were doubtful; they wanted people from Bezalel or the museum to fax them something immediately so that they would give me the visa.

"You've been in Israel for too long." "But I love Israel!" What did the trick was the Connaught scholarship letter saying I have 15,000 dollars from Canada to complete my dissertation. This time, HM refused to take off his Anarchists Against the Wall pin. I was in and out of the ministry in less than two hours, called M, and had coffee and breakfast with her. Then, relieved and immensely happy, I came back to Ramallah. When I arrived home, Jenna had forgotten to leave me the key. She was unreachable by cell phone, so I crashed for a bit at Shadi and Ihab's. Afterward, I sat on the sidewalk reading my new Houellebecq (*La Possibilité d'une île*, it's good, but not as good as others I've read) until Jenna finally showed up and let me in. I felt such a huge relief having renewed my visa that I took up my New Year's resolutions: to work harder at learning Arabic and finishing my thesis. To travel to Haifa, Akko, Jenin, Balata; to spend a few days in Hebron. Perhaps to visit Jericho—we will see. Relief, relief. Breathe in.

I'VE BEEN SPENDING LOT OF TIME at Zan with F; things are getting strange: he's been drinking waaaay too much and trying to talk me into going home with him almost every time we meet. And I have considered it. I won't deny I am tempted to love him; I desire him, I love his hands, and I want him to touch me, but he is such a drunk. I also don't want to become another of his foreign conquests (he's had lots of girlfriends!). Ruthless seducer. I think I have reached him at a layer beneath his seductive surface, and he's been opening up. I think he's had to change his lines because I don't buy his usual ones. He's been teaching me the fine art of cursing in Arabic, so he's become my teacher, guide, companion, and suitor. I feel really close to him, and we don't know what to do with the tension and the love and the ongoing companionship. "I know how much I need you, but do you realize how much you need me?" he asked me the other day. Of course I do. And then I had to leave Zan, because if I had stayed, I would have loved him. It's been many evenings at Zan, working together, having endless conversations, sharing childhood memories, making plans for the future, discussing daily frustrations, sharing everything, cigarettes and arak, talking about (pre-Islamic) Arabic literature, Mahmoud Darwish, cursing at stupid gringos.

I haven't written a lot about my new roommate, Jenna, from New York, doing graduate studies at an Ivy League school, doing research in Ramallah because she is working at a conference for economic development that will take place the coming June. I think she's a cutter, I saw the marks on her arms; she also smokes a lot of hash. She asks me for permission to do things around the house like smoking and bringing friends over—I don't want to be her mom! Katie has been gone for about ten days, so the energy in the apartment is different. Friends of hers came to get her because she was so depressed she couldn't leave her bed for way too many days in a row. They tell me she's in a facility recovering from PTSD. Jenna has a boyfriend in Bethlehem, which is why she decided to stay and work for important Palestinian people. She's their English translator, and they don't treat her very well. I told her that's the foreigner or white or single woman tax to be reckoned with here.

Things are not looking very bright lately, but neither are they dark, they are just quiet. Near-normalcy is felt, although the peace talks are a joke and everyone knows it. They are building settlements across the West Bank like crazy. Angela Merkel recently visited Israel without paying a visit to the West Bank, and this means completely siding with Israel. Canada took Israel off its list of human rights violators. Palestine keeps shrinking and shrinking, and we all just want some space to keep moving on with our lives. Condoleezza Rice asked Obama to pressure Olmert to remove checkpoints but to keep those necessary for Israeli security.[146] The law regarding Route 4370, a highway that Palestinians will be forbidden to drive on, has been approved by Israel.[147] Quiet insanity, neither sumud nor resistance, only Gaza holds on. Massive repression has followed, disquieting soothing quietness.

Last night, two guys who work for National Geographic dropped by at Zan. They are in the area to do research for reportage about Arab Christians. They have a beautiful Palestinian woman as their native informant and main contact. They asked us a lot of questions about Zan: when does it get full, what kind of people come here, etc. They were surprised I have a wireless connection. Rachel Corrie's parents also came to town yesterday to accompany the staging of her play, to promote her book, and to talk about their daughter. I couldn't make it to the play. Why are these parents who have lost a child to this war, so active but other parents aren't? Rachel Corrie's parents are here to discuss the legal battle they've been fighting against the American government regarding the conditions of her autopsy and transport back to the US, and about how their daughter's death led them to become activists. Said and F said, "Activism is a colonialist luxury, colonialism comes with its cure." F is opening up about his opinion about foreigners and NGOs, about their adrenaline-seeking curiosity. According to him, people who came to Palestine in the 1990s were much more interesting.

It is true that with things feeling relatively quiet (after the Second Intifada and the Israeli invasion, I mean), more and more people are coming to the West Bank. In one week, about seventy people joined the Yahoo group RamallahRamallah. I posted the sublet for Katie's room and I got at least five people interested.

Then I ended up at Zan with F again. We had a conversation about his alcoholism; I shared some of my experiences. Of course, he is in complete denial, lately sparing the beer and going straight to lots of arak, probably blaming me for it. Lately he talks about being foolish around me, about his golden laughter, laughing about wanting me, and I want to tell him: I am tempted to love you but I can't, I can't go home with you blurry, when you're just half there. I want you whole, not in denial, running away from yourself. You are addicted to evading yourself. Running away from the reality that you are not too dangerous for them (or so you think) so you get to be spared, not imprisoned, not killed. Last night you left with your dignity intact after seven araks, Mustapha was making comments about your drinking, you left when you had to go and I missed you, but I thanked you.

The night before (or two nights before?) we sat with a bunch of Qattanites and this beautiful, beautiful woman in her early forties in charge of some cultural center in Jerusalem who'd just gotten out of prison because last Sunday, a bunch of people gathered in the Palestinian National Theater in East Jerusalem to launch Jerusalem as the cultural capital of the Arab world in 2009. Of course the Israelis didn't like this, so they shut the theater down. To keep the gathering going, the crew moved to a coffee shop. There, they started to sing the Palestinian national anthem and then arrests came. Huda was imprisoned for two days. She told us that she had been interrogated by some guy who spoke good Arabic. Her wrist was bandaged, and she'd come out as a hero to celebrate her release, to tell her story, and to be consoled by friends. I was blown away by this beautiful woman, but then I felt estranged from the conversation, not because everyone was speaking Arabic (with F occasionally providing good subtitles) but because we were all women (except F) and women's talk is gossip, so gossip there was, including a review of AH's wedding: beautiful *hafla*, he looked *ktir marbsut*, and I just wanted to puke, and, of course, I didn't get subtitles for this, which got me into a really bad mood.

I've had such a bad headache since yesterday, I thought I was going blind. The bright morning light felt like it was blinding me further, and my right eye just couldn't focus. I felt like I was seeing through wet glasses and the drops were blurring the focus. It hurt, and I was scared of going blind. I had been writing my suicide-bomber-as-witness paper, which was due in a couple of days. Spring had come, but after two days passed, it got too cold again. Yesterday F and I had a discussion about how to empower people if they have been educated to be narrow-minded. Ken Loach's film from 1970 about a girl that gets sent to a mental hospital came up. The connections linking us to social structures and social behavior are the first to harden up in the brain and are therefore the hardest to change. The girl from the movie gets to make a clean slate through electroshock therapy, which was the solution in the 1970s. In her case, the social-neuronal structures hadn't hardened enough, and that is why she had been questioning them, rebelling against them. Javier T. made a beautiful film (or so I hear) for the Whitney Biennial based on Diderot's *Letters to the Blind Man*, and we must be connected in the noosphere somehow as I'd been thinking about blindness for a few months now, connecting Godard's inquiry into seeing/reading/knowing. Javier T. had eight blind people encounter an elephant and then describe their experiences. It's apparently the most charming piece of the whole biennial.

So the National Geographic Americans from yesterday at Zan found this Mexican wearing wrestling boots living in the West Bank incredibly exotic and felt uncomfortable when I told them that Ramallah feels like Tijuana visually, not in spirit but also because of its closeness to another place you need to cross to. I told them it reminds me of the steep contrasts one feels going back and forth between TJ/San Diego. Dirar was having a conversation with Mustapha Abu Ali (who then joined F and me for drinks, of course) about his life in Haifa, about segregation between Jews, Druze, and Arabs, about al-Birwa, his village (which is the same village where Mahmoud Darwish is from). Mustapha asked him lots of questions about al-Birwa and his family and his life in Haifa. I am not sure how often Mustapha has been to '48 Palestine, but he seemed to know it very well. It seemed that the conversation was, for Mustapha, like getting news from an old friend from home. The lost became very present, I could feel their nostalgia, and I was very touched. Mustapha wanted to know who the good filmmakers of today are, and I gave him a list. He told me that he is not interested in the kind of cinema that tells a story (of course! Fiction is useless from his militant filmmaker's point of view). I liked his film *They Do Not Exist* (1974) very very much; I compared it to Rossellini, but he doesn't like him! He said he's pretentious.

In these apparently quiet times, Palestine is working hard to get her pieces together, again, with renewed force, looking at education and at what is going wrong, at culture and what is going wrong. Ali complained they're backward, and I told him: you don't even want to hear about the Mexican mediocre postcolonial/colonial crisis that's been going on for the past three centuries. At least in Palestine people know my mother tongue is Spanish when I say I'm from Mexico, which is hardly the case in many so-called developed countries. We spoke about the Cortázar short story and we wondered why people kept the keys to their homes when in "Casa tomada" the narrator throws the key down the sewer. Because Palestinians thought the displacement was temporary: they were sure they were going to return in a few months. The key has become the symbol for *Al-'awda*, and they pass it on from generation to generation.

Today the sky reminds me of Mexico City, it's gray and dusty. I miss the unbearable blue blue blue of the Palestinian sky. F gave me *The Way of the Peaceful Warrior*, a book that was apparently really important for Hussein

Barghouti, and for F too. Yesterday he was in a really sad mood; there had been a workshop for Ramallah teachers at Qattan in which they screened and discussed a Jordanian film about catcalling. F told me that the workshop attendees agreed that women who are insulted on the street deserve it because they are not properly dressed. That depressed him; then, Shadi was around sending waves of negativity and cynicism. I suppose that, in spite of having many privileges, it is very difficult to be an Israeli Palestinian. They're fully immersed daily in racism and aggression and so they need to cultivate their own in order to be able to speak back, to reduce their feelings of bitterness, displacement, and alienation.

I should go back to Haifa and visit Maria, Dirar, and Dabdoub, then make my way up to Akko and Nazareth. I would also like to spend some time in Jenin. I was supposed to go with Yousef, but lately I just don't have the patience for him. Besides, we're both broke, so we postponed the trip until further notice. Beirut is calling me louder and louder as well—will I make it to Sarajevo in August with Nora? We'll see. Toronto in September, Mexico in October, New York in November? And when will I come back to Palestine? I feel less enthusiastic about my nonacademic writing, I don't know why. F is trying to convince me that my uneasiness is a good sign.

Why did I come here? To get a political education, awareness, to come to protests. Apparently this is what attracts people to Palestine: the highly politicized environment, where everything is inevitably a political statement. Now Palestinians in the West Bank are a bit disappointing because they have stopped actively resisting occupation. Is this a sign that they have they given up? Of course not! Although there is a general feeling of defeat, there is mistrust of Abbas, people are fed up with the situation and wish to lead normal lives. Gaspar, the animation teacher, came from Hebron, and I might catch up with him later. The Swede completely disappeared from the landscape (I am not surprised), and I got a glimpse of the sexy Bombay cameraman who came here to shoot for L. They filmed Zacharia Zbeidi in Jenin. Silvia, back in Mexico, wants me to put together a proposal to her museum-director friend in Haifa for a solo show; she said that would give me an excuse to have an Israeli residency permit. But I told her I'm retiring from the art world. What will I do when I get my life back once I'm done with the damn PhD?

I WATCH THE LOVE AND CARE with which Abu Aljaz prepares coffee. He spends some good five minutes preparing the *kemkha* (foam) because he knows I like it. *Bint al-yamani* is another name given to coffee. To prepare it, you need to boil water first, add as many spoons as you wish, depending on the desired thickness, and let it boil again. When you add the coffee, foam rises, and you can increase the amount of foam by spinning the spoon. Once the foam is formed, you must carefully pour it into the cups, then you let the coffee boil one more time and serve it with love.

S (the Swedish activist) tells me her horror story about crossing the border last night: a 20,000 shekel fine after a weeklong stay at Allenby and a denied entry. I pay a visit to the Jelazone cultural center during a course for animation special effects. Passing by, I hear that, as the Olympics are approaching, there might be a war with Lebanon.

Apollinaire: "Artists all, above all, are those humans who fight to be inhuman."[148] Gilles Deleuze: "Si vous êtes pris dans le rêve de l'autre, vous êtes foutu" (If you're trapped in the other's dream, you're fucked).[149]

I want to write about F's sisters' wedding, but I'm not sure about what. It took place in an indoor party room where men and women were segregated. While the women danced and danced, the men smoked and gossiped in a room on the floor above. Everyone drank remarkable amounts of sugary drinks. How do they do it, putting up with each other without getting intoxicated with alcohol? Does the sugar rush do the trick? Tzikriat and I were the only women smoking in our room. The little girls had the best time, dancing nonstop; they graciously extended their arms, exuding sweetness and femininity, swinging their hips as well. The wedding ended early (no comparison with Mexican weddings, which can start at 1 pm and end the next day at 6 am), and what I enjoyed the most was when the men came up to the women's area and stood in line to congratulate the bride and groom. That's when the single ladies did their shopping.

THE DAUGHTERS OF THE GREAT Sheikh or Imam of Jerusalem invited me over to their home for lunch. The youngest is a volunteer at Qattan; the oldest is pursuing an MA in sociology and literature focused on Ghassan Kanafani at Birzeit University. Kanafani is known to be the first Palestinian writer—that is to say, the first to describe the history of the Palestinian condition. Kanafani was also active member of the PLFP; he claimed responsibility for a terrorist attack in Lod in 1972, and that same year, it is heard, the Mossad murdered him in Beirut.[150] I found a book of his short stories, which had been published in the 1970s, at the Jerusalem Hotel bookstore.

N and B live with their older brother, who is single and owns eight turtles that live on the rooftop. The turtles are very bourgeois, as they are fed *jiar* (with the heavy snows the price of cucumber went up, as has the price, generally, of everything). Their parents left to live in Jerusalem when the wall was built. The sermons of the great Imam of the Al-Aqsa Mosque were transmitted every Friday on Palestinian television. In another attempt to displace the Palestinian capital away from Jerusalem, two weeks ago the Friday sermons began to be broadcast from a mosque in Ramallah.

We were joined at their home by a neighbor and one of B's classmates from a village near Betunia; the neighbor told me that his mother wears the traditional *Fuṣṭān* and that he has spent the last fifteen years going in and out of Israeli jails. The conversation during the gathering was mostly in Arabic; I listened and fished for words here and there. The sisters are gorgeous, with huge clear eyes, sharp elegant features, and feminine curls. The older brother offered me cigarettes, a kind of small cigar made of tobacco from Hebron; they were very good. N prepared filled zucchini or *Kousa Mahsi*, virgin rumballs, and mango juice. Being the daughters of the great Imam didn't turn out to be easy. N was dying for a new kitchen and trying to evade pressure from her sister; her friends also pressured her to pursue a prestigious master's degree. After all, their mother is a prominent translator and Qur'an scholar; they show me proudly a copy of one of the books she has published.

I help translate a text AH will read during the opening of the contemporary dance festival, and a line surprises me: "We will receive those who don't
know the occupation but who will return home full of love and gratitude."
I'm not sure what to think. I despise those who confuse vulgarity with freedom, who ignore the difference between terror and revolution, between being
radical and being reactionary, those incapable of laughing at themselves and
closed off to change. The screams of the tortured ones, and the survivor's
guilt of the privileged; aesthetics after Auschwitz: A kind of bad metaphysics
of beauty? Attempts to find moral substance in what is human, or to tran-
substantiate horror?

LAST SATURDAY I GOT A VISIT from the Swedish journalist. I felt spied on because he came by unannounced, and because he said he knew where I lived because he once saw me leaving one of my neighbors' apartments wearing golden shoes (I was headed to F's sister's wedding, but I was wearing a golden blouse, not golden shoes). He told me about his life in Hebron, that he now spends his days in the market chatting people up. At the beginning they didn't trust him and accused him of being a spy (I heard that about him from a couple of locals). To earn respect he applies certain tactics: when he gets together with the *shababs*, he confessed, he spends his time discussing sex. He tells me they dream of getting two hundred shekels or more to visit the prostitutes in Bethlehem (who are, on average and according to him, fifty years old). He told me that the *shababs* watch porn all day and have fantasies about young virgins. He was curious about what it is like for me to live in Palestine as a woman from Mexico. Adhaf Soueif, the Egyptian writer, reflects in a chapter from her book *Mezzaterra* on foreign women in Egypt and how they carry the stigma of being "easy." Apparently, foreigners in the Middle East have an "available" sign tattooed on our foreheads, leading many to make shameless passes as they confuse freedom with vulgarity. We went out for chicken and, from there, to Al-Kasaba to see the French dance troupe Danse de Signes perform. Amazing dancers, but mediocre choreography. And we didn't end up in bed.

SWEDISH LUBRICANT, ORANGE UNDERWEAR, a gallery of mismatched earrings, a new set of sheets and a stove, fancy face cream, a lonely sandal. Traces in the cave of passersby.

"Do you know who I am?"

"*Shuai*," he said, feeling that anything could be the wrong answer, as he heard a *poooong* coming out from her eyes. After a while she softened her facial expression and her eyes caressed his. "A bit, some," he finally answered.

"What is it that you see in my eyes?"

"I see a river of love. What do you see in mine?"

"Only suffering is visible to my eyes."

"I see lusty, drunken eyes."

"Then you haven't really seen. You haven't seen me. You can't see."

"OK, go crucify yourself again. But do it right this time, Pedro Juan.[151] What is it that you see in my eyes?"

"I see doubt."

"That's weird. You should see my love for you in them."

"I'm not a passerby, neither are you."

"Neither am I."

[ . . . ]

"My boobs hurt."

"Yeah? Why?"

"I'm not sure, I'm ovulating so it's normal. But they're bigger and more sensitive than usual. And they miss you."

"And I them. Maybe you should leave them here."

"Yeah, on the wall, as part of your little memorial, next to the photograph of your mother, the New Poets, Hussein Barghouti, your blurred Korean calligraphy exercises, and the photo with your friend Nigel; framed between two different earrings of the kind in orientalist fantasies (from two different women, I suppose) and the cheap orange Scandinavian silk slip (from H&M?) hanging from the corner by those beautifully calligraphed poems."

"No, that's where your bra will go."

"I don't know where else my boobs could hang." (Tears start flooding her eyes; she gives up and stays still with the coffee cup between her folded naked legs, staring at it and turning it around to make the liquid cool more quickly. Craving its sweet taste, she feels bitter and sad inside, curses her boobs because they do hurt like hell. "Are you going to work?"

"No, I'm staying home today. It's one of those days in which it is hard to put up with the world out there."

A heated discussion about evolution and development follows. "Things are neither better nor worse, they just change. I'm a natural product of Islamic culture of the past fourteen centuries and to 'evolve' means to have the possibility to discuss with others the problems of the world (although I admit that what remains of Islamic culture is completely decadent)." Being enslaved to daily habits makes a change in his routine a source of intolerable anxiety and horror: that is the meaning of suffering for him. He tells himself: "To find ways to make the world more bearable for myself, instead of staying coiled in arrogance looking toward an unreachable ideal, I need to accept my own (physical, intellectual, economic, and social) limitations and to keep on walking." That day, he is not up to facing the world because he refuses to interact with a distorted version of himself. The mirror she had placed in front of him had created an additional layer of pain, making his addiction and his inability to deal with life evident. Above all, he did not want to hear from her that Marxism is a dead ideology that needs to be reinvented. Condescendingly and with love, those around him are used to helping him maintain his illusions while keeping their distance. After all, he thinks he is much better than them because he is above everyone, so nothing they could say could question his moral authority. He constantly feels the urge to construct beautiful things; once he does, he destroys them and enjoys watching them crumble with Wagnerian fury, demonizing the loved object, letting pride and fear win over desire. He then starts over again, dragging others to wallow in the shit with him, the shit of survivor's guilt and impotent desperation. What do masculine self-destruction, punk self-degradation, rock self-annihilation, and anarchist terror have in common? Do they relate to one another?

**DARLING,**

I thought about you a few days ago

My sister and I went to see a film at the Hot Docs festival—*The Art Star and the Twins*—and Vanessa Beecroft sort of reminded us of you b/c of her naiveté, passion, and lovely freckles, funny no?

i hope you're not offended by the comparison (she doesn't come out as the most reasonable woman in the movie)

Love,
M.


**DUNNO HOW TO RESPOND TO** this. What did I do wrong? How is Palestine comparable to Sudan? Adopting Sudanese twins to moving to the West Bank? I am just speechless! Am I naive and unreasonable? Passionate and lovely? This is very frightening. I am mute with ire. Me a Vanessa Beecroft playing United Colors of Benetton? At least the documentary is critical of Beecroft's endeavors. I do a quick Google search and find out that the documentary follows Beecroft to Sudan, where she adopts malnourished orphan twins. Then, the camera follows the actress to Venice while she puts together her project for the Fifty-Second Venice Biennial: *Still Death! Darfur Still Deaf?* is a performance in which white women wearing full black body makeup lie on their stomachs on a platform on the ground. There, they are bathed with bucketfuls of blood thrown at them by a white woman (without black makeup). The artist is interested in investigating—according to the documentary's trailer—whether women in any way ended up being psychologically or physically affected by the war; if they were not, whether they had been sexually attacked by a family member or had undergone any other type of violence. In the trailer, Beecroft states that she wanted to adopt the two

FIG. 9. Vanessa Beecroft and the Sudanese Twins, 2008, courtesy of the artist.

babies because they were malnourished. While she states this, we see one of babies sucking from a white breast. "For some reason, I was blessed with real milk, so I spent about ten days nourishing them. If they had me since then, they might not have thought that they didn't have a mother. Why not extend our wealth to someone else?" Kidnapping and fetishizing the black babies. Where to begin to link colonial exploitation with white condescendence?

"To live better" is a slogan that goes well beyond populism. "The right to happiness," another propagandistic neoliberal right-wing slogan, is a right granted through credits and by the privatization of public services. For Horkheimer, fascist thought demands that subjects "be reasonable." Living in Palestine is unreasonable, so, like Vanessa, I am not being reasonable. But what is *not reasonable* is the daily suffering to which Palestinians have been subject for the past fifty years. Asymmetrical military force, psychological warfare, oppression through infrastructure and the economy subject them every day to Israel. *This is not reasonable!* The Israeli security apparatus *is not reasonable* (just as it is not effective, I hear). The intensity of the violence *is not reasonable!* Perhaps it is not reasonable to be exposed to the danger that living in the Occupied Territories implies? I feel endangered in Israel. Palestinians are subjected to Israeli irrationality. Palestinian life is irrational; that is why its people sometimes make irrational choices. I am irrational for having come to live in an "intractable" place, as observers have described it.[152]

BOREDOM, CLAUSTROPHOBIA, DOUBT, solitude, feeling overwhelmed by the balding red hills that make me nauseous with their dust and overbearingness that makes my mind want to flee through their curves. F's house is inhabited by some twenty semiwild cats; Tiresias, the kitten that was born blind, died yesterday and ended up being butchered by his mothers and siblings. He'd been agonizing for the past two weeks, and three days before he expired we had begun to feed him milk with a syringe until he began to refuse it. The mothers had given up for a while and stopped feeding him; they got busy helping the strongest kittens to survive. Tiresias's head was much bigger than his body; he remained disoriented at the edge of an old couch, all the time trying to avoid falling over. His siblings spent a lot of time cuddling him. We all knew he was going to go today, but we didn't want to find him dead. It came to worse than that because we found him torn to pieces: a chunk of head here, a leg over there. There was no blood, only some of his hair scattered on the couch. We supposed that animals cannot distinguish between a piece of fresh meat and the body of an animal of their own species. Or that pulling him to pieces was a means of burying him collectively.

The animal world is, to our eyes, wild and violent. Why did we feel sorrow, disgust, and horror when we saw that the other cats had devoured Tiresias? Do these feelings arise because we are used to anthropomorphizing animals? Take, for example, Werner Herzog's *Grizzly Man* (2005), for which the German director edited hundreds of hours of video footage that had belonged to Timothy Treadwell, an American man who devoted the final years of his life to documenting and protecting grizzly bears in Alaska. Treadwell spent many summers interacting with the bears, and on his last trip he decided to stay for two weeks longer than usual with his girlfriend, and this is when the bears devoured both of them. What puzzled the people who found traces of their bodies was that the huge mammals hadn't killed them to feed themselves but instead had viciously attacked the couple. One of the explanations for the extreme violence of the attack was that the creatures felt disoriented and threatened by the humans' unexpected presence in their territory. In the film's voiceover, Herzog juxtaposes his own (Romantic) vision of nature with Treadwell's. He discusses the sublime, dark, horrendous, and incomprehensible aspects of natural forces, which contrast with the American man's perception of the bears he keeps trying to humanize, attributing emotions and intentions to them. For the German filmmaker, nature is dark, it is horror. So is violence.

And I think about ways in which the kind of violence operative at a whole other dimension is internalized in the occupation, into what no one wants or can see or is capable of sublimating. A very raw form of violence is felt in Jenin. We get there quickly, in less than an hour; there were no checkpoints that would stop us, and the *servīs* (collective taxi) driver was going at full speed. I tend to get sick during car rides, but this time I fell hard asleep on the road. When we go to Jenin *balad* (the city), I was a bit disappointed because there wasn't much to see. The city has been completely destroyed, and most of the buildings are new: a mall, a hideous tower, a sad marketplace, tiny filthy restaurants. The city's edges are made up of wheat fields of a hundred colors ranging from intense green to ochre yellow. On the horizon, two Israeli settlements are visible. The occupation does not *seem* too close there, but the incursions are surely felt. People downtown greet us in Hebrew. With his long hair and rebellious Western ways, Yousef could pass for a foreigner. We find a nice restaurant and order hummus.

"Where are you from?" a young boy standing in line to buy ice cream asks us as we pass.

I stop and order one for myself and answer: "From Mexico."

A kid next to him exclaims: "Márquez? Márquez from the Barcelona?"

"*Aiwa* (yes). He's a distant cousin of mine."

"*Walla*? Máquez *ibn 'ammik*?" (Really? Márquez is your cousin?)

"Prove it! Come play soccer with us for a while."

Outside a dry cleaner's shop a kid calls me *sharmuta*. I curse right back at him in Arabic, and he disappears in half a second. I think about the scene in *Nervus Rerum* in which the camera wandering, or rather floating, through the Jenin refugee camp runs into a tiny boy who stares furiously and yells inaudible things at it, then goes into a house to grab a plastic gun with which he threatens the camera.

We get to the Freedom Theater and run into Zacharia Zbeidi, the leader of the Jenin resistance in 2002. According to the legend, when he surrendered his weapons, Zbeidi negotiated an arrangement with the Israelis as other members from the brigade were killed or incarcerated. Some swear he's a collaborator—who isn't around here? Legend says that for a while he was together with an Israeli activist and journalist, Tali Fahima; he is also one of the most active members of the theater. I was told that he made many people angry because in an interview with the PNA he spoke very badly of them. We watched him get into Juliano Mer-Khamis's jeep. Juliano is the son of an Israeli Jewish woman (Arna) and a Palestinian man. In the 1990s, Arna founded a theater workshop for children in the Jenin refugee camp. After working with them for a decade, Arna died of cancer. During the Second Intifada, Juliano made a documentary, *Arna's Children*, editing footage of Arna's workshop together with images from the kids, now grown up. Most of Arna's students had died as martyrs, others went to prison, all had taken up arms. Zbeidi was one of the survivors who remained free. After the global dissemination of the documentary, Juliano got subsidies for the theater, and what used to take place in a tiny apartment became full-blown theater in a first-rate building, with rooms for rehearsals, seminars, offices, and an apartment for guests and residents. The Jenin theater troupe has done international tours and is one of the bastions of Palestinian cultural resistance. The theater is controversial in Israel as in Palestine: in Israel because it constitutes an image of progressive pacific resistance and in Palestine, especially for radicals and Muslims, because it pacifies armed resistance and corrupts young people with Western habits, like not segregating the sexes.

In 2011, three years after I visited the theater, Juliano was murdered by an unidentified commando right outside of the theater while carrying his one-year-old son in his arms. No one claimed the attack, all the groups are suspects. His widow, Jenny Nyman, a Finnish activist, was left to her own devices, pregnant with twins. She remained in Jenin to continue Juliano's work. The same year Juliano was murdered, theater producer, director, and actor François Abou Salem, founder of the Jerusalem Theater, killed himself. Globally, we mourned for two luminaries of resistance, experimentation, radicality, and hope in Palestine.

Zacharia Zbeidi starts up Juliano's jeep and fully accelerates just to advance the vehicle, propelling the car forward thirty-five centimeters, dangerously approaching the theater's gates. After the mishap, he recovers his characteristic nonchalance and states with a smile:

"What is this? It's completely crazy!"

"It's a display of Apache love," I hear someone around there say.

Zacharia disappears behind the dust that the jeep's acceleration leaves behind, and we hear squealing tires when he takes a turn onto the refugee camp's main avenue. The frenzy of Zacharia's driving contrasts with the paralysis of the camp, the feeling of waiting to return, for a country, for a future.

While opportunities diminish, boredom and violence increase as children become adults and the quality of life degrades visibly for every succeeding generation. Palestinians are systemically reduced to shadows of what they once were, soaked with hope and violence for lack of a future.

I think about Pedro Páramo in Ramallah or Jenin, like Comala. Halfway between life and death, Comala is a kind of purgatory in which souls continue their earthly suffering, incapable of finding consolation or the certitude of eternal punishment. Comala is a wasteland, the barren zone in which nothing can grow. The living are not welcome, and no one can escape. There is no one in Comala, only fragments of living beings, lamentations and wailing are heard, loose fragments of their old inhabitants. There is silence and the momentary illusion that death can be vanquished, or at least suspended. The chief crumbles like a pile of rocks. After the revolution, Comala remains arid and lonely.

"Mi madre siempre vivió suspirando por Comala, por el retorno, pero jamás logró volver."

"Su cara se transparentaba como si no tuviera sangre y sus manos estaban marchitas y apretadas de arrugas. No se le veían los ojos."

"Llanuras verdes, ver subir y bajar el horizonte con el viento que mueve las espigas, el rizar de la tarde con la lluvia de triples rizos. El color de la tierra, el olor de la alfalfa y el pan. Un pueblo que huele a miel derramada."

"El pueblo está lleno de ecos. Tal parece que estuvieran cerrados en el hueco de las paredes o debajo de las piedras. Cuando caminas, sientes que te van pisando los pasos. Oyes crujidos. Risas. Unas risas ya muy viejas, como cansadas de reír. Y voces ya desgastadas por el uso. Todo eso oyes. Pienso que llegará el día en que estos sonidos se apaguen."[153]

El bien, quisimos el bien:
                              enderezar al mundo.
No nos faltó entereza:
                    nos faltó humildad.
Lo que quisimos no lo quisimos con inocencia.
. . . . . . . . . . . . . . . . . . . .
                    Y lo más vil: fuimos
el público que aplaude o bosteza en su butaca.
La culpa que no se sabe culpa,
                              la inocencia,
fue la culpa mayor.

OCTAVIO PAZ[154]


**DEAR M,**

I suppose you can imagine why I haven't responded to your emails, and why I choose to write to you as opposed to returning your call. I am absolutely baffled and only a little less speechless by the note you sent me from Toronto comparing my decision to live in Palestine with Vanessa Beecroft's trip to Sudan. You wrote that she sort of reminded you of me because our naiveté, passion and freckles, and because she is not reasonable. I think the "lovely freckles" part really helps to veil some passive-aggressiveness here . . . Yes, M, I have never felt so insulted, both as a scholar or as a person. Your analogy is very stupid, although your unconscious link between Sudan and Palestine sort of gives me hope. It also seems that your assertion shows that you didn't see—and really didn't want to see—the irony in my New Year's postcard. I'm afraid I have not told you enough about my reasons for coming here, but this has been out of a basic respect and a tacit understanding that we would not discuss the political situation of your country. Respect and mutual understanding are the basics for friendship, and calling me "Passionate and lovely" is only condescending and belittling. The main question of my dissertation is how to speak and act in the name of others, and I naively assumed that after having known me and my work for the past five years, this is what would come to your mind when you see a white person acting politically, ethically, and even as a tourist in "third world" or war zones. How does asking the question of how to speak and act in the name of others during my prolonged visit to Palestine compare to breastfeeding malnourished black babies? I am not white, and I am not making images of black bodies spread out in pools of blood, nor am I aestheticizing violence through a conscious reference to Yves Klein's misogynist blue performative paintings from the 1960s. I thought that from reading my work it would be clear to you that it is at the crossroads of postcolonial and geopolitical thought, focusing on how the West and the North have related to the East and the South in the past forty years, specifically on the question of Palestine.

Here's what Beecroft said: "For some blessing I had real milk, I spent about 10 days nourishing them. If they had me since then they might have not thought that they didn't have a mother. Why not extend our wealth to someone else?" Please tell me how this statement relates to my dissertation or to the reasons I have expounded elsewhere about my choice of moving here. Here is the list of reasons I wrote back in December, which is a bit distant from how I see my prolonged visit to the West Bank now. Here it is regardless, if you care to take a look:

**Linguistic:** I wanted to stop saying "Ramallah" and learn how to pronounce "Ramallah."

**Cynical:** Outsourcing; it's cheaper to live here than in Canada. Besides, Canada is too cold and too low-intensity and I discovered I can think better in high-intensity places. I was too bored in Toronto.

**Guilt trip:** I am an Israeli in Mexico and I knew no guilt before coming here. I am guilty because I am innocent.

**Ethical:** I felt a responsibility to get to know the state of affairs firsthand in order to write and speak about it. I wanted to go beyond taking the obvious pro-Palestinian position of the consensual liberal Left. Nobody disagrees on the wrongs that are done here, and yet there is still a big misunderstanding in how the conflict is understood in terms of humanitarian "ethics," as such an approach obliterates the social and political aspects of the occupation.

FIG. 10. Self portrait as: "This is another chapter in the sad saga of the radical intellectual projecting her fantasies in a foreign exotic uprising that allows simultaneously satisfaction of her emancipatory desires and a secret 'masochist' yearning for hard discipline and masculine oppression."

**Intellectual:** I wanted to get out from the ivory tower of academia and move into practice; to be able to do empirical research in order to better understand the images of the conflict produced both from the inside and from the outside.

**Autobiographical:** Tijuana is not Ramallah is Tijuana (Mexican/American relations, American occupation of Mexico in the 1830s and its outcome today).

**Strategic:** To explore my fluid identity, to decenter myself, and to find a discursive position to address Godard's Eurocentric approach to the question of Palestine.

**Irrational:** A microchip lit up in my head after my first short visit; all I could think of was to come back.

**Political:** Revolutionary singularities shared between Mexico and Palestine; mapping out the question: What is there to be done, today? As a child of NAFTA and globalization, I am interested in exploring the passage from political interventions in the 1970s to cultural and solidarity tourism today.

**Politically correct:** To initiate a transversal dialogue (from the South to the East) as opposed to the usual dialogue between North and South or between East and West.

Two people have advised me to let your analogy pass as an expected trait of the current Israeli levity and denial. I really don't know what to do, but I'm open to discuss this further with you. In the meantime, good luck with everything.

Yours, Gardi.

PS: I have a forthcoming piece where I address some of the concerns specifically relating to contemporary art. I'm attaching it here, in case you're curious.

HEARTBURN THE FIRST DAY, EXHAUSTION on the tenth, unusual pains, different from PMS, soreness in my breasts right away. Some nausea on Saturday. I'm behind three days. Terrible pain in my lower back. I took antibiotics for a UTI. The home test was positive. Two or three days before conceiving I dreamt that I gave birth to a boy, feet first. I experience a too-wide range of emotions: happiness, sadness, plenitude, lightness, confusion: a basic instinct tells me that F is not the right one, and neither is my current situation. I feel terrified with the thought of being pregnant alone in the cold Canadian winter. Maria congratulates me and L gives me a reality check: don't feel like superwoman or believe you can do it on your own. "I've met too many single mothers struggling and too many disastrous marriages," she tells me. F is sad because he doesn't have much to offer us as his story repeats itself for the nth time. It's the kind of bad repetition, dystopian, evil, traumatic. To procreate to hold on in a different and stronger way to the land, procreating as a form of resistance.

I wake up to the sound of a liquid spilling on an object on my bedside: one of the cats is peeing on my suitcase and on my good shirt. With an agitated whisper, I send him off outside. I have the habit of always leaving my suitcase where I can see it, to remind myself that no home is permanent. The cat's pee was a declaration, a claim, a total expression of resentment for my imminent departure. L and W remind me of a general doctor whose office is down Rukab toward Ramallah Tahta, across from a yoga and tae kwan do place. It turned out that he speaks Spanish because his wife is from South America and he lived in Colombia for a while. We began talking about differences between Latin America and the Arab world. "It seems like women have more rights and freedom there than here; parents meddle more in their children's lives. . . ." The solution he offered me consisted of getting an injection, waiting for a week, and then inducing the abortion with some pills. I went for this option, which felt safe and easy to me. When I told F about my decision, he shakily made coffee with salt instead of with sugar and told me we had spilled honey on the pavement.

My roommate says she's feeling depressed and plans on leaving soon; she's in pieces, I can tell. I notice my hormones begin changing when she leaves me a five-hundred-shekel debt for March; forget about April, May, and June. I feel a mad need to cry.

I spent Sunday at L and W's. L tells me W had a psychotic episode and that he has anxiety all the time. I'm anxious too, as I wait for the imminent bleeding and pain. I stay over and W gets me two bags of Doritos; the serotonin makes me feel better. L takes the guitar and begins singing Joni Mitchell songs to me, and a repertoire she's composed herself. "Don't take my heart for ransom," is about being stood up in a city, alone and sad.

I do not want to think of F and his Wagnerian destructive impulse. I tried very hard to keep things together, but, in the end, with no results. W cooks a delicious kufta for dinner, I watch him prepare it very delicately; it turns out with thousands of subtle and hidden flavors. Then, he tells us the story of the radio station he had in Hebron, which ended transmissions after ten months on air when the police invaded the headquarters saying that their radio waves had interfered with a nearby airport. Things became violent, and W ended up in jail. His partner in the radio station was a millionaire orphan who has been arrested many times in Jerusalem for getting involved in fights; W's brother is purging a hundred-year-old sentence for having murdered six Israeli soldiers in cold blood in Hebron's old city.

I began my farewell to Ramallah the night dead life exited my body last Tuesday, when I traveled to Jerusalem to meet Marianne and Jürgen to bring them over to Ramallah. That day, I show them the *muqāṭaʿ*, the old city, the martyr posters hanging across the Orthodox church, the Qattan Foundation. The previous night F had taken us to a restaurant he used to go to with his friend that was murdered by the IDF in 2005. The place, it turned out, is the hidden hangout of fatehawi, reserved for men; *al-ṭayba* and arak are served there. Afterward, we tried to get to the *ḥamām turky* by foot, but we got lost. We stopped at a car mechanic to ask for directions, and the owner ended up giving us a ride there. It turned out he imported cars from Germany and was a Christian. Jürgen complimented the car, and indirectly its owner. We got off at the *ḥamām*; L joined us later, and we stayed soaking our souls for about three hours. W came to pick us up in his car, and he and L invited us over to dinner at their place. They cook a beautiful *za'atter* chicken, and when we are back home, I realize that I am very happy to receive my guests, my adored Marianne and her new partner.

The next day I take them to Hebron, and, while riding in the *servīs*, we meet a Palestinian who lived in Germany and who is also in the automobile business. Gladly, he offered to be our guide in the city; he spoke perfect German and was very kind to us. He had spent twenty years in Nuremberg, and he told us about his life there as if there were no difficulties or racism for migrants. I'd never seen the old city of Hebron like that, with many shops open. We even managed to enter the Abraham Mosque, a site in dispute. Aside from being a mosque, the monument houses the tombs of Jewish prophets, and that is why Israeli settlers have occupied half of the building. They can be spied through the opposite door leading to Abraham's tomb, seen wearing their Orthodox clothing. I had previously been able to enter neither the Muslim nor the Jewish section—it is an exceptionally beautiful place. I notice that our host guide feels ashamed for showing us around his city, where the streets are occupied by settlers and IDF checkpoints. He refused to drive us past the settlements surrounding the city so Jürgen and Marianne could see them. Maybe because of shame or fear. On the way back from Hebron we only had to cross one checkpoint. The hosts were lovely and the food was good, and I'm happy these two didn't have to see the uglier part of Hebron. My German friends have seen enough for a day.

W grew up in a home near the Hebron mosque, which was destroyed in the 1980s by the Israelis, so the family had to find another one. Eventually the family left and settled in Ramallah. The family is composed of siblings with four different mothers. His stories are insane: getting kidnapped and beaten up by soldiers and settlers, tortured at checkpoints, having his home invaded and posing as gay so they'd leave him alone, being shot in the leg. He tells his stories laughing! Marianne and Jürgen got a dose of W's stories on their second night in Ramallah. According to F, all is quiet in the West Bank because of the Bethlehem economics conference taking place these days. There is a huge billboard between Bethlehem and Ram where you can read: "Welcome Palestine Visitors." The conference will place the West Bank for sale and subject it to neoliberal interests and forces; its goal is to attract investors, to open the zone up to import/exports, to establish export processing zones (EPZs), and to offer nonskilled labor. The land and resources are for sale for the highest bidder, all monitored and administered by Israel. Nation-states mediate social relations and the law in the West; here it is the rule of the tribe, the police, the National Authority, the Israeli army. Too many layers of overlapping authority.

*El País*: Seven dead police officers in a shootout in Culiacán, Sinaloa.

Anxiety, uncertainty, sadness, hope, love. Mixed feelings, Palestine is under my skin, Palestinian blood mixed with my blood, the thought is too overwhelming. I feel a great desire to breed life and to create the most significant connection possible for a woman. Understanding womanhood and the core of sexual difference is beyond him; I can't make him understand the feeling of your body changing and how the changes are unforeseen, new feelings, hormones flying, body growing slowly wider, becoming a nest. Then, I feel the relief of my body coming back to normal. Another birthday is coming up. I feel far away and close to myself and I was remembering how I found myself about a year ago. I had gotten lost in the anxiety academia had given me. Misguided ambitions impeded my brain from thinking, acting, getting an overview. Now I'm realizing that the world looks so much more different from this part of the world. War stories, life stories, no hope, death drive, no long-term plans, not even mid-term plans, the tyranny of incertitude creeping into everyone's skin, but then it all feels so quiet and peaceful, lots of unveiled young girls on the streets, walking around, enjoying the weather, the light has changed in Ramallah. The bright summer light is finally back, with its overwhelming blue sky, and my eyes have trouble getting used to it. The comfort of having family-like friends around and the pleasure hosting gives me makes me want to set up a base, settle. But I also feel like I'm not done traveling yet, getting to know the world. After the cat pissed in my suitcase I washed it, but it still stinks. I need to prepare my departure, FedEx things to myself in Canada, and it is all painful and confusing and relieving to know I can escape the tyranny of incertitude here, the boredom, the claustrophobia, slowly wanting to start moving across, up, and down again, my mother is blackmailing me for not coming to my brother's civil wedding and engagement party in Mexico, but it is partly her fault, how she raised us not to feel any solidarity, she didn't teach us to be there for each other, *drôle de famille*. Telenovela material.

Yesterday afternoon, L and W came to kidnap me: we picked up W's brother, Ahmad, and his wife Rita. We hiked a mountain whose name I can't recall, near Birzeit, transformed into a public space after a writer donated the terrain. It consists of a chunk of woods surrounded by mountains, some of them bald, others exuberant green; I see more than three hills with their tops flattened with imitations of Californian suburbs on top. We can hear cars passing by on the Israeli highways, and we can see the security patrol's lights. A settlement is being built on the nearest hill: there are some thirty or so campers and a trailer. I'm not surprised they want it all, it's so beautiful. The Sabbath prayers are heard competing with the Palestinian muezzin. We roast chicken, kufta, garlic, onions, and tomatoes. We smoke hash and drink wine. We laugh and find an energy different from the depressive madness of Ramallah.

The next day I meet M in Jerusalem; she wanted to apologize for our "Beecroftgate." I missed her but was still angry at her for thinking Palestinians had brainwashed me. She suggested that we meet at the bookstore at the American Colony Hotel. "The best in English in all of Israel," I told her. I was a bit depressed after talking to her; she finally realized that being passive is a form of action, that passivity is complicit with all forms of power, that her taxes are invested in settlements. The problem is assuming that every Palestinian is a potential terrorist willing to threaten your beautiful protected lifestyle, protected by your suppression and repression and compression of your guilt and panic. We had a long conversation. She felt judged by me, she confessed. I tried to take up our talks as usual, but when she started saying things like "I thought Palestinians had brainwashed you," "I am relieved to learn this is not your life project," "Today is Shabbat and I went to southern Tel Aviv where it felt very strange, foreign, and surprising to see all those immigrants having a picnic in the park." At least she came to East Jerusalem, a place rarely frequented by Israelis. She apologized some five times, and said something like: "When I'm done with my thesis I will find a way to make this place more livable."

Palestinians complain that there are too few swimming pools, no rivers, only Lake Tiberias, the Dead Sea, the Mediterranean Sea, and the Red Sea, all out of their reach, they had been kidnapped from them. In Mexico something similar happens because of pollution, but no one mourns those lost bodies of water or lack of access to them.

I thought about passing by to say farewell to Khadijeh, who decided to leave for Amman for two months to recover. When I get there, she gives me two beautiful watercolors. She is balding and looks very ill. She only wanted to see me for fifteen minutes; she seemed depressed, vanquished, cancerous. Warm but distant. I told her about the essay I want to write about the documentary on her archive. She tells me about the failure of the political project as analogous to the failure of her marriage.

When I get home, I hear that W had thrown up and that he was feeling sick. My new roommates had moved in two weeks ago. L and I had a long discussion about the history of colonization. According to her, British colonization (which she knows because she's of Hindu origin) was preferable to that of the French. "Look at what the British did in North America, in the Middle East. India's was a mere economic colonization; language, body, soul were not colonized. There was no explicit genocidal project and neither was a new religion or culture imposed." At night, I help F injecting the cats. Lucas and Mishmish are better. Farah's eyes are still swollen, one of them bleeds, she doesn't seem better at all. The newborn kittens got sick with an infection

that killed most of the litter. One, two at the most survive. I suggested injecting them with antibiotics to see if we can save a few more.

I visit with Neta, Yael, and a handful of Italian and Australian activists to
discuss the roads that communicate five small Palestinian villages in which
some fifty thousand persons live. The villages are on a belt around East Jerusalem and are surrounded by seven settlements. These latter are interconnected through route 334, forbidden for Palestinians, for whom a special road
to connect them with Ramallah has been built (they can access Jerusalem,
but only through crossing Qalandya).[155] This road goes under highway 334 and
connects populations living in something like bubbles, or in the holes of a
Gruyère cheese, smaller versions of the Gaza Strip, spaces whose access is
completely controlled by the Israel army, with entries and exits that are narrow and thus easy to block, with control towers and infrastructure like water
and electricity that is easy to cut in the eventuality of needed punishment.[156]

Every stream/current of the wind blowing at night has a name.

It is true that the idea that "others need our help" is analogous to the logic
of the conquest of what today is Latin America. Colonizers brought not only
a catastrophe, but also a "remedy": to save the unfaithful through religion.
Devastation and genocide coexisted with "salvation." The secular missionaries of the twenty-first century, tourists reinforcing human rights, must be
conscious of this history. There is a great contradiction in this kind of tourism: on the one hand, citizens from privileged countries and in the globalized world must assume the responsibility of the privilege they enjoy. On the
other, many do so inspired by having a "good conscience," a mental state that
can be intoxicating, with the adrenaline unleashed by the state of exception
blinding them to the reality of the situation. Perhaps the key lies in the way
of considering and addressing others, sympathizing with them in the most
profound sense of the word instead of "making them others." It is problematic, however, to use empathy and pity as political emotions because, when
doing so, we hinder others from defining themselves as autonomous and politically constituted communities. Not charity or heroism, but political work.

Kinds of extreme tourism: Houellebecq writes about sexual, spiritual, bellicose, lonely, cultural. What is the difference between the impossibility of
loving what is not familiar to us (Freud) and desiring it (Genet, Levi-Strauss)?
Who is that third who always walks on your side? When I count, there's only
you and I. But when I look forward, there is always someone else walking on
your side, sliding into a brown coat with a hood. I'm not sure if it is a man

or a woman walking with/around/between us in this listless hole among the hills, under that pale moonlight.

While redundant populations on the margins across the globe survive through the informal economy, without being capable of imagining better lives, only desiring them, the middle classes are aware that social mobility cannot be realized without the right tools: learning languages, acquiring cultural capital, and, above all, giving their children better prospects. Social mobility projects and social distinction, class consciousness through specific consumption practices: the small global bourgeoisie acquire symbols of Western modernity. The First Intifada's culture of austerity and self-sacrifice had eradicated nightlife and ultradisciplined forms of military training. In the process of understanding an abstract art installation, a Bach cantata, a Maghrebi film with French inflexions, cultural practitioners and those adept to the new sensibilities consume their membership in a new social category with a sharp consciousness. In contrast, during the First Intifada, the nationalist movement had promoted a whole culture of austerity and resistance that had censored popular music, weddings, dancing, and other traps of "normalcy," promoting seriousness with regard to the sacrifices of martyrs, prisoners, and the wounded. Only folklore was allowed. A decade later, new ideas began to be articulated with the collapse of the nationalist consensus and the erosion of the culture of resistance. Resistance was translated to culture.

When the austerity era ended, your ideals expired and you began living in a space of abjection (or in the place where abject things live). The abject is letting go of something we want to keep. Fluxes and bodily waste, pee, shit, hair, which are reminders of what you have lost. Those traces remind you that you cannot bear the world today, you say you're hung over from your hangovers, you get depressed and stay home. Stop complaining! (And his voice echoes the voice of his father while he silences his mother by forcing her to understand the obstacles of her own life.) I feel like an observer of my own emotions, trying to neutralize them, anesthetizing myself from whatever you make me feel. You accuse me of not belonging because I can't deal with a tiny piece of shit and you demand that I accept you as you are, that I understand love as an invitation to the life-space of an other, and you mention that loving you in your complete abjection would be really to love you. "I am not going to change! This is what I am!" I look at you and feel sad while I scan the room and make a list of the traces other passengers in your life have made to better the space. In the end, it's you on your own in your abject space, what is visible are the traces of failure, the tyranny of entropy, a badly digested depression, idealized alcoholism, a mystified lifestyle that transforms you into a parasite wanting to be recognized by claiming responsibility for everyone you believe in. But in truth, you don't need us and that is why you shatter the arak glass on the ground and go to sleep in the other room. War is going to be waged, and it is no longer against normalization. Nor will the cultivation of negation free Palestine. To console the prisoners, the dead, their mothers. It is the time to act out; we don't have the luxury of wallowing in pain. We can overcome the pain. I forbid you to feel any guilt. You can offer me the gift of your repentance, but never of your guilt. Abjection as a psychological condition, as a dark revolt against being, targeted against a threat that seems to emanate from an exorbitant outside, or from a within thrown beyond the field of the possible, the tolerable, the thinkable. It is there, very close, but it cannot be assimilated. Because you cannot come to terms with your losses. You reject what you desire and possess the certitude protecting you from shame, a certitude sustained by your pride. The vertigo of repulsion caused by the tyranny of entropy and of the cats, filth, and dust, gets you out of yourself toward a place where you can protect yourself from your own ghosts. That little piece of shit is your absolute other: that which you have cultivated as marginal, something that does not belong here, like me, but that opposes me. The abject opposes the I and your abject space is opposed to your being, which makes you abject in turn. Meaning stops being produced. I feel like the void is sucking me up, your abjection is contagious, your brutal rejection of life wants to stick to me. When you stop birthing yourself, you become something else and the price is your life. Your pain is infectious.

# Encounter with Mahmoud Darwish at the Grand Park Hotel in Ramallah

SALLY CONNECTS US THROUGH THE Palestinian writer Ziad Khaddash, who joins us to drink a beer at the Grand Park Hotel. Darwish says he accepts the meeting with me because he wants to discuss the role he played in Godard's film *Notre musique*. He speaks of the filmmaker with admiration; he tells me that during the shooting, he only uttered the lines Godard told him to say, that was it. The scene in which Darwish appears is a reenactment of an interview that took place in Amman in 1996 between Darwish and the Israeli poet Helit Yeshurun while Darwish waited to get a permit from Israel to live in Ramallah. Both discuss their status as "victims." Darwish declares: "Palestinians are famous because we have an enemy that the whole world has their eyes on: the Jews." For the remake of the interview in *Notre musique*, Godard substitutes Yeshurun's voice, that of a mature poet, with Judith Lerner, a fictive character, a young woman looking for answers around the conflict. Later on in the film, American Native peoples recite passages from Darwish's poem "The Red Indian's Discourse." We speak about the asymmetry introduced by Godard, I think, to tone down the Israeli poet's arrogance in the original interview. Darwish answers: "I just spoke the lines written on the script Godard gave me." Afterward, the poet mentioned an encounter he had with Octavio Paz in the 1980s; we talked about his position as "official poet" and representative of the Mexican state in 1986, of his resignation as protest against state repression in Tlatelolco. Darwish tells me that in the 1980s, an issue of the Palestinian journal *Al-Karmel* was devoted to

Mexican poetry, translated by Syrian writer Ikram Antaki. We spoke about the universality in Shakespeare. I feel intimidated and hyperconscious for being a woman, which I try to erase by saying smart things, but I'm not very good at it. I am surprised by Darwish's elegance, and by his being a gentleman. Three weeks after our meeting, Darwish died of a heart attack in an operating room in Houston, Texas. I remain mute; when *This Week in Palestine* asks me to write an obituary recalling our encounter, I can't do it.

I GET TO THE VILLAGE at around one o'clock. Next to the mosque there is a community center where all international visitors gather. Everyone but me came from First World countries like Germany, Spain, France, Canada, and the US. A mad Irishman and two lost Koreans were also there. After waiting for some fifteen minutes talking to Maria—the girl from Galicia who says she has no country and that there are no nations, that Palestinian women should also join the protest, that the *shabab* should not throw stones, and that national identity does not exist—I join the meeting at the community center, during which we receive the following instructions: "Cover up your face if tear gas is cast; if you feel sick, sit under an olive tree and wait for it to pass; if rubber bullets are shot, do not duck because they aim at the feet; above all, do not throw stones, we are here to protest in peace with the Palestinians and, if we can, to be their shields against the attacks from the Israeli soldiers." When the Friday prayer ended, the demonstration began. There were about forty locals and an equal number of foreigners. Most remain below the trees demarcating the road, about 1.5 kilometers long, leading to one of the access points for the gate (which is not a wall yet). The area surrounded by the gate is shaped like an inverted pear; on its belly there is a hill and a Palestinian house. The gate is bordered by a road used by the army. That's where a jeep parks, to the right of the home and five hundred meters away from where I was standing. At the gate there were two more jeeps. We came down chanting slogans and carrying posters, which, frankly, were terrible, with images of wounded Palestinians and activists in past demonstrations. When the vanguard of the protest—composed in its entirety by *shabab*—arrives at the gate, they begin throwing stones to the soldiers. Soldiers counterattack with sound bombs for twenty minutes (for the past four days I've had a head and ear ache because of the detonations). Afterward, they begin to throw tear gas—around three hundred canisters, I am told—and the cartridges flare up some of the olive trees. The *shabab* do not stop throwing stones from their strategic hiding places among the trees. Two press vans are also hidden near the house; suddenly, everyone starts running and there is a moment in which almost nothing is visible because there is so much tear gas. The wind is blowing against us, there are some ten soldiers shooting up to fifteen gas bombs at once. Cartridges start falling near me, as close as thirty centimeters from my feet. I run to the opposite side and one of the Palestinians lets me and Maria know that we have to look up to avoid the cartridges. He gives us each a Kleenex with alcohol to cover our mouths. Some thirty canisters are shot at a group of Palestinians waving a Palestinian flag some three hundred meters behind us. The whole thing lasts for about two hours, until someone decides that the protest has ended. Ibrahim's brother—wounded last week by a cluster bomb—had been previously wounded in a confrontation with the IDF in 2000 and, since then, he has been using a wheelchair. With pride, he shows Maria and me the home he is building with his own hands to inhabit with his unknown future wife. He goes up and down the road in his wheelchair picking up the cartridges scattered on the road. The tear gas bombs fired up some of the terraces of olive trees. The *shabab* kept on throwing stones from the gully, very close of the soldiers, protecting themselves behind the old olive trees, the ones offering generous cover, with thick trunks, so wide that they cannot be surrounded by someone's arms. An older Palestinian man was wearing the Palestinian flag as a cape and kept running up and down the road. Someone gives me another piece of cotton with alcohol to reduce the effect of the tear gas. Cartridges begin to rain again; I run, feeling disoriented. Rubber bullets are shot at the *shabab*. An American with Asian traits asks me to take a photo of him capturing the Israeli tank at the bottom of the hill. "Nothing like this can be seen in the US, like the police attacking people." No comment. After a while, a journalist encourages us to go back down because the shooting has apparently diminished. "Come on! They need us!" Confused, gassed, and scared, most decide to remain up, some go back to the village. I go further down the road, but when the shooting begins again, I go right back up to observe how a group of *shababs* stands waving the Palestinian flag for five minutes under a rain of ammunition and a spicy fog. Ibrahim invites us over to his place to drink tea; some five Israelis that speak a bit of Arabic come with us.

I'M AFRAID I LEFT EVERYTHING HALF DONE: the description of the trip with Rebecca through the West Bank, the farewell to F and Ramallah, Sally's generosity. I arrived Monday night as if I had dreamed the red earth, the soldiers, the tanks, my friends' love. The first thing I did was to find Palestine in Toronto, to contact Sally's friends so that they would welcome me to Canada. The crossing back was uneventful. M had asked me to come by to see her in Tel Aviv before getting to the airport. ("So that I am able to lie better to the airport's security services in case they call me," she tells me.) I left F in *duwwar as-sa'a*; I watched him walk away toward Zan, clutching his gut cramp and ulcer. For the last days we were depressed, nearly completely in silence, making love but not a lot (Saturday night a literal fuck confused me). I was terrified of the possibility of undergoing an exhaustive search by the Israeli security services at Ben Gurion. I dodged the interrogation successfully, although I got a "Security level 5" sticker glued to my passport. My suitcases were checked; the tedious precaution of emptying my computer's hard drive from all Palestine-related information, as well as having mailed a lot of my belongings, paid off. The security guards pass a little cloth that is able to detect gunpowder or chemical explosives over my suitcases. As I check into my flight, the gate agent frowns when she realizes I am traveling to Canada on a Mexican passport. The fact that I don't have a return ticket to either Israel or Mexico makes her hesitate in giving me a boarding pass. When exactly did airlines become the border police? I show her my expired student visa and the letter that states I'm a student in Canada.

After a four-hour flight, I land in Budapest and head toward the shuttle bus that will take me to the thermal baths at Szechenyi. Once there, as I sink down in a hot water tub I feel my chest slowly decompressing, then my back, as if my soul could finally breathe fully after remaining crushed for many months. The hot water relaxes me, and I feel my energy recharging; I feel the tension that had occupied my body in Israel-Palestine evaporate. I arrive in Toronto, I am interrogated at the passport control, I do what I can with the papers I'm carrying, and I go in. I feel disoriented and sad; I wait until the everyday of the city embraces me, and I begin savoring life here again. Yet my head is a tangle of ideas, and I feel dislocated. How can I retain what I see from here, but coming from there, now?

Dear Gardi,

I am still in Gotheburg (a beautiful and green city), Sweden, with my sister. Of course you feel disoriented, it is a big change from Palestine to Toronto. It will take you time to find your space. But I am sure that, although you are so far away, Palestine and her people will always be part of you.

Love,
Sonia

I got this note from Sonia this morning. She made me cry. Indeed, Palestine is under my skin. I feel like I need to recover my strength, to decide the direction my project is going. I am shaken up by seeing this abysmal difference. Confusing. The priorities of privileged people are arranged according to the stress and anxiety they live. Hyperproductivity. I miss you, Ramallah. I am overwhelmed and mortified. I try to find the pieces of Palestine inside me and see how I've changed and how those transformations will be reflected in my life here.

How can we go through the images' surface, through information and deliver the world?

We don't live in the world we want to; this is a world in which a New York Cuban artist and academic, CF, an artist with an international reputation, carved a career—with acerbic criticism—through performance art and writing on racism in North America. Yet she warned me during her brief visit to Ramallah: "If you are infected by Palestine, you will be rejected by the art world." Speaking to Canadians is also difficult because they are a bit morbid toward Palestinians, war, reality elsewhere. JG asked me about the shocking things I lived over there. Definitely, I wasn't there to experience the adrenaline, to see soldiers on their Humvees and jeeps. To get tear gas thrown at you is extreme; to see a youth arrested in a village is extreme. To experience the generosity of people in extreme adverse conditions, their solidarity, after having lived the ugly side of their society, is extreme.

Silvia is right: we get panic attacks because we have lost the capacity to exteriorize ourselves, to be in the world outside of ourselves. That is why we have decided to shut down in introspection, but such captivity leads us to explode in panic.

Europeans in the West Bank bear a new middle-class orientalism, with the mission of "educating Palestinians"—for example, telling teenagers in Bil'in not to throw stones—or they want to impose their Western feminist visions, or sermonize about the dangers of religion or generally act condescendingly.

In *The Good Terrorist*, written at the demise of the Cold War, Doris Lessing tells the story of Alice, a woman who spent fifteen years living in a squatters' community, assuming the role of the housewife sustaining the home, doing reproductive labor. Of middle-class origin, Alice faces the contradictions of her education and life choices. Her mother describes her as someone who has taken a long time to grow up. Her choices, although she doesn't realize it, have ruined the lives of the people around her: Philip's, her parents'. Alice is willing to do everything for the home where she's squatting. In fact, she gives everything up to maintain it, even herself and all her money. The house becomes the symbol of home and family warmth, opposing the logic of squatting, which should function as an extension of the Communist Party. Lessing is not very empathic with her characters; they reminded me of Godard's *La Chinoise*, but fifteen years later. The squatters are in their mid-thirties, and the author gives us her opinion of them: they are parasites looking for something that will not bear fruit. In two hundred pages, Lessing narrates how Alice gets enough money and then fixes the home, gets electricity, and makes other repairs. She also devotes some pages to describing the heroine's relationship to Jasper, her lover for fifteen years who has become more and more distant. The novel ends when the squatters commit a terrorist attack. The characters are almost a caricature of squatters in the 1980s. Alice's character is shallow and defined by the forces she grapples with and that place her at the center (negotiating, dealing with other squatters, finding money, feeling guilt about her mother, and so on). Lessing offers us a portrait of the useless, dysfunctional, and wasted lives of the characters from House 43 who attend protests for fun; their beliefs are so deeply rooted in their natural habitat that they revolve around the failure of two individuals to be accepted as IRA or Russian militants and around other squatters' success in becoming spies. Their souls have been crushed, and reality escapes them.

Sensations pass as if they were fixed stills of my impressions of Palestine parading before my eyes. I had forgotten what reality is like here. I am sad because you are lost and broken, and my love will never be powerful enough to restore your willingness to live, your willingness to be with me, to build a life together. Your brain has been invaded by clouds; thousands of kilometers away I hear how you bite your fingers to stop yourself from calling me and shortening the distance, listening to my voice for even a few minutes. The headline from the *Globe and Mail* today is "Sewage as Fertilizer, Is It Safe?"

"Clintonomics" is the historical period in the economy during which the Democrats embraced the neoliberal ideology of privatization. At the same time, the humanitarian Left—together with an army of globalized cultural producers—scour the globe in the search for meaning.

In *Torpor*, Chris Kraus defines trauma literature as descriptions of experiences that were not fully registered at the moment of the event. The person who remembers the event is no longer the person he or she was at the time of the experience. The direct object of the question "Who, exactly, is experiencing the event?" falters. To be traumatized is to be possessed by the image of an event. Trauma is also numbness, paralysis: it leaves no trace of any kind, only a void. Emotion is blocked because the emotion takes you to what you think can overwhelm you. In that state, future life is predicated upon the past, conditioned by the past.

Just like the train journeys during the Holocaust were designed to humiliate and break the passengers, the network of checkpoints, roads, borders, and the wall are conceived to humiliate and break Palestinians down. The words *apartheid* and *occupation* are insufficient to describe the situation in the West Bank and Gaza.

## AUGUST 7, 2008

Your emotions are unstable and it is possible that while I write these lines, you've decided to forget me in someone else's arms. And just because you don't let me remind you not to forget that I love you, and that my love contains a promise, that my heart is yours as long as you want it. Just let me know when you don't want it anymore. You need to live in order to be able to die. You need to be able to enjoy in order to suffer.

## AUGUST 8, 2008

It is alarming news, I'm afraid, *habibti*. I got a note from F earlier today telling me he was hospitalized yesterday because of a panic attack. He's either having a massive breakdown or it could also be that he's not drinking while he's there and his body and psyche need the alcohol and the deprivation is causing him anxiety (he needs his arak, I'm afraid). I don't know what else to do aside from reassuring him and urging him to forward me a number where I can reach him . . . Any luck finding someone who could help him in Ramallah? I'm afraid if this worsens (it's not the first time this has happened), he might end up getting the wrong kind of help . . . his brother might be the angel—it's happened twice that I haven't heard from F for a few days and then emailed his brother asking him to get F to email me (to his work address, as I don't have his personal one and I'm not sure he has had access to it), and the next day I've had emails from F. I'm hesitating about whether to take for granted that his brother is reading his work messages and just email him sharing the urgency . . . I'm sorry I know this is extremely disturbing, distracting and painful . . .

About a matter in my dream
I became the flute of myself and I will play it until my mouth
Becomes a butterfly
A matter in your absence
To be continued
(from F)


YESTERDAY, DURING THE FLIGHT TO Boston, I visualized two mad images in my head that I could not reconcile. The man sitting to my right was reading an article in the *Boston Globe* about the approval of a new settlement in the West Bank, and about how Israeli settlers had confronted and beaten up Palestinian people near Nablus. I could not help crying. I had spent three days in the cradle of white privilege—Harvard, Wellesley, MIT—and had read about Condoleezza Rice's foreign policies based on the idea that the United States is not an empire, but a republic that disseminates global democracy. A world subsumed to US interests and ideology in which we are all either citizens or noncitizens and in which the imperialists make themselves responsible for the good of the planet. The idea depresses me a lot, especially after having visited this niche of privilege. I spent the weekend with my godmother and her Wellesley friends; we visited the city and the El Greco and Velázquez exhibition, also the Anish Kapoor retrospective. We took walks in the parks lush with gorgeous trees, towering pines and weeping willows. The city was verdant, with gigantic old houses. It all felt inflated, even the new Frank Gehry building at MIT, enormous in comparison with the one he made at the Dusseldorf port. Even inside it, the pieces of furniture are gigantic; they exude this kind of American grandiosity, the culture of excess. The world, like a Botero painting, scares me. I think about Birzeit when walking around MIT; seeing the privileged kids here, and those living in refugee camps in Palestine.

We do the Boston Duck Tour. The Duck is the World War II equivalent of army Humvees: huge and heavy vehicles that can go as fast as eighty kilometers per hour and can navigate in water. A dozen of them take people around the city. The guides are the worst; they mix entertainment with information and pseudohistorical facts. My godmother spoiled me a lot in Boston, and I feel lucky she looks after me. I bought a lot of books at the MIT bookstore: *Aliens and Anorexia* by Chris Kraus, Boris Groys . . . slowly, I find my brain; seeing art helped. The first page of *Aliens and Anorexia* is an imaginary dialogue between Andy Warhol and Ulrike Meinhof: two opposing characters in a dialectical synthesis transposed to a psychic state. Meinhof is the legend who transformed political action into tragic poetry and Warhol became a clone of himself. They meet by chance.

I am still sad. I cried a lot yesterday. I saw Wong Kar-wai's *2046*, three love stories interwoven by a fiction writer: a man who gets on train 2046 and in which nothing changes, everything is the same, and that takes him to forgetfulness. So people get on the train to forget. Sometimes the choices we make in the past will inevitably determine the decisions we will make in the future.

Show at Heather's gallery; "Palestine"; urban space; Majd's match tower/camera obscura; Nora A—Eyal Weizman; Eshrat's piece; otolith/v-tape; reading by Chris Kraus; hollow land (Eyal Weizman); urban planning, cityscape; the spaces in which we live (critique of Torontonian projects of "beautifying the city"); (Stan Douglas's photographs of Cuban ruins?) Said: in "Panic of the Visual," I once evolved a kind of typology, a kind of pedagogical typology of thinkers who proceed according to temporality and are gripped by it, and that World includes Derrida, Lukács, and then what I will call the spatial tradition, going back to Lucretius, but including Vico and Gramsci; and there the conception of society is essentially territorial, and, therefore, in criticism and philosophy there's a whole question of how you cover one with the other, and how you move between different segments of a contested geography. . . . The contemporary universality of the Palestinian experience, which is also about territory and contested space and dispossessions, which means you have to do certain things because you don't have the space or the place. It's hard to regain some substitute or equivalent for space if you don't have it in the first place. And the relationship between language and space becomes an issue, above all, the notion of writing and distance, which very much informs my thinking about matters of exile and displacement. *Speaking from a place* (what does this place we speak from look like?) Narrative as spatial; with temporal elements, but more of space. Hollowness as exile, hollowness as the condition of landscape.

# You're Trapped in a Maze of Tiny Little Passages, All Different

MADNESS AND VERTIGO make it hard for you to catch your breath, and the ensuing paralysis is a symptom of a panic attack, an angst trip. You find yourself in a maze of tiny little passages, all different. You think of Kafka and his characters lost in bureaucracy; of Beckett undergoing a panic attack. You walk by the Richard Serra in Terminal 1 at the Toronto Pearson Airport, which reminds you of the fraction of the wall toppled down in the Gaza Strip; but also the appearance of equilibrium disorients you because the sculpture shatters perceptual space: it offers a crooked, paralactic perception.

That morning you had scheduled a series of meetings. A little routine, as you usually navigate toward Robarts (the library), you get there early and spend the whole day writing. First thing, you took your computer to the technician; luckily repairs were still covered by the one-year warranty. The mishap had taken your sleep the previous night. The keyboard failure was not uncommon for that version of MacBook, and the cute guy at the Apple Store said he'd order the part and change it. You continued your way on your rollerblades, late for your first appointment of the day: 9:00 AM, breakfast with a group of videoactivists who would gather with the goal of putting together a project to support the West Bank with Canadian video art, "The Olive Project." Since 1967, over two hundred thousand olive trees on Palestinian lands have been torn down by Israeli forces. This fact inspired a campaign of hundreds of international and Israeli volunteers to protect Palestinian olive farmers and help them harvest, but also to prevent settler theft and destruction. "The Olive Project: Two Minutes for Peace and Justice," by the Hard Pressed Collective, is a video that contributes to that effort. In total, the project encompasses four video programs from twenty-three collectives and videoartists from all over the globe, who responded to the call to make two-minute-long videos in solidarity with the Palestinian olive harvest. They can take any angle, style, or approach, and they are required to show olives, olive trees, or products derived from olives. Combining brevity with impact, these veteran videoartists have produced documentary and experimental pieces, with factual, ironic, militant, and funny discourses—olived creativity.

You get to Boom, a coffee shop with a Mexican theme that serves Latin food in general, specializing in breakfast. You're about forty minutes late, but the last time you got together with this group everyone was late so you don't worry too much. You sit down and wait for half an hour. You suspect that the reason no one appears is because there's a failure in your brain; perhaps the meeting was really scheduled for the next day or the previous one? You can't connect to the internet (you didn't have your cell phone on you and, back then, you didn't own a smartphone anyway) to reread the message setting up the breakfast. After waiting for thirty-five minutes and drinking two cups of really bad coffee—it makes you very thirsty—you rollerblade to College Street to find a restaurant-coffee shop with internet. You're not in luck. Five blocks later, you find one. "I'm sorry I don't have time to drink coffee, but I'd be eternally grateful if you let me connect to your internet for a few minutes," you say. The girl behind the counter, grouchy, gives you a small piece of paper with the network password. At 10:15 you find out that the breakfast is taking place somewhere else: at the Beaver, on Queen and Gladstone, on the other side of the city. You decide to catch the end of the meeting. Fifteen minutes later, you arrive to find a crew shooting something inside. You're not allowed in, but one of the guys from the crew lets you know that your friends are waiting for you at the Gladstone, a block away. When you get there, everyone is already leaving, but not without letting you quickly recite your intellectual-political-academic credentials. You describe briefly your project and emphasize the aspects you think would impress them. One of them, whose exhibition is opening that night, invites you for a preview. You accept with curiosity. He lists all the contacts he had from the West Bank and sums up his career as you cover three blocks: Halifax, Whitney Program, San Diego, Banff residency, individual and collective exhibitions.

You look at the work for ten minutes, then excuse yourself and run to your second appointment, at 11:00 AM at Hibiscus, on Harbord. It's about 11:15 and you thought you'd be a little late but it wouldn't matter, considering that M is not very punctual. You were rollerblading on the streets as fast as you could and felt the sweat in the hot and humid Toronto summer. At Berkeley, close to College, the wheels of one of the skates gets stuck in a crack in the pavement. You leap through the air, ducking your head to avoid a car fender and landing on your back. A cyclist passing by stops and asks you if you're all right.

You get up, it's 11:28, you get to Harbord and Bathurst at 11:31 AM. You go all the way up to Spadina looking for Hibiscus Café; you ask a couple at a restaurant about it, but they don't know it. Then you remember that there was a nice coffee shop at Christie, next to the park by the dog run; you go there. You arrive at 11:40 AM (still a decent belatedness); when you read the name of the restaurant, Linux, you begin to worry about your mental health, suspecting there's something very wrong. Again, you look for an internet connection to check your email and see exactly where you will find your friend. You skate back to Spadina, where you're certain you can catch the university's Wi-Fi. You finally reread M's email from the previous day, where she suggests to meet at Hibiscus in Augusta. Fuck! Toward Kensington Market. You write a quick apology: "I'll be there in 10 minutes. I just fell twice rollerblading on my way there." The second time you're lucky enough there were no cars passing by on your left because they would have run you over for sure. You breathe. You recover. You keep on going. You get to Augusta and you go up the street looking for Hibiscus. Mexican, Thai, Cuban . . . the papusas place. No Hibiscus. You ask two passers-by about it, and each points in an opposite direction. After going up and down the street some five times, you sit down to find another internet connection and read your friend's email again: "See you at the organic coffee shop I like, Hibiscus, at Augusta 238." You were only three doors away from the place. You feel pain on your head and neck, and relief you didn't stand her up completely. You send her another email: "Dear, ignore my previous email, I'm undergoing brain failure, I'll see you at Hibiscus at 1." You realize you feel a lot of disquiet and anxiety, and that time is running out to do all the errands you had planned that day, as you have an appointment with your friend JP at 2:30 PM to see the new Julian Schnabel film, *La Scaphandre et le papillon*, being released at TIFF. After seeing M, you won't have time to return the videotapes due that day, so you decide to leave your stuff at Hibiscus: "I'll be back in twenty minutes, thanks!" You run to the library, drop the films off, and are back at 12:57; you feel relief that the brain failure is probably temporary. You sit down to drink your coffee, which is already cold, and you find a new email from M: "Dear, I called you this morning at 8:30 to change our meeting to 11:30 at L'Expresso on St. George and Bloor."

# Finally, *Awdati*

## *(I Go Back, My Return)*

AFTER A YEAR OF ABSENCE, my body molds quickly back to the Ramallah topography, to the undulating rhythm of the red earth hills and the dry green of the mutilated olive trees. The days in which traces of desert storms coming in from the east decide not to impregnate the city's atmosphere, I manage to glimpse the plateau and, further back, the Mediterranean, on its kidnapped horizon. The atmosphere softens up when the sea wind blows toward us. If you look, turning around a little bit in the opposite direction, the seemingly inexorable barrier appears, winding along the hill with diplomatic credibility that threatens to appear and, as usual, the invading demography that yells immediately: "Holocaust!"

The compass aims toward Mahmoud Darwish's tomb, northeast of Jerusalem. Or is Jerusalem northeast of the tomb of the first Palestinian poet? In any case, his remains lie inside a pyramid reminiscent of I. M. Pei's Louvre. When did the crystal pyramid become a universal symbol for high culture? The tomb is right across from the Qasser al-Thaquafa (or Culture Palace), where an image of smiling and greeting Yasser Arafat seems to tell the visitors: "Ahlan ua sahlan!" The figure is magnificently photoshopped so he can appear in front of the Al-Aqsa Mosque; it must be mentioned that the work is extraordinary, as Arafat's shadow is perfectly outlined on the immaculate white of the temple's floor. The city breathes dust without luxury. It's Qatar, Kuwait, or Dubai in a *tiers monde* version. The eternal dust that won't settle, a trace of the bombs remaining from many years ago. The popular corners and those unkept, vestiges of torn martyrs' posters dissolving on the walls next to almond buds that forgot to bloom the previous spring, the secret stairs to shorten the roads, the *shabab* overflowing with testosterone, shouting innocent obscenities in English they heard on television. The sonorous cartography encompasses many languages, with the persistent sound of a Caterpillar hitting hard rock, excavating the foundations of a foreign chain hotel. Are those really the foundations or are they bunkers for the rich? Whistles intensify in frequency and become the sound of zooming, unmanned planes that fly over the city at least once a week: more as a reminder of the intrusive foreign presence than as a threat. Fridays, from the *'ins* (Bil'in and Nil'in), the sounds of stones being thrown, rubber bullets shot, and tear gas canisters launched can invariably be heard, preceded by the ardent, shouts of enthusiastic foreign activists and by the pastoral melancholy of the muezzin that propagates waves of guilt and denunciation through the summer winds. Meanwhile, under the pretext of a security threat and through real estate battles and urban design, Palestine becomes more and more an archipelago of barely concatenated territories.

At Blue, the Stammcafé of the new season, I recognize the sweet well-being of contemplative decadence. Some foreigners compare it to a Parisian dump from either the 1920s or 1960s. The more I spin around possible analogies, the image that comes to my mind in the 1920s is a parade of masked *gueules cassées*. In the 1960s, I see Maoists and their antibourgeois revolutionary airs, *démodé* existentialists, wine drunks, and solitary poets experimenting with hallucinogens. Then I think of Paris under German occupation, and I imagine with expectation the scene of underground resistance . . .

The walls are light blue in honor of the bar's name; an Irish flag hangs from one of them. Other walls display a collection of photographs of Hollywood stars: from Marilyn Monroe to George Clooney. There are no tables but comfortable wide sofas, and many consider the Stammcafé to be their own living room where they receive guests, welcome passersby, and observe lovers and collaborators intertwined without discretion. Politics, economy, local jokes, offers of work or bed, art and culture. Worlds crossing paths permeated with a soft, blue light with breath smelling like arak, *al-ṭayba*, or mint tea. We'd rather not discuss the music: the invasion of teenager's tastes in the background is drowned by discussions of culture wars.

Foreigners working for NGOs distribute responsible budgets on ephemeral projects, appeasing consciences and recycling rich countries' taxes to generate short- or medium-term well-being for the dispossessed. The energy of people carrying out redemptive missions makes this diplomatic-humanitarian-capitalist presence feel more like Lawrence Durrell's Alexandria than Malcolm

Lowry's Cuernavaca, right before the disaster and the loss of sense. In truth, however, these people are on an unconscious trip to save themselves, destined to fail. The characters painted by Durrell and Lowry are on the verge of abyss or desperation. Don't get me started on Paul Bowles. At the end there is nothing to win or lose, and their spiritual adventure of indefinite contours is inspired by the temptation of having access to an inaccessible reality *there*, manifest in an exuberant sensibility lacking compassion, full of interested responsibility that corrupts and intoxicates in the process of fulfilling itself.

Ramallah exercises a spiritual and psychological influence on its inhabitants; it propagates the collective desire for prosperity and the guilt of normalizing the occupation to be able to make it through the day. The temperament of the city (evidently from a masculine perspective) has been compared to a young woman forced to become an adult by prostituting herself. The guilty call for the movement of things I am trying to describe in alternating breaths of nostalgia, melancholy, cynicism, freedom, cultural movement, desperation, prosperity, and exhaustion—the "Ramallah Syndrome." Calling it a syndrome is not the first time that a comparison is drawn to a discourse from the enemy: for example, the transposition of stereotyped history of a Holocaust survivor (or one of their descendants, preferably from the United States) that comes to Switzerland to claim the bank accounts stolen by the state and, of course, gets them with interest. A similar script was recently repeated not long ago in Ramallah—in a film where the grandfather's money is lost. But more than inspiring films (that appease consciousness, tirelessly speaking truth to power, or whipping nostalgia, about culture for culture's sake and in the name of visibility and civilization), Ramallah is condemned for being the product of a spatial order effectuated by the Oslo Accords.

As headquarters of the PNA, it has given way to relative prosperity and a middle class. Since the 1990s, all functions of the national capital have been transferred from Ramallah to Jerusalem—clearly Palestine has been ceaselessly "transferred" since 1948. This series of transfers and the expansion of the middle class have as a collateral effect what is called the "mirage of normality." And this mirage is known as the "Ramallah Syndrome," the result of the passage of merchandise, people, culture, and funds propelled by globalization, by the bubble created by the support of NGOs. This relative prosperity is accused of veiling the occupation. The fact that it's a syndrome implies "overidentification with a pathological landscape." A "normal" landscape painted not by the collective desire for freedom, but by national assertion materialized in relative "development" and "economic progress."

Ramallah is a colonial city unlike most others. The UNRWA's slogan is: "Realizing the humanity of Palestinian refugees for the past sixty years." Such a slogan posits humanity, infrastructure, schools, and hospitals as the same things: the agency veils the real-estate battles, the business of information, the diplomatic circus, and this is how it extracts moral and monetary surplus value from its interventions. And who else, aside the UNRWA and its Western infrastructure, gives Palestinian refugees the status of "humanity"? Walter Benjamin's modernist shock today is provoked by something different than technological capitalist alienation; it is the shock of "dehumanization" of some men against others, and that is the root of the crisis of empathy and compassion that has destroyed ethics and responsibility for others.

How do we remember, exercise, be compassionate again, soften the gaze beyond scandal and indignation? To have buried empathy is not having a heart and mouth when speaking. Suffering is reserved for only a few; it makes others impatient before the monopoly of torment. And is this conflict not sold to those who enter easily into shock in the struggle for the monopoly of torment? On the one hand, there's the torment of maintaining one's own dignity, and, on the other, there's hubris justified by a history of forced exile. I read a newspaper story about a man who survived a fatal fall into the Atlantic on Flight 447 from Rio de Janeiro to Paris. He could tell his own story because he missed the flight. In the post-Titanic era of demands and compensations, the obsession with details of a fallen aircraft, the tireless search for the black box are reminiscent of Holocaust movies, focusing on certain fears and phobias. Another passenger was unable to tell her story, although she, too, missed the flight: she died a week later in a car accident in Austria. This is how the extraordinary goes a step beyond sensationalism.

Are the many easy smiles here veiling their pain by embodying the tragicomedy of the occupation? How many degrees of happiness mark the symptoms of Charcotian hysteria? A quote by Jean Genet giving voice to a fedayeen: "In sum—he points out—they invade us, stifle us and they would like to hug us. They say they are our cousins. They are sad when they see us turn our backs to them. They must be furious with us and with themselves."[157]

FOR ONE OF MY TRIPS leaving Palestine through the Ben Gurion Airport, right next to Tel Aviv, I hired Abul Hafez, a cab driver who lives in Ramallah. He has Israeli citizenship, which offers him the advantage of entering and exiting the West Bank relatively easily to work in Israel. Abul Hafez had already driven me once to Tel Aviv, where I accompanied my professor, RC, who was going to spend a few days there. That time Abul Hafez took us out from Ramallah through the checkpoint near Betunia, passing Modi'in. That alternative crossing to Qalandya, forbidden to Palestinians residing in the West Bank, is preferred by '48 Palestinians (Palestinians with Israeli citizenship, who make up 20 percent of the population), business people, diplomats, and all kinds of foreigners. It is a quick and easy crossing, yet that time we were stopped some twenty minutes while the soldiers checked our car. I felt responsible for whatever happened for my professor—after all, I had found the driver, who instead of coming to get us in an Israeli cab had picked us up in an old battered car. That immediately inspired mistrust in R, although Abul Hafez was F's trusted driver. After what seemed an eternity, and after having shown our papers, even those of the driver and his companion, they let us pass, to my relief. Once I dropped off RC and was back in Ramallah, F told me that Abul Hafez was the father of another taxi driver doing a life sentence at an Israeli prison for having driven a militant to blow himself up at a restaurant in Tel Aviv during the Second Intifada. I was muted. I wasn't sure if he had put us at risk or not, if the soldiers at the checkpoint recognized his identity, if he was blacklisted. Then I understood F's gesture of normalizing resistance. Abul Hafez was not the father of a monster but a member of a people in struggle.

A few weeks later, I would hire Abul Hafez to drive me to the airport. That time, to my relief, he did appear in an Israeli cab, although that exit from Israel was the most difficult and terrifying I'd ever gone through. I must say that in spite of the terror and paranoia that the Israeli surveillance and control apparatus gives me (in my case more psychological than physical), I have a privileged status to enter and leave Israel because of my origins. People of

Arab origin (let alone Palestinians or Muslims) and prominent dissident Jews are routinely denied entry. Sometimes they spend days in detention centers before being deported.[158] Young non-Jewish women are always viewed with suspicion, and this time I was no exception. I've always been successful with the border agents except for the first time I crossed, when two young soldier girls opened my suitcase and were literally horrified by my Palestinian para-phernalia and Arabic books, and they interrogated me for nearly three hours. Right before my flight left, they led me to the boarding gate. Luckily, that time I did not have my laptop with me; the airport's security agents routinely copy suspicious visitors' hard drives, access their social media, and examine their digital photos. Sometimes laptops are returned to their owners broken.

This time, when I got out of the cab, I paid and thanked Abul Hafez, who accompanied me to the entry. Three seconds after I stood in line to put my suitcases through the X-ray machines (the routine process before checking in), an agent came up to me and began bombarding me with ques-tions: "Where are you traveling to? Where are you from? Why did you visit Israel? What are your friend's names? What Tel Aviv bars do you usually go to? How long were you here? Have you got weapons on you? Why did you go to Morocco? What is your father's name? Your grandfather's? Where are they from?" Once in Toronto, my friend Elle explained to me the complex functioning of Ben Gurion's surveillance apparatus: at the first entry—by car—you are asked to hand in your boarding pass and passport, that's when you get racially profiled. The passenger drop-off area is located under huge windows, where a team of surveillers watch the comings and goings below. Another agent—the guy who had begun making me nervous—enacts the third filter. I did not want to tell him I was coming from the Occupied Terri-tories. At some point during the interrogation I ran out of alibis. Before he asked me the phone number of an Israeli contact and after he asked me, "But what exactly do you do in Israel?" (by then it had become evident that I had come and gone many times), I had an epiphany and said, in desperation:

"The truth is, I, a few years ago, I met an Israeli in Paris, and we fell in love. Then I moved to Tel Aviv for a few months but things fell apart."

The agent then asked: "Did you see that person during your stay this time?"

I answered: "I haven't seen Gila in a long time; I know about her through common friends."

When he heard I was in a lesbian relationship with an Israeli, the agent let me go immediately; I suppose his decision follows Israelis' indoctrina-tion to tolerate homosexuals visiting their country, as Israel's brand is "Gay Paradise."

# From Ramallah to Tel Aviv

I HAD BEEN SEARCHING AROUND the city for the drawings of Mahmoud Darwish made by Ernest Pignon, and I finally found one of them while riding on the *servīs* from Ramallah to Qalandya, where I would cross to go to Jerusalem and take a bus toward Tel Aviv. Darwish appears in a poster, drawn in real life, on one of the walls bordering the checkpoint. I recognize the image because of his glasses and shape. Pignon plastered the posters in places he deemed emblematic in the West Bank and Israel, as well as in the ruins of the poet's village, al-Birwa, toward the interior, very close to Akko. He wanted to do the same in Gaza, but he was not authorized without getting an explanation.

With his absence I formed his image.[159]

Once in Tel Aviv, S takes me to visit her friend, the painter's Hanan S.'s studio. He makes portraits of objects using a nonsaturated colored paste, amalgamated on the canvas with egg. The objects are as material as they are transient: cigarettes, books, or dollar bills. Tobacco that is consumed as smoke by a breathing body, text that becomes knowledge evaporating in memory, the dollar's fetishistic dematerialization in financial fluxes. The paintings, like money, are hiding the abstraction that materializes them. Money is the universal and abstract measure of exchange, the expression of commodity value that hides work relations and the amount of labor that has been invested in them. In addition to these ethereal-material objects that represent visual games hidden in still lives, the artist has created a series of paintings with naked bodies of a middle-aged African woman who served as his model. The painter translated her figure to nude masculine bodies seen from behind wearing a kippa, and into squatting feminine bodies, evoking the figure of an exile in the desert who does not know where to go. Hanan is also known for painting cityscapes in which smoke from recent explosions metastasize in the sky. The last two series that I'm describing evoke something of the Israeli fear of becoming refugees again, either being expelled by sea or being bombarded by the Arabs. Here and there, ghosts everywhere. Mark Fisher wrote a book on pop culture in which he explains the presence of ghosts in contemporary culture as the coexistence of two temporalities in the collective imaginary: There is the superficial frenzy of novelty and the perpetual movement that coexists with ecstasy and anachronism. As a consequence, recognizable forms persist, giving way to a vague and obstinate feeling of the past that doesn't invoke any specific historical moment. The future is canceled, expectations deflated. Fisher explains this imaginary construction of the present grounded in a past without history through Jacques Derrida's concept of *hauntologie*, a kind of haunting in which nothing has a purely positive existence: all that exists is only possible because of the series of absences that precede and surround it. Fisher links haunting to loss, and specifically to pending mourning. If mourning is the slow and painful retiring of the libido from the lost object, in melancholia, the libido remains attached to that which disappeared. In order for the mourning to begin properly, it is necessary to conjure the death away, to make sure there is no return. In the Palestinian imaginary as in the Israeli, there is a refusal to bury the bodies, an insistence on hanging onto the ghosts. That specter is what enables the acceptance of mediocre solutions, lost futures, and false choices.[160]

As I transit from one side to the other, the ghosts of my own dislocation add up—not only specters of imaginaries but of affects and sensibilities. It doesn't have much to do with moving from one urban center to another. Rather, crossing the wall means going from depressed lockdown to euphoric paranoia, from being constantly surrounded of reminders of the occupation to experiencing a near-normality punctuated by seeing soldiers walking down the street or navigating checkpoints to go into restaurants.

After we visit the painter in Tel Aviv, we sit down for a *café a fuchs* in the old house of Hayyim Nahman Bialik, the nationalist-Zionist poet who arrived in the city in 1924. The café is on a street where there are seven museums constituting a modest enclave of cultural sophistication. Old friends of S join us, and I hear that the punk anarchists and dissidents from the 1980s are now buying chunks of the old city in Akko, which has become a fashionable weekend place. The population in Akko is mostly Palestinian, and pogroms have been documented there since 2008. In October of that year, there was very intense persecution against Muslims by Israelis who tried to stop them from celebrating Ramadan.

Bialik's poem "El Hatzipor," or "To a Bird," symbolizes the nineteenth-century nostalgia for Zionism. Before Ben-Yehuda reinvented the biblical language to make it colloquial, this was the first poem ever published in Hebrew:

### "To the Bird," by H. N. Bialik (1891)[161]

Greetings to you, kind bird, upon your return
From the hot lands back to my window
Back to your pleasing voice, My soul perishes
In the winter when you leave.

Sing, tell me, my beautiful bird,
About the wonders of the distant land.
Is it full of evils and hardships also
There in the hot beautiful land?

Will you bring me regards from my brothers in Zion,
From my brothers far and near?
O happy they are! Do they know
How I suffer, O suffer, from grief?

Do they know how many accusers I have here,
How many, so many, rise up against me?
Sing, my bird, of the wonders of the land
The spring is coming, but to stay forever.

Bialik gazed east in search for freedom as Jews were suffering the violence of Russian pogroms. The promise of a warm, faraway land where Jews could virtuously work in the wheat fields became part of the Zionist narrative and the basis for the kibbutzim until the 1950s. That narrative was exchanged for the image of a modern Israel, of the "only" democracy in the Middle East, with transparent elections and tolerance toward the LGBT+ community. With regards to the latter, Israel is a gay tourist destination well known to Westerners; in 2016 the Tourism Ministry even announced the investment of $11 million NIS (Israeli shekels) with the goal of positioning Israel as a liberal country.[162]

The state's promotion of open dissent is complemented by the public display of tensions between different sectors of the population. This gives the illusion of democracy, or at least of a balance between fundamentalists and liberals. But, in reality, there is no balance: the settlements are a constituent element of both Tel Aviv and Jerusalem, a phenomenon that is comfortably ignored, though the settlers are slowly acquiring political capital. After visiting in 2011, I returned to Israel in 2015. I was surprised by the warmth with which my friends M and Y received me. They were now worried about the situation and said they were planning to leave the country. As educated liberals, they had seen the country, its institutions, and public opinion being gradually taken over by religious fundamentalists. For years, settlers received state subsidies to occupy key areas in the West Bank and religious Israelis enjoyed support to establish education and community structures grounded in religion.[163] "We will be another Iran in a few years," my friends tell me.

Sitting among members of the old Israeli left condemning the attacks against Gaza, sipping coffee at Bialik Café, I thought about similarities in the distribution of life forms and of making a living across the world. Originary and rural populations are forced to urbanize or move to suburbs, and they lost the means to sustain life. Real-estate speculation and gentrification lead to precarity for the middle and lower classes. And in Israel, the expulsion of Palestinians is made invisible at the same time that Palestinian enclaves undergo Israelization. The cosmopolitism and "recovery" of traditional neighborhoods fueled by economic prosperity and sustained by a real-estate bubble is intended only for the leisure of the privileged classes.

Nobody asks me what life is like in Ramallah, so I listen attentively to the sophisticated critical reflection in the conversation that reminds me of Ari Folman's film *Waltz with Bashir* (2008). In the movie, one of the characters compares without irony the whistling sounds made by rocket-propelled grenades with arrows shot by North American Indians; *falafel* is referred to as "Israeli food"; and the 1980s hit "Lebanon, Boker Tov," a song of desperate love inspired by the mission of a young soldier stationed in Beirut during the siege in 1982, is one of the movie's theme songs. *Waltz with Bashir* is a kind of animated documentary that follows the main character, Ari, as he tries to thread together a narrative from the memories he repressed during the Lebanon war, which now manifest in vague nightmares and blurry visions of the massacre in the Palestinian refugee camps at Sabra and Chattila. Ari does not remember his role in the massacre or even if he was present. But he feels that his recurrent nightmare of dogs chasing him is telling him something he suppressed from the war. To recover his memories, he goes looking for his battalion companions and discovers that he was in the second or third ring of the siege surrounding the refugee camp, and that he shot flares into the sky to facilitate the massacre by the Lebanese Christian Phalange. Those who praise the movie argue that discussing the Lebanese civil war in Israel is taboo, yet the film considers Israel's role in that war and the massacres against Palestinians. And, indeed, at some point the main character questions the role that Ariel Sharon played in the war and the massacres; the film also realistically depicts soldiers watching porn, killing innocent civilians and dogs, and getting drunk or high. In *Waltz with Bashir*, moreover, a comparison is drawn between the Lebanon war and the Holocaust, and between Israeli soldiers and Nazis. At the same time, the film draws the figure of the shooting-crying-guilty-traumatized Israeli soldier, a character conflicted about participating in the war. This figure feeds into the image of the IDF as a "humanized" army, with compassionate and comprehensive soldiers acting in the name of their country's security. From that point of view, trauma and war are filtered through a prevailing ideology derived from consumerism, which affirms pain and trauma as accidents, something that we can or should avoid, and thus that we should seek to forget or relativize pain. War is emptied out of meaning at the ideological level, and what comes to be implanted is an ethical ideology that assumes that there is an a priori absolute evil that justifies the imposition of an essentially defensive ethics. Ethics here implies protecting or preventing a potential terrorist intervention in the name of collective interest. The collective fiction of absolute evil, therefore, is the intellectual justification of the status quo.

According to John Berger, however, the root of terrorism is not absolute evil, but desperation rooted in passivity, bitterness, and a sense of the absurd emanating from the feeling that neither one's own life nor the lives of others count or have meaning. That is why martyrdom is the search for transcendence. Berger also describes that the IDF is not there to bring security to Israel and its citizens, but rather has de facto become an army of conquest that guarantees uninterrupted theft of Palestinian lands. Thanks to the constant presence of the army, the siege on the territories tightens its grip more and more.[164]

*Waltz with Bashir* ends with archival footage of the refugee camps after the massacres in Sabra and Chattila; it shows Palestinian women desperately wailing over rotting butchered bodies invaded by flies. This event was masterfully described by Jean Genet, who emphasizes the power of the written word to testify using a photojournalistic image in his text, "Four Hours at Chattila" (1982). Genet argues that photojournalist images desensitize us toward the victims and the documented situation. Notably, *Waltz with Bashir* absolutely depersonalizes the enemy, neither comprehending nor expressing interest in their ordeal, to the degree that it appears in the film only as a hoard of aggressive dogs. In the kingdom of hubris, the "simulacrum" of the event (its vague memory as a distant dream) is confused with the real event; the alterity of the enemy means its absolute depersonalization. This is because in order to keep on moving forward, the subject of hubris must resist the temptation to impose an absolute truth about its role and the meaning of the war. In the first scene of the movie, we see a hoard of dogs running furiously along the emblematic Rothschild Boulevard in Tel Aviv until they stop to bark under Ari's window. The hoard is an ambiguous figure that generates incomprehensible anguish and guilt and from which the enemy has been abstracted.

Curiously, or rather "coincidentally," the film was released in North America on December 25, 2008, two days before the three-week-long attack against Gaza known as Operation Cast Lead. The war was laid forth as a response to missiles launched from Gaza into Israel and to illegal arms traffic from Egypt.[165] This conflict is distinguished by having introduced new weapons and legislative technologies: what Eyal Weizman calls *lawfare*, a form of war based on manipulating international law to prevent actions from being defined as war crimes or human rights violations.[166] During Operation Cast Lead, around fifteen hundred Palestinian lives were lost and thirteen Israelis were killed.[167] The controversial Goldstone Report was written when the war ended, gathering expert testimony and knowledge to identify human rights and international laws violations on both sides.[168]

In 2003, on the eve of the US invasion of Iraq, the DVD of the classic *Battle of Algiers* (1962) by Gillo Pontecorvo was released, putting images of counterinsurgent war in the Arab World into the Western imaginary. Similarly, the image of suffering Israeli soldiers with a critical consciousness from *Waltz with Bashir* populated Western cinemas, right when the Gaza Strip was being bombarded with white phosphorous bombs. These particular bombs smell like garlic and illuminate the sky with gigantic spider webs of light. They are the new napalm, a rain of jellyfish flipping in the air; colorless fireworks that penetrate the skin until the phosphorous stops burning, sometimes once it has gone all the way through bone. After this war, some survivors began to develop strange skin bumps, formed by the impact of bone and tissue fragments from other victims, now embedded in their bodies like organic ammunition making the dead live inside the living.

At Bialik Café, the enemy is the uncivilized religious fanatic terrorist; in spite of that, "your son is very well looked after in the army." (Every Israeli citizen is forced to do military service for three years.) An army of soldiers who shoot while crying, who cultivate their humanity with no conscious colonizing or annihilating purpose in mind because they act in the name of security, against the fear the enemy provokes in them. Fearing the fiction of absolute evil obliterates alterity and causes the world to forget to practice compassion. The pain that produces ugliness—caused by the gradual negation and obliteration of a whole people—should not be confused with the revulsion caused by hearing that the army looks after Israel's children. I think about the lines Mahmoud Darwish speaks in Godard's movie *Notre musique*: "The end will come when they beat us in poetry."

# *Avatar* in Palestine

ON FEBRUARY 12, 2010, for the protest against the apartheid wall in the West Bank village of Bil'in, five Palestinian, Israeli, and international activists dressed up as characters from James Cameron's film *Avatar*. Afterward, they posted a video statement on YouTube, comparing the Palestinian struggle to the ordeal of the Na'vi in the film.[169] Peaceful demonstrations against the construction of the wall and the expropriation of Palestinian lands by Israelis have taken place in Bil'in, a village nine kilometers away from Ramallah, every Friday since January 2005.[170] And every Friday, the IDF responds with violence using sound bombs, firing plastic bullets, and launching tear gas canisters against the demonstrators, often at such close range that the canisters and rubber bullets cause serious injury or death.[171] In Bil'in, as in the adjacent town of Nil'in, to demonstrate is to risk one's life. Bi'lin and Nil'in are adjacent to the Israeli settlement of Modi'in Illit, and the construction of the wall has been justified as a security measure to protect the settlers against Palestinians. In addition to the weekly protests, the Palestinians have taken legal action to stop the construction and expansion of the settlement and of the wall. In 2008, the town of Bil'in sued a Canadian construction company in the Supreme Court of Israel in hopes of stopping the construction of fifteen hundred homes in Modi'in Illit.[172]

According to the press release published on the Friday the protestors dressed up as characters from *Avatar*, they sought to symbolize "united resistance against imperialism of all kinds." The action won considerable visibility in Israel and some press coverage abroad. The Hollywood iconography presented the Palestinian struggle in terms that were well-known to many

Israelis (*Avatar* had been a huge success in Israel). The analogy between the Palestinian struggle for political self-determination and the Na'vi's ordeal in *Avatar*, however, is confusing. Perhaps it's more palatable for Palestinians to be compared to the Na'vi people, who, along with their environment, were being destroyed by foreign agents, rather than being perceived as terrorists, their struggle to defend their territory being delegitimized by their means to fight. But because the hegemonic narrative of the occupation is justified in terms of security and religious conflict, Israelis would hardly identify themselves with the colonialist power in *Avatar*. The Palestinians' situation, although it can definitely serve as model and example of resistance for populations across the world who are being dispossessed and displaced by resource extraction projects or the destruction of the commons, their situation is far more complex than that of the Na'vi people in Avatar. This is due to the fact that Palestinians have been the direct object of repressive and destructive policies on behalf of Israel, as well as being cogoverned, as I have discussed, as noncitizens.

The activists' effort to present the conflict to Israelis and Palestinians from a different point of view——as an instance of dispossession by accumulation—occurred at an unprecedented impasse: negotiations had been frozen, Netanyahu preached fascism, Iran was considered a lethal menace to Israel, and settlements kept on expanding. The two-state solution had already become impossible because of the ongoing expulsion and oppression of Palestinians, the fragmentation of the West Bank, the expansion of settlements and the tightening of the siege over the Gaza Strip. In parallel, the West Bank and Gaza were more divided than ever because they were being governed by two different state apparatuses serving divergent interests—the Palestinian National Authority and Hamas—and because the occupation differs in each area. As a consequence, their resistance strategies have diverged and fragmented. For instance, Salam Fayyad, the PNA's finance minister, established a neoliberal policy using the economy as a means to "free the territory," substituting prosperity and foreign investment for political self-determination.

Gaza, for its part, has been deliberately reduced to abject destitution: once productive and self-sufficient, it has now been impoverished and made dependent on humanitarian aid. This is due to the siege Gaza has faced since 2006, and to the Cast Lead Operation in 2008–2009, in which the IDF fired missiles, damaging and destroying homes and infrastructure to such a degree in Gaza that productive activity was completely extinguished. According to Noam Chomsky, four hundred trucks were needed each day to alleviate food shortages in 2010.[173] Moreover, the naval blockade led to the collapse of Gaza's fishing industry. It has been extremely difficult to reconstruct infrastructure and homes, and pressure from the European Union and the United States to end the blockade has been insufficient.

In this context, the protesters in Bil'in used *Avatar* to represent not only Palestinians, but all Indigenous peoples who are being dispossessed and displaced across the world. In this way, a kind of anti-imperialist internationalism was tenuously drawn, abstractly linked to an unnamed struggle against the destruction of originary peoples' forms of life. A well-known example is the fight against the construction of the Belo Monte Dam in Brazil, planned to fulfill Brazilians' electrical needs before the 2014 World Cup and the 2016 Olympics. Building the dam, however, meant destroying the way of life of twenty-five thousand inhabitants of eighteen tribes.[174] In Mexico, hydroelectric dams are presented as a symbol of development and clean energy; they are framed as a way to mitigate the climate crisis. However, it is well-known that transnational companies are the beneficiaries of these megaprojects. Many of the planned dams, such as the Picachos Dam in Sinaloa, end up being built against the will of originary peoples. In the Mexican state of Guerrero, inhabitants who would be affected if La Parota Dam were constructed have been resisting since 2003.[175]

In another example of organized resistance, campesinos and farmers are protesting against El Zapotillo, a dam project in Jalisco which threatens to flood and destroy the villages of Acasico, Palmarejo, and Temacapulín.[176] Generally, the government offers housing and relocation to the concerned populations, but they would be in principle severed from their agricultural lands and would thus be obliged to change their forms of life. In this manner, the dam projects are instances of transnational companies stealing public resources while the government destroys indigenous and *campesino* communities, which are considered to be redundant populations disconnected from global processes. Dam projects are also an assured means to uproot undesired populations and to separate them from them vital resources like land and water.

In India, the Naxalites are a Maoist guerrilla group fighting to defend their lands, which are mineral-rich forests targeted by transnational companies for exploitation. The Hindu state considers the group to be terrorists and a threat to national security and has made major military operations to repress them. The Naxalites control Dantewara and Chhattisgarh, and the government has responded by attacking them with thousands of troops.[177] Denying them the ancestral right to sustainability, the Hindu state has criminalized their means of making a living. We could draw a link between these instances

of dispossession and destruction across the globe and the Palestinian struggle, considering Arundhati Roy's statement that the Indian government has
imported Israeli armament and that the Mossad has trained thirty elite officials to assassinate the leaders of the Maoist organization.[178]

The comparison between the Naxalites, Indigenous groups resisting the
construction of hydroelectric dams in Brazil and Mexico, the Na'vis of *Avatar*,
and the Palestinians reveals that what they have in common is the theft of
their lands, the exploitation of natural resources, the groups' imminent ex-
tinction, and the use of Israeli weapons and techniques as means to repress,
displace, and control them. Noam Chomsky, for instance, has linked naval
attacks of the Gaza Strip and the discovery of natural gas fields on Gaza's
coast. The naval blockade, in addition to destroying the Strip's fishing industry, has enabled Israelis to take control of the shale gas fields. The fields are
currently exploited by British Gas, and the gas is sold by the Israel Electric
Corporation. The fields could be a considerable source of income for Gaza,
but the fact that the Gazans have no control over the resource testifies to the
fact that Israel has implemented a matrix of control to exploit the Palestinian commons.[179] As Israeli settlements expand and their needs increase, the
living conditions of Palestinians deteriorate and the possibilities for self-
determination become less and less viable.

That is why the comparison between Palestinians and the Na'vis in *Avatar* is on track but not quite appropriate. In the case of the Palestinians,
land theft is being carried out in the name of development, free trade, and
modernization in a complex network that involves Palestinian, Israeli, and
foreign actors as well as NGOs closely tied to the occupation. For instance,
the policies of dispossession are covered by the ethnic-religious aspects of
the conflict that posit Palestinians as threats to Israeli democracy. That is
to say, focusing on ethnic and religious differences hides a process of accumulation of land and resources to support the long-term survival of Israelis.
This is why representing Palestinians as Na'vi peoples from *Avatar* offers us
a confusing and depoliticized image of the conflict. But this is nothing other
than, first, a sign of the postmodern symbiosis of culture and politics: politics as a simplified summary of itself based on the destruction of a sense of
history as cultural pastiche and, second, a product of the collapse of political
representation and its substitution by simulacra and by becoming spectacle.

The adoption of a politically correct Hollywood discourse in the Bil'in
protest also hides brutal racism. In the narrative of the film, a retired marine
is sent to infiltrate an aboriginal tribe of blue-skinned beings living harmo-
niously with nature to convince them to allow a foreign company to extract

natural resources from their lands. The invader falls in love with an aboriginal princess and ends up becoming one of them, transferring his soul from his human body to its avatar and joining them in their battle to expel the colonizers. We could interpret the movie as the confrontation between two worlds: a world of colonial imperialism (or the ordinary world) and a fantasy world inhabited by aboriginals living in a pure or spiritual relationship to nature. When the hero falls in love with one of the aboriginal women, the film addresses the utopian hybridization of the two worlds by evoking a narrative of the white man as a ruler who unites with the indigenous princess (as in the case of Malinche and Pocahontas). In that regard, the film is ideologically conservative. However, as Slavoj Žižek argues, we don't need to escape from social reality to live in a fantasy, as the hero does. Rather, what becomes urgent is to *change* the fantasy to enable it to fit into reality and from there, take action.[180]

The narrative of the film is aligned with political correctness in the sense that a white man sides with the aboriginals and struggles for the conservation of the environment against the "military-industrial complex" of the imperialist invader. The aboriginals in this narrative can only be saved or destroyed by human beings—that is, they can choose to be the victims of imperialism or to play the role that the fantasy of the white man has given them. The film is therefore based on idealizing the lower classes and representing the cruel selfishness of the rich like a cartoon—a kind of superficial Hollywood Marxism. At the same time, it evokes the reactionary myth of the privileged person undergoing a crisis resolved by a brief and intimate contact with the life of the poor—all to camouflage his vampire-like exploitation. Aside from the brutal racism, the adoption of the politically correct discourse of *Avatar* by the pro-Palestinian protesters in Bil'in also hides the narcissism of the external sympathizer and the violence inherent in spectacular images of political processes. The action, moreover, was not an act of resistance in itself: it was an act of counter-information and symbolic visibilization, but it was not politically effective. Instead, the action deprived Palestinians of the "right to resist" to defend their common forms of life and their commons.

The action makes evident that it is indispensable to create strategies to resist the disappearance of ways of life, to protect that which already exists, or to protest against that which has been lost or is about to be lost. The action reflects the gap between real politics and a spectacle-saturated public sphere—where such political actions get lodged. The long-term outcome of this gap is the slow transfer of political action and resistance to the sphere of the media. For example, in April 2010 James Cameron protested, along with

Sigourney Weaver, against the construction of the Belo Monte Dam in Brazil. In 1989, Sting had protested against the construction of the same dam in an effort to dissuade foreign investors from financing the project.[181]

This trend to combine spectacle with political action is best represented by Arnold Schwarzenegger's governorship of California. According to Jean Baudrillard, Schwarzenegger's masquerade obfuscates political processes with a grotesque parody of democracy converted into a rational power exercise, in which politics becomes an interplay between idols and fans that will die at the hands of spectacle.[182] For Baudrillard, the search for power through an image implies the perishing of the return of that image. Politics in the space of the media, in other words, is a parody of the systems of representation as well as a form of self-cannibalization. And this form of sensible or *celebrity* politics oscillates between, on the one hand, populism, political insurrection, misogyny, and racism as exemplified by politicians like Berlusconi, Netanyahu, Sarkozy, and Trump, and, on the other, a version of capitalism with a human face that seeks the democracy of Obama and Lula—the latter of whom lobbied for the construction of the Belo Monte Dam.[183]

We can conclude that the image of the Bil'in demonstrators dressed up as characters from *Avatar*, aside from reducing the Palestinian struggle to a struggle for the commons and obscuring other aspects of the occupation, put into circulation social-democratic and Christian ideas as spectacle but without real consequence. At the same time, in its mise-en-scène of the "What to do?" of today, it reveals that citizens of privileged countries now travel to the other side of the world to challenge global capitalism only to return and subject themselves to local capitalism. This shows that there is no alternative to global imperialism and that it can only be opposed locally, by carrying out local insurrections against global administration in a bid to expand and extend zones of opacity within the maps of empire.[184]

I FEEL THE ENNUI of having to think too much about cultural differences, experiences of trauma, and matters of translation. Last year I wrote a really long text to share some of my impressions with you, images of the neighborhood where I had been staying in Toronto last summer. But then it felt futile and even banal to send it because you live in a place where people fight to resist and to rebuild what has already been lost. It is the opposite here, where life is built on a promised future of progress and immediate satisfaction.

Missing you feels like my worst hangover. I felt it for the first time exactly a year ago, in the same house that hosts me today. The hangover feels like thousands of paper cuts moving from within my gut all the way through my skin. I feel nauseated, and a weight on my chest hinders me from breathing. But last year many more things weighed on me: uncertainty about when I would see you again, a feeling of being overwhelmed by the greatness of this love, a bit of fear about where we would take it. I notice on my feet the same marks the sun left last year, traced by the leather sandals I bought in Old Jerusalem for 100 shekels. I am wearing the gray dress you like so much, and the *masbaha* (Muslim rosary) threaded with a green string, which I just recovered from one of the boxes I had in storage at my old roommate's home, is hanging around my neck.

On my return this time, I repeat a series of actions similar to those I completed last year: I go to the same shop to buy a used bike (last year's was stolen), I admire the flowers blooming in the garden (Toronto never seemed greener to me), I stay in the same neighborhood, inhabited by sophisticated young people who worry about curating their own lifestyle as well as about the world in general. I walk through the same galleries exhibiting handmade things called art and sold like expensive toys that will hang from halls or rest on shelves inside nearby condos. I avoid, like last year, getting on the streetcar; it feels unsafe, as if it came from Krakow in the 1970s. Public transportation in Toronto is unlikely to improve because the city is right next to the biggest car factory in North America.

I sense an abyss opening up between last year and this one; some of my past fears are fulfilled but take an unexpected turn. The pieces of the puzzle are clearer, the future less uncertain, there is hope on the horizon: a life together, a life together. Suddenly I realize I am leading a double life, like a spy; I juggle between disparate worlds, that go from lumpen to privilege and all the nuances in between. I don't shift from one place to the other, but move every time with new eyes, opening up wider with every movement.

I go to dinner at JG's. Famous filmmaker AE shows up with his gorgeous, fabulous, and exotic wife. I listen attentively to their debate about the format of television divided into series or soap operas, two different strategies for telling stories. She sexily peppers her sentences with French. What's the best way for characters to seduce the public, to make the public desire their everyday visits via the television? A guy from the Canadian Arts Council wants to chat me up, and to me the whole thing feels completely decadent. They talk about canoeing and kayaking, two very exotic sports that the Canadians stole from the Indigenous population. The seven furies traverse my chest; I inhale and exhale slowly. I feel the rawness of my skin. Will I ever feel "normal" again? Or maybe not so angry?

I still can't blame you for anything, but I can tell that your vengeful soul will act not in my name but against me. To prove yourself, you find a way to betray me ("I loved you so hard I had to cheat on you," you told me years later). Without being completely subject to my love, you projected all your neuroses onto your computer screen. After purchasing a ticket to visit you, I find out that you've decided to leave me again. For the first time, I consider the threat seriously. I tremble, because I had announced that I'd be arriving eleven days later, but you write to me:

I suggest that you save money and not buy that ticket, to me it is obvious that all the things you left behind in your life and the things you still want to do in life are a fantasy, and your plans have nothing to do with me. For a time, I thought we could work, but no longer. So use the money that you will save on your ticket and go somewhere else where you can see or try to live what is locked inside you. And believe me when I tell you this with love and prophetic sadness. And here are the first lines of the *Era of Prophecy*:

It is good, but not good enough
To keep me hanging
Amongst the threads of what you pretend
And what I see

It is good, but not good enough
For me to turn my gaze elsewhere
From the sad black sun of my dream
Mao is dead
And so are we

Farewell

Without emails to explain or discuss or blame, just make arrangements for someone to come collect your stuff. With all the love I can give you at this time.

I don't know what to make of this, except that I believe that it's your paranoia talking, not your heart. Until then, I had ignored your attempts to break up with me, but I don't want to force things anymore. I suspect something is going on with someone else, with that woman whose gaze clouded over when one night at Blue you introduced me to her as "your girlfriend." Possibilities open and close, a door swings, there is doubt, fear. What is to be done when love appears to be on the crack of failure? I could try to save it, concentrate on a professional career, go back to writing, invent a new plan to run, change the ticket, try to forget until I get tired of staring at that crack of failure, although it's already been covered by greenery . . . that will dry up in the Fall. Or attack, take revenge, seek to wound. Wait, breathe, wait, breathe, don't give up on going back just yet, not now. What would make me take another road would be treason. Not his paranoia attack. It would be so much easier to go back than not to go back.

The next day you insist on the separation, you change the channels and the terms of communication. My head hurts just there where it hurts when you piss me off. I feel something breaking inside me that debilitates me, my will to keep us together vanishes while my head fills with doubt and fear. You're clinically paranoid, and that really hurts me.

When love is reciprocal, it is singular. When it becomes a desire to possess, it becomes redundant and loses its meaning because it is reduced to the social content of desire. I had found an island in your arms, arms that chain, a country in your eyes, eyes that lie. To break something to get to the other side. The desired being becomes invulnerable, and when this feeling is multiplied by two, it becomes possible to run almost any risk. When desire is reciprocal is a double plot to face and defy all other plots that determine the world. It is a conspiracy times two. The plan is to offer the other a truce from the pain of the world. Not happiness, but a truce for a bodily inclination toward pain. That is why desire is inconceivable without a wound. The conspiracy to create a space of exception together, a space for unmitigated pain, is love. The exception happens when love offers a shield and one opens up oneself fully, physically and spiritually. From the beginning, there are two bodies involved, and when the exception is achieved, both are covered in love. That is how desire moves toward the plenitude of silence, of darkness, where everything is peaceful. The sirens scream at the end of the street. As I remain in your arms, nothing can hurt me.

# NOTES

1. See "Israel Legalizes Nine Settler Outposts in Occupied West Bank, *Al Jazeera*, February 13, 2023, https://www.aljazeera.com/news/2023/2/13/ israel-grants-authorisation-to-nine-settlements-in-west-bank; and Reuters, "Explainer: Israel, Annexation and the West Bank," *BBC News*, June 25, 2020, https://www.bbc.com/news/world-middle-east-52756427.

2. Allan C. Brownfield, "To Silence Critics of Israel, the Term Anti-Semitism Is Being Trivialized," *Washington Report on Middle East Affairs*, July 25, 2022, https://www.wrmea.org/israel-palestine/to-silence-critics-of-israel-the-term-anti-semitism-is-being-trivialized.html.

3. See "Living Conditions in Gaza 'More and More Wretched' over Past Decade, UN Finds," *UN News: Global Perspective Human Stories*, July 2017, https://news.un.org/en/story/2017/07/561302-living-conditions-gaza-more-and-more-wretched-over-past-decade-un-finds; Jacob Kagon, "The Deterioration of Quality of Life in the Palestinian Territories," *Center for Israel Studies*, November 3, 2017, https://edspace.american.edu/ studentisraelity/the-deterioration-of-quality-of-life-in-the-palestinian-territories; and Dima Qato, "The Politics of Deteriorating Health: The Case of Palestine," *International Journal of Health Services* 34, no. 2 (2004): 341–64.

4. See "Israeli Forces Storm Holy Site of Al-Aqsa Mosque on Eid," *Democracy Now*, August 12, 2019, https://www.democracynow.org/2019/8/12/headlines/ israeli_forces_storm_holy_site_of_al_aqsa_mosque_on_eid.

5. See "Temple Mount Clashes: Jordan Condemns 'Blunt' Israeli Violations as Jews Allowed in Holy Site," *Haaretz*, August 11, 2019, https://www. haaretz.com/israel-news/2019-08-11/ty-article/.premium/clashes-erupt-in-temple-mount-between-israeli-forces-and-muslim-worshipers/0000017f-f86d-d47e-a37f-f97db3340000.

6. "Ultra-nationalist Jews Storm Al-Aqsa ahead of Israeli Flag March," *Al Jazeera*, May 29, 2022, https://www.aljazeera.com/news/2022/5/29/settlers-storm-al-aqsa-compound-ahead-of-israeli-flag-march.

7.  "Palestine PM Says Israeli Flag March 'Crossed All Red Lines,'" *Al Jazeera*, May 30, 2022, https://www.aljazeera.com/news/2022/5/30/palestine-pm-says-israeli-flag-march-crossed-all-red-lines.

8.  "Israeli Far-Right Group Calls for Dismantling Dome of the Rock on 'Jerusalem Day,'" *Middle East Eye*, May 18, 2022, https://www.middleeasteye.net/news/israel-palestine-jerusalem-far-right-dismantling-dome-rock.

9.  "Israeli Ultranationalists March in Show of Force in East Jerusalem," *PBS*, June 15, 2021, https://www.pbs.org/newshour/politics/israeli-ultranationalists-march-in-show-of-force-in-east-jerusalem.

10. Daniel Estrin, "A Look at the Gaza Strip, 2 Months after a Devastating 11-Day War with Israel," *NPR*, August 1, 2021, https://www.npr.org/2021/08/01/1023393358/a-look-at-the-gaza-strip-2-months-after-a-devastating-11-day-war-with-israel.

11. Bethan McKernan and Quique Kierszenbaum, "Clashes in Jerusalem as Israeli Nationalists March through Muslim Quarter," *Guardian*, May 29, 2022, https://www.theguardian.com/world/2022/may/29/jerusalem-israeli-parade-old-city-flag-march.

12. Alice Speri, "Israeli Forces Deliberately Killed Palestinian American Journalist, Report Shows," *Intercept*, September 20, 2022, https://theintercept.com/2022/09/20/shireen-abu-akleh-killing-israel.

13. See Ariella Azoulay, "The Collaborator, She Doesn't Exist," in *The Civil Contract of Photography* (New York: Zone Books, 2008), 406–23.

14. Azoulay, "The Collaborator," 268, 314, 322, 324.

15. "Israel Passes Law to Strip Residency of Jerusalem's Palestinians," *Al Jazeera*, March 7, 2018, https://www.aljazeera.com/news/2018/3/7/israel-passes-law-to-strip-residency-of-jerusalems-palestinians; and "Israel Passes Law Allowing Deportation of Palestinian Prisoners," *Al Jazeera*, February 16, 2023, https://www.aljazeera.com/news/2023/2/16/israeli-law-allowing-palestinian-prisoner-deportation-a.

16. "Dugin and the Discourse of Deception," *EU vs DiSiNFO*, January 13, 2021, https://euvsdisinfo.eu/dugin-and-the-discourse-of-deception.

17. Maayan Lubell, "Bibi Times: Netanyahu's Tangled Relationship with Israel's Media," *Reuters*, November 23, 2015, https://www.reuters.com/article/cnews-us-israel-netanyahu-media-insight-idCAKBN0TC1DP20151123; Oded Yaron, "How Fake News Is Threatening the Upcoming Elections in Israel," *Haaretz*, September 15, 2018, https://www.haaretz.com/israel-news/2018-09-15/ty-article-magazine/.premium/the-online-dangers-threatening-fair-elections-in-israel/0000017f-e1e1-d38f-a57f-e7f37e850000;

and Oliver Holmes, "Facebook Penalizes Netanyahu Page over Hate Speech Violation," *Guardian*, September 12, 2019, https://www.theguardian.com/technology/2019/sep/12/facebook-disables-netanyahu-page-bot-over-hate-speech-violation.

18. Natan Sachs and Kevin Huggard, "In Israel, Benny Gantz Decides to Join with Rival Netanyahu," *Brookings*, March 27, 2020, https://www.brookings.edu/blog/order-from-chaos/2020/03/27/in-israel-benny-gantz-decides-to-join-with-rival-netanyahu.

19. "Address by PM Netanyahu at Bar-Ilan University," *Ministry of Foreign Affairs*, June 14, 2009, https://www.gov.il/en/departments/news/address-by-pm-netanyahu-at-bar-ilan-university-14-jun-2009; and "Netanyahu Speech: An Attempt to Evade Foreign Pressure," *Emirates Center for Strategic Studies and Research*, June 28, 2009, https://www.ecssr.ae/en/reports_analysis/netanyahu-speech-an-attempt-to-evade-foreign-pressure.

20. "Address by PM Netanyahu"; "Netanyahu Speech."

21. Akiva Eldar, "Netanyahu, Master of Alternative Facts," *Al Monitor*, January 31, 2017, https://www.al-monitor.com/originals/2017/01/israel-benjamin-netanyahu-amona-settlement-bedouin-arabs.html.

22. Ruth Eglash, "Netanyahu Apologizes to Israeli Arabs for Comment Widely Criticized as Racist," *Washington Post*, March 23, 2015, https://www.washingtonpost.com/world/netanyahu-apologizes-to-arab-voters-for-comment-widely-criticized-as-racist/2015/03/23/93417f1c-d18c-11e4-8b1e-274d670aa9c9_story.html.

23. "Military Occupation," The Practical Guide to Humanitarian Law, Médecins Sans Frontières, https://guide-humanitarian-law.org/content/article/3/occupied-territory.

24. Yaron Steinbuch, "Palestinian Officials Recall UAE Ambassador, Slam Israel Peace Deal as 'Betrayal,'" *New York Post*, August 14, 2020, https://nypost.com/2020/08/14/palestinians-recall-uae-envoy-call-peace-deal-a-betrayal.

25. "Repression and Injustice in the United Arab Emirates," Free speech, Amnesty International UK, May 18, 2020, https://www.amnesty.org.uk/united-arab-emirates-uae-free-speech-repression-injustice-censorship.

26. David Patrikarakos, "What Do Arabs Think about Israel?," *Jewish Chronicle*, February 4, 2021, https://www.thejc.com/comment/opinion/what-do-ordinary-arabs-really-think-about-peace-with-israel-1.511527.

27. Antony Loewenstein, *The Palestinian Laboratory: How Israel Exports the Technology of Occupation Around the World* (Melbourne: Scribe, 2023).

28. "La marcha zapatista llega hoy a la capital para intentar lograr la aprobación de la Ley de Derechos Indígenas," *El País*, March 10, 2001, https://elpais.com/elpais/2001/03/11/actualidad/984304201_850215.html.

29. Mike Gonzalez, "Zapatistas after the Great March—a Postscript," *International Socialism* 2, no. 91 (Summer 2001), https://www.marxists.org/history/etol/writers/gonzalez/2001/xx/postscript.htm.

30. Chris Arsenault, "FBI Targets US Palestine Activists," *Al Jazeera*, October 3, 2010, https://www.aljazeera.com/news/2010/10/3/fbi-targets-us-palestine-activists.

31. "They Still Have Painted What They Saw: Children's Art Censored in Oakland," *Global Exchange*, September 23, 2011, https://globalexchange.org/2011/09/23/they-still-have-painted-what-they-saw-childrens-art-censored-in-oakland.

32. Ed Pilkington, "University Denies Tenure to Outspoken Holocaust Academic," *Guardian*, June 12, 2007, https://www.theguardian.com/world/2007/jun/12/usa.highereducation; Or Kashti, "Bar-Ilan Lecturer Reportedly Denied Tenure Due to Views," *Haaretz*, September 24, 2010, https://www.haaretz.com/2010-09-24/ty-article/bar-ilan-lecturer-reportedly-denied-tenure-due-to-views/0000017f-f7da-d47e-a37f-fffead980000; "Steven Salaita, Rejected by U. of I. over Israel Tweets," *Chicago Tribune*, March 6, 2019, https://www.chicagotribune.com/opinion/commentary/ct-perspec-steven-salaita-israel-university-illinois-tenure-0308-20190306-story.html; and Ilan Pappé, *Out of the Frame: The Struggle for Academic Freedom in Israel* (London: Pluto Press, 2010).

33. Robert Booth, "Israeli Attack on Gaza Flotilla Sparks International Outrage," *Guardian*, May 31, 2010, https://www.theguardian.com/world/2010/may/31/israeli-attacks-gaza-flotilla-activists.

34. See Azoulay, *Civil Contract of Photography*.

35. "Exigen peritajes para esclarcer muerte de niño en Puebla," *Sistema Integral de Información en Derechos Humanos, Centro Prodh*, July 29, 2014, http://centroprodh.org.mx/sididh_2_0_alfa/?p=35478.

36. "B'Tselem's Investigation of Fatalities in Operation Cast Lead," *B'Tselem – The Israeli Information Center for Human Rights in the Occupied Territories*, September 9, 2009, https://www.btselem.org/download/20090909_cast_lead_fatalities_eng.pdf.

37. "Muere Juan Francisco Kuykendall, activista herido durante #1DMX," *Aristegui Noticias*, January 26, 2014, https://www.972mag.com/watch-idf-fires-tear-gas-canisters-directly-at-protestors; and Natasha Roth-Rowland, "WATCH: IDF Fires Tear Gas Canisters Directly at Protesters," *+972*

*Magazine*, March 24, 2015, https://www.972mag.com/watch-idf-fires-tear-gas-canisters-directly-at-protestors/.

38.  Nathalie Khankan, *Quiet Orient Riot* (Oakland, CA: Omnidawn, 2020), 62.

39.  Nick Aikens, "Picasso in Palestine: Taking a Modern Masterpiece to Ramallah," *Frieze*, July 6, 2011, https://www.frieze.com/article/picasso-palestine.

40.  See Mahmoud Darwish, *Memory for Forgetfulness: August, Beirut, 1982*, trans. Ibrahim Muhawi (Berkeley: University of California Press, 1995).

41.  Marian Houk, "More Subtle than It Seems: The Mystery of Arafat's Death," *+972 Magazine*, November 18, 2018, https://www.972mag.com/more-subtle-than-it-seems-behind-the-mystery-of-arafats-death.

42.  Robert Barron, "Palestinian Politics Timeline: Since the 2006 Election," United States Institute of Peace, June 25, 2019, https://www.usip.org/palestinian-politics-timeline-2006-election.

43.  See Azoulay, *Civil Contract of Photography*.

44.  "The Nakba Did Not Start or End in 1948," *Al Jazeera*, May 23, 2017, https://www.aljazeera.com/features/2017/5/23/the-nakba-did-not-start-or-end-in-1948.

45.  Amena El Ashkar, "Palestinian Refugees in Lebanon Denounce New 'Inhumane' Work Restrictions," *Middle East Eye*, July 23, 2019, https://www.middleeasteye.net/news/palestinian-refugees-lebanon-denounce-latest-work-restrictions.

46.  Michael C. Hudson, "The Palestinian Factor in the Lebanese Civil War," *Middle East Journal* 32, no. 3 (Summer 1978): 261–78.

47.  Ann Mosely Lesch, "Israeli Settlements in the Occupied Territories, 1967–1977," *Journal of Palestine Studies* 7, no. 1 (Autumn 1977): 26–47.

48.  Eyal Weizman, *Hollow Land: Israel's Architecture of Occupation* (London: Verso, 2009).

49.  Mark Oliver and Simon Jeffrey, "Soldiers Evict Gaza Settlers," *Guardian*, August 17, 2005, https://www.theguardian.com/world/2005/aug/17/israel4.

50.  Claire Parker, "Jewish Settler Population in West Bank Passes Half a Million," *Washington Post*, February 2, 2023, https://www.washingtonpost.com/world/2023/02/02/jewish-settlers-west-bank-half-million.

51.  "The Oslo Accords/Oslo Process," Glossary Term, Anti-Defamation League, September 1, 2016, https://www.adl.org/resources/glossary-term/oslo-accordsoslo-process.

52.  "A Performance-based Road Map to a Permanent Two-State Solution to the Israeli-Palestinian Conflict," *United Nations Peacemaker*, April 4, 2003, https://peacemaker.un.org/israel-palestine-roadmap2003.

53.  Amnesty International, *Israel's Apartheid against Palestinians: Cruel System of Domination and Crime against Humanity*, February 1, 2022, https://www.amnesty.org/en/documents/mde15/5141/2022/en.

54.  Eyal Weizman, "Walking through Walls: Soldiers as Architects in the Israeli-Palestinian Conflict," *Radical Philosophy* 136 (March/April 2006), https://www.radicalphilosophy.com/article/walking-through-walls.

55.  Weizman, "Walking through Walls."

56.  Weizman, "Walking through Walls."

57.  Weizman, "Walking through Walls."

58.  "Israel/Palestine: Unlawful Israeli Airstrikes Kill Civilians," *Human Rights Watch*, July 15, 2014, https://www.hrw.org/news/2014/07/15/israel/palestine-unlawful-israeli-airstrikes-kill-civilians.

59.  Nida'a Yousef, "Under Scrutiny: Allegations of Use of Human Shields by Palestinian Armed Groups and the International Criminal Court Investigation," *Law for Palestine*, August 2, 2021, https://law4palestine.org/under-scrutiny-allegations-of-use-of-human-shields-by-palestinian-armed-groups-and-the-international-criminal-court-investigation.

60.  The 1994 Oslo II Accord established the administrative division of the Palestinian West Bank into Areas A, B, and C as a transitional arrangement, pending a final status agreement. The divisions persist: Area A in which the Palestinian Authority administers civil and security matters; Area C, which includes all Israeli settlements and two thirds of the West Bank's fertile agricultural land, where Israel administers both civil and security matters; and Area B, where the PA administers only civil matters. While Area C is a continuous territory, Areas A and B are fragmented into 166 separate enclaves. "Areas A, B, C," Visualizing Palestine 101, https://101.visualizingpalestine.org/resources/glossary/areas-a-b-c.

61.  European Union, Office of the European Union Representative (West Bank and Gaza Strip, UNRWA), *One Year Report on Demolitions and Seizures in the West Bank*, March 23, 2023, https://www.eeas.europa.eu/delegations/palestine-occupied-palestinian-territory-west-bank-and-gaza-strip/one-year-report-o_en.

62.  Hasan Ibheis and Khaled Ayad, "The Separation Wall in the West Bank," *Al-Zaytouna Centre for Studies and Consultations*, 2012, https://www.dohainstitute.org/en/ResearchAndStudies/Pages/The_Separation_Wall_Israels_Complete_Apartheid.aspx.

63.  Linah Alsaafin, "The Colour-Coded Israeli ID System for Palestinians," *Al Jazeera*, November 18, 2017, https://www.aljazeera.com/news/2017/11/18/the-colour-coded-israeli-id-system-for-palestinians.

64. B'Tselem, The Israeli Information Center for Human Rights in the Occupied Territories, "Restrictions of Movement," November 11, 2017, https://www.btselem.org/freedom_of_movement.

65. Sami Miaari, Asaf Zussman, and Noam Zussman, "Employment Restrictions and Political Violence in the Israeli-Palestinian Conflict," *Journal of Economic Behavior and Organization*, no. 101 (May 2014): 24–44; Ruth Margalit, "Israel's Invisible Filipino Work Force," *New York Times*, May 3, 2017, https://www.nytimes.com/2017/05/03/magazine/israels-invisible-filipino-work-force.html.

66. Cheryl Rubenberg, "Israel and Guatemala: Arms, Advice and Counterinsurgency," *MERIP* 140 (May/June 1986), https://merip.org/1986/05/israel-and-guatemala; América Profunda, "De la Franja de Gaza a las Favelas de Río de Janeiro: Israel globaliza la experiencia del terror," *Avión Negro*, February 23, 2023, https://avionnegro.com.ar/latinoamerica/de-la-franja-de-gaza-a-las-favelas-de-rio-de-janeiro-como-israel-globaliza-la-experiencia-del-terror; Rachel Stromousa, "Will the US Stop Importing Israeli Torture Techniques?," *Haaretz*, September 18, 2016, https://www.haaretz.com/opinion/2016-09-18/ty-article/.premium/will-the-u-s-stop-importing-israeli-torture-techniques/0000017f-e99d-d62c-a1ff-fdff06f30000.

67. "Israel's Occupation: 50 Years of Dispossession," Amnesty International, June 2016, https://www.amnesty.org/en/latest/campaigns/2017/06/israel-occupation-50-years-of-dispossession.

68. Mohammed Najib, "Palestine Runs Dry: 'Our Water They Steal and Sell to Us,'" *Al Jazeera*, July 15, 2021, https://www.aljazeera.com/news/2021/7/15/water-war-palestinians-demand-more-water-access-from-israel; and "Merokot's Involvement in the Israeli Occupation," Who Profits: The Israeli Occupation Industry, December 2013, https://www.whoprofits.org/flash-report/mekorots-involvement-in-the-israeli-occupation.

69. Peter Beaumont, "What's Driving the Young Lone Wolves Who Are Stalking the Streets of Israel?," *Guardian*, October 18, 2015, https://www.theguardian.com/world/2015/oct/18/knife-intifada-palestinian-israel-west-bank.

70. "Israel Removes Metal Detectors from al-Aqsa Compound," *Al Jazeera*, July 25, 2017, https://www.aljazeera.com/news/2017/7/25/israel-removes-metal-detectors-from-al-aqsa-compound.

71. John Kerry's Full Speech on Israeli Settlements and a Two-State Solution, published December 28, 2016, available at: https://time.com/4619064/john-kerrys-speech-israel-transcript; Carol Morello and Ruth Eglash, "Kerry Harshly Condemns Israeli Settler Activity as an Obstacle," *Washington Post*, December 28, 2016, https://www.washingtonpost.com/world/

national-security/kerry-address-middle-east-peace-process-amid-deep-us-israel-strains/2016/12/28/d656e5fa-cd0a-11e6-b8a2-8c2a61b0436f_story.html.

72. "'Stay Strong Israel,' Trump Tweets as Settlement Row Flares," *France 24*, December 28, 2016, https://www.france24.com/en/20161228-israel-trump-tweet-settlement-jerusalem-kerry.

73. David Smith, "Republican Senators Introduce Bill to Move US Embassy in Israel to Jerusalem," *Guardian*, January 4, 2017, https://www.theguardian.com/world/2017/jan/03/us-embassy-israel-jerusalem-republican-bill.

74. Committee on the Exercise of the Inalienable Rights of the Palestinian People, *The Status of Jerusalem*, (New York: United Nations, 1997), https://www.un.org/unispal/wp-content/uploads/2016/07/The-Status-of-Jerusalem-Engish-199708.pdf.

75. My good friend and Arabic literature expert, Nathalie Khankhan, pointed out to me that the old classical love poem is called *ghazaal* (gazelle). The beloved in the old *Qasida*, or love poem, is called *ghazaal* because her eyes are just as beautiful as gazelle eyes.

76. I am referring to Sekula's piece in Dokumenta 12 (2007), a photograph of a Mexican worker at the Ford factory in Detroit over which he imposed the famous sentence from the fourth movement of Beethoven's Ninth Symphony, the "Ode to Joy": "Alle Menschen werden Schwestern" (All humans will be sisters). Following Slavoj Žižek, "Ode to Joy" represents a magic moment of ecstatic brotherhood. As such, it is an "empty signifier" that can stand for anything, from being an ode to the brotherhood of all people, to being played in 1938 for Hitler's birthday. In the German Olympic Games in 1972 it was played whenever the German team of athletes from East and West won a medal. See "The Disturbing Sounds of the Turkish March," *In These Times*, November 6, 2007, http://www.inthesetimes.com/article/3393/the_disturbing_sounds_of_the_turkish_march.

77. Ronen Eidelman, "Turning a Dead Giraffe into an Idea," *Maarav*, September 11, 2007, http://www.maarav.org.il/archive/classes/PUPrintf1cb.html?id=1010&lang=ENGz.

78. "There it is truthful," or "There it is for real." All translations are my own unless otherwise noted.

79. The play was performed for the first time in February 1972 at the Capannone in Milan. The script is published in *Le commedie di Dario Fo* (Turin: Einaudi, 1977).

80. See Roland Barthes, "Diderot Eisenstein, Brecht," in *Image, Music, Text* (New York: Hill and Wang, 1977), 69.

81. Mónica Baptiste G., "Traces of Death, in the Work of Teresa Margolles," *Mediamatic*, https://www.mediamatic.net/en/page/378691/traces-of-death.

82. Theodor Adorno, *Minima Moralia: Reflections from Damaged Life*, trans. E. F. N. Jephcott (New York: Verso, 1974), 115–16. Adorno further argues that zoos defy animals' freedom by making boundaries visible, inflaming the longing for open spaces. For him, there is a link between zoos and Noah's Ark, as animals displayed "in couples or as 'specimens' defy the disaster that befalls the species *qua* species" (116). Further, he draws a link between zoos, civilization, and nineteenth-century colonial imperialism, in their common striving to dominate nature.

83. Here I evoke a pathology described by Frantz Fanon in *Black Skins, White Masks* (New York: Grove Press, 1994), what Said calls the "Spectre of Comparisons," a double specter or inverted telescope through which one can see oneself only by way of the gaze of the colonizing culture. See as well Benedict Anderson's reading of José Rizal's novel *Noli me tangere*, in which the main character returns to Manila from Europe, where he was educated, and can only see Manila through the European lens, simultaneously close and far.

84. Fredric Jameson, *Postmodernism, or the Cultural Logic of Late Capitalism* (Durham, NC: Duke University Press, 1991), 411.

85. As defined by Foucault (in 1979), intervention is a manipulation of the social in order to introduce additional freedoms, a kind of Keynesianism, as an ensemble of "liberogenic devices" that seek to produce freedom through economic development. The problem here is that such devices may lead to exactly the opposite of what was intended, becoming instead the mainspring of control. Michel Foucault, *The Birth of Biopolitics: Lectures at the College de France, 1978–1979* (New York: Palgrave, 2008), 67, 69.

86. The name Katyūshas comes from the rockets made by the Soviet Union under Stalin. But I think today it has become a general term for a kind of "mobile" artillery. I am not sure if they are homemade or not (as is the case for the qassam rockets).

87. Lucretius, *On the Nature of Things*, trans. Cyril Bailey (Oxford: Clarendon Press, 1948), 74.

88. Alain Badiou, *Being and Event* (London: Continuum, 2007), 97.

89. Amira Hass, "Israel Makes It Increasingly Difficult for Palestinians' Foreign Spouses to Stay in the West Bank," *Haaretz*, September 13, 2017, https://www.haaretz.com/middle-east-news/palestinians/2017-09-13/ty-article/.premium/israel-makes-it-hard-for-palestinians-foreign-spouses-to-stay-in-w-bank/0000017f-db2e-d856-a37f-ffeeedf30000; and Al Jazeera Staff, "New Israeli Rules on Foreigners Visiting West Bank Stir Outrage," *Al Jazeera*, April 27, 2022, https://www.aljazeera.com/news/2022/4/27/new-israeli-rules-on-foreigners-visiting-west-bank-stir-outrage.

90.  Sylvère Lotringer, "Introduction: The History of Semiotext(e)," in *Hatred of Capitalism, a Reader*, ed. Chris Kraus and Sylvère Lotringer (New York: Semiotext(e), 2001), 16.

91.  See the Freedom Flotilla Coalition website, https://freedomflotilla.org.

92.  "Yasser Arafat's Welsh Human Shields," *BBC News*, October 7, 2003, http:// news.bbc.co.uk/2/hi/uk_news/wales/3169690.stm; "Welsh Activist inside Besieged Church," *BBC News*, May 5, 2002, http://news.bbc.co.uk/2/hi/uk_ news/wales/1969332.stm.

93.  "Israel: Killing of Thomas Hundall by Israeli Soldiers," *Asian Human Rights Commission*, April 13, 2003, http://www.humanrights.asia/news/forwarded-news/FA-04-2003; "Gaza Activists' Killing Was Murder," *Al Jazeera*, April 10, 2006, https://www.aljazeera.com/news/2006/4/10/gaza-activists-killing-was-murder; Antonella Ciancio, "'Dismay and Sorrow' in Hometown of Italian Activist," *Reuters*, April 15, 2011; Jessica Kwong, "Former UC Berkeley Tree-Sitter Injured in West Bank," *DailyCal*, March 13, 2009, https://web.archive. org/web/20100725102435/http://www.dailycal.org/article/104844/former_ uc_berkeley_tree-sitter_injured_in_west_ban; "Emily Henochowicz Speaks Out: Art Student Who Lost Her Eye after Being Shot by Israeli Tear Gas Canister in West Bank Protest Discusses Her Life, Her Art, and Why She Plans to Return," *Democracy Now!*, August 5, 2010, https://www. democracynow.org/2010/8/5/exclusiveemily_henochowicz_speaks_out_ art_student.

94.  Immanuel Kant, "The Contest of the Faculties," in *Kant: Political Writings*, ed. H. S. Reiss (Cambridge: Cambridge University Press, 1991), 182–83.

95.  The Al-Aqsa Martyrs Brigades are a secular coalition of armed Palestinian groups in the West Bank.

96.  Jonathan Lis, Yair Ettinger, Amos Harel, and Haaretz correspondents, "Eight Killed when Terrorist Opens Fire in Library at Jerusalem Yeshiva," *Haaretz*, March 6, 2008, https://www.haaretz.com/2008-03-06/ ty-article/eight-killed-when-terrorist-opens-fire-in-library-at-jerusalem-yeshiva/0000017f-ef39-dc28-a17f-ff3fce710000.

97.  Hussein Al Barghouti, unpublished fragment from "What the Gypsy Said."

98.  Sliman Mansour (1947) is a Palestinian painter considered to be an important figure among contemporary figures in his country. His work gave visual expression to the cultural and political concept of *sumud*.

99.  Adam Robert Green, "Economic Peace in the West Bank and the Fayyad Plan: Are They Working?," *MEI*, January 1, 2010, https://www.mei.edu/ publications/economic-peace-west-bank-and-fayyad-plan-are-they-working; Raja Khalidi and Sobhi Samour, "Neoliberalism and the Contradictions of the Palestinian Authority's State-Building Programme,"

in *Decolonizing Palestinian Political Economy*, ed. Mandy Turner and Omar Shweiki (London: Palgrave Macmillan, 2014), Adam Hanieh, *Money, Markets and Monarchies: The Gulf Cooperation Council and the Political Economy of the Contemporary Middle East* (Cambridge: Cambridge University Press, 2018).

100. The title of this section, "Don't think this is the next Chiapas," is from the training manual of the International Solidarity Movement (ISM).

101. From Goethe's *Faust*.

102. Andrew Buncombe, "Rachel Corrie Was Killed in Gaza by the IDF: 20 Years on, Her Parents Are Still Fighting for Justice," *Independent*, March 17, 2023, https://www.mei.edu/publications/economic-peace-west-bank-and-fayyad-plan-are-they-working.

103. Henry Weinstein, "Activist's Parents Sue Caterpillar Inc.," *Los Angeles Times*, March 20, 2005, https://www.latimes.com/archives/la-xpm-2005-mar-20-fg-corrie20-story.html; Ed Pilkington, "Families Cannot Sue Firm for Israel Deaths," *Guardian*, September 19, 2007, https://www.theguardian.com/world/2007/sep/19/usa.israel; Harriet Sherwood, "Rachel Corrie Lawsuit Result 'Dangerous Precedent' Say Human Rights Groups," *Guardian*, August 28, 2012, https://www.theguardian.com/world/2012/aug/28/rachel-corrie-dismissal-dangerous-precedent; Ruth Pollad, "Israeli Army Cleared of Activist's Death," *Sydney Morning Herald*, August 28, 2012, https://www.smh.com.au/world/israeli-army-cleared-of-activists-death-20120828-24ya2.html.

104. Judith Butler, *Frames of War: "When is Life Grievable?"* (New York: Verso, 2009).

105. "Near is and difficult to grasp, the God. But where danger threatens, that which saves from it also grows." Friederich Hölderlin, *Patmos: Das scheidende Erscheinen des Gedichts* (Munich: W. Fink Verlag, 1999).

106. Mustafa Khalil al-Sayfi, "Trip in the Ruins of Al-Walaja, Rihla Fi Atlal Al-Walaja," in *Nakba, 1948 and the Claims of Memory*, ed. Ahmad H. Saadi and Lila Abu Lughod (New York: Columbia University Press, 2007).

107. Ian Black, "'Haifa Is Essentially Segregated': Cracks Appear in Israel's Capital of Coexistence," *Guardian*, April 19, 2018, https://www.theguardian.com/cities/2018/apr/19/haifa-is-essentially-segregated-cracks-appear-in-israels-capital-of-coexistence.

108. Elisa Greco, "Africa, Extractivism and the Crisis of This Time," *Review of African Political Economy* 47, no. 166 (2020), 511–21; Henry Bocanegra Acosta, Jorge Enrique Carvajal Martínez, "Extractivismo, derecho y conflict social en Colombia," *Revista Republicana*, no. 26 (Jan.–June 2019), 143–69.

109. B'Tselem, The Israeli Information Center for Human Rights in the Occupied Territories," "Background on the demonstrations in Bil'in," B'Tselem, January 2, 2013, https://www.btselem.org/demonstrations/bilin.

110. *Mutasha'il* is the name of Emile Habiby's novel, combining pessimist with optimist. In English the title was translated as *The Pessoptimist*. I would have translated it as *The Opsimist*, as they did in Hebrew. The main character of the novel, a Palestinian from Haifa who became an Israeli citizen after the Nabka, is a kind of Candide or Svejk, who thinks he lives in the best possible world, in spite of all the disgraces he has to go through. As Habiby's novel became very popular quickly, *mutasha'il* became a commonly used word in Arabic.

111. Luc Boltanski, *La Souffrance à distance: Morale humanitaire, medias et politique* (Paris: Métailie, 1993).

112. "Tahta" is the low side of Ramallah where the old city is located, also known as "Low Ramallah."

113. Slavoj Žižek, *The Parallax View* (Cambridge: MIT Press, 2008), 264.

114. Jacques Derrida about *Izkor* by Claude Lanzmann in *Ecografías de la Televisión* (Madrid: EUDEBA, 2007) 132.

115. Hannah Arendt, *What Is Politics* (Barcelona: Paidós, 2005), 57.

116. "Israel Kills Hamas Leader's Son in Gaza," *CBS News*, January 15, 2008, https://www.cbsnews.com/news/israel-kills-hamas-leaders-son-in-gaza.

117. "Israeli Strike Kills Gaza Civilians," *Al Jazeera*, January 17, 2008, https://www.aljazeera.com/news/2008/1/17/israeli-strike-kills-gaza-civilians-2.

118. Zaatari and Raad, born in the 1960s, are Lebanese video artists whose works address archive, history, and personal memory in relationship to the civil war in their country. Noureddine is a filmmaker, also from Lebanon and a decade younger, whose filmic proposal addresses the trauma and senselessness of the war in Lebanon.

119. Rory McCarthy, "Hamas Says It Was behind Suicide Blast in Israel," *Guardian*, February 6, 2008, https://www.theguardian.com/world/2008/feb/06/israelandthepalestinians.international

120. Gilles Deleuze, "Les Intércesseurs," in *Purparlers (1972–1990)* (Paris: Les Éditions de minuit, 1990), 187.

121. José María Marti Font, "Discutir sobre el velo es un error; el debate es sobre moral sexual," *El País*, February 12, 2008, https://elpais.com/diario/2008/02/13/internacional/1202857204_850215.html

122. Serge Daney, "Le thérrorisé (pédagogie godardienne)," *Cahiers du Cinéma* 263, no. 3 (January 1976).

123. W. Andrew Terrill, "The Political Myth of the Battle of Karameh," *Middle East Journal* 55, no. 1 (Winter 2001): 91–111.

124. Britannica, s.v. "National Convention," accessed July 15, 2023, https://www.britannica.com/topic/National-Convention.

125. Mahmud Darwish, in an interview with Israeli poet Helit Yeshurun, published in *Hadarim*, no. 12 (Tel Aviv, Spring 1996), translated to the French in *La Palestine comme métaphore* (Paris: Actes Sud, 1997), 117–18.

126. See Hannah Arendt, *Sobre la violencia* (Madrid: Alianza, 2013).

127. Jacques Rancière, *The Politics of Aesthetics: The Distribution of the Sensible*, trans. Gabriel Rockhill (London: Verso, 2004).

128. Semiocapitalism is a term coined by Italian philosopher Franco Berardi (Bifo) to describe the current form of capitalism grounded on cognitive labor and in the production and dissemination of signs. In this phase of capitalism, the basis of production passes from merchandise to languages and forms of communication from which surplus value is derived.

129. Ben White, "Bedouin Transfer Plan Shows Israel's Racism," *Al Jazeera*, September 13, 2011, https://www.aljazeera.com/opinions/2011/9/13/bedouin-transfer-plan-shows-israels-racism.

130. Charles Bybelezer, "Israeli Government Again Asks Court for Delay in Demolishing Khan al-Ahmar," *JNS*, February 1, 2023, https://www.jns.org/israeli-government-to-respond-court-order-to-demolish-khan-al-ahmar.

131. Zora Ahmed, "Prawer Plan Buries the Two State Solution," *Al Jazeera*, December 11, 2013, https://www.aljazeera.com/opinions/2013/12/11/prawer-plan-buries-the-two-state-solution; Harriet Sherwood, "Israel Shelves Plan to Forcibly Relocate Bedouins from the Negev," *Guardian*, December 12, 2013, https://www.theguardian.com/world/2013/dec/12/israel-shelves-plan-relocate-bedouin-negev; "Max Blumenthal on 'Goliath: Life and Loathing in Greater Israel,'" *Democracy Now!*, October 4, 2013, https://www.democracynow.org/2013/10/4/max_blumenthal_on_goliath_life_and.

132. "The Prawer Plan: Ethnic Cleansing in the Negev," Institute for Middle East Understanding, November 27, 2013, https://imeu.org/article/the-prawer-plan-ethnic-cleansing-in-the-negev.

133. "Palestinians in Israel Strike after Deadly Negev Raid," *Al Jazeera*, January 19, 2017, https://www.aljazeera.com/news/2017/1/19/palestinians-in-israel-strike-after-deadly-negev-raid.

134. Eyal Weizman, *The Conflict Shoreline* (Göttingen: Steidl Verlag, 2016).

135. Weizman, *The Conflict Shoreline*.

136. Dima Abumaria, "Palestinian Women: Increase in Council Representation Not Enough," *Jerusalem Post*, January 15, 2021, https://www.jpost.com/israel-news/palestinian-women-increase-in-council-representation-not-enough-655544.

137. Eyal Weizman, *Hollow Land: Israel's Architecture of Occupation* (London: Verso, 2007); Hannah Arendt, *The Human Condition* (Chicago: University of Chicago Press, 1958), 63–64.

138. "Ciudad de México tendrá 10,000 cámaras de vigilancia en 2011," *El País*, February 2, 2008, https://elpais.com/internacional/2008/02/29/actualidad/1204239601_850215.html.

139. "Israeli Minister Warns of Palestinian 'Holocaust,'" *Guardian*, February 29, 2008, https://www.theguardian.com/world/2008/feb/29/israelandthepalestinians1.

140. Allegra Stratton, "Israeli Air Strike 'Destroys Gaza Ministry,'" *Guardian*, January 18, 2008, https://www.theguardian.com/world/2008/jan/18/allegrastratton.

141. "Bare Life" exhibition at the Museum on the Seam in Jerusalem, https://www.mots.org.il/bare-life,

142. "8 Die in Terror Attack on J'lem Yeshiva," *Haaretz*, March 7, 2008, https://www.haaretz.com/2008-03-07/ty-article/8-die-in-terror-attack-on-jlem-yeshiva/0000017f-f550-d887-a7ff-fdf42a550000.

143. Francesc Relea, "Del campus al campamento," *El País*, March 12, 2008, https://elpais.com/diario/2008/03/12/internacional/1205276404_850215.html.

144. Raphael Ahren, "Netanyahu: Economics, Not Politics, Is the Key to Peace," *Haaretz*, November 20, 2008, https://www.haaretz.com/2008-11-20/ty-article/netanyahu-economics-not-politics-is-the-key-to-peace/0000017f-f49d-d47e-a37f-fdbd12a10000.

145. "Industrial Zones in the Occupied Palestinian Territory," Who Profits: The Israeli Occupation Industry, June 19, 2019, https://www.whoprofits.org/dynamic-report/industrial-zones.

146. "Rice Pressures Barak on Roadblocks," *Al Jazeera*, May 5, 2008, https://www.aljazeera.com/news/2008/5/5/rice-pressures-barak-on-roadblocks.

147. Construction of the road began in 2005 and ended in 2017, and the road was opened in 2019. Cécile Galluccio, Antoine Mariotti, and Irris Makler, "The 'Apartheid Road': West Bank Highway Sparks Controversy," *France 24*, April 2, 2019, https://www.france24.com/en/20190204-focus-israel-palestinian-territories-apartheid-road-highway-4370-jerusalem-segregation.

148. Apollinaire, quoted by Jean-François Lyotard, *The Inhuman: Reflections on Time* (Cambridge: Polity Press, 1993), 2.

149. Gilles Deleuze, "Qu'est-ce que c'est l'acte de creation?," presented at the FÉMIS, May 17, 1987, https://www.lepeuplequimanque.org/acte-de-creation-gilles-deleuze.html.

150. Sheren Falah Sabb, "The Tragic Life of Ghassan Kanafani," *Haaretz*, October 11, 2022, https://www.haaretz.com/middle-east-news/palestinians/2022-10-11/ty-article-magazine/.premium/the-tragic-life-of-pflp-member-and-author-ghassan-kanafani/00000183-adf8-d3b1-a9f3-fff802550000.

151. Reference to the writer Pedro Juan Gutiérrez, representative of the "Dirty Realism" movement in Cuba.

152. A professor back in Canada also described my PhD project as "intractable."

153. "My Mother always longed for Comala, to go back there."

"Her face was white, as if she had no blood, and her hands were withered and covered with wrinkles. Her eyes were sunken so deep into her face they were almost invisible."

"Seeing the horizon rise and fall as the wind moves the corn stalks, the afternoon rippling as the heavy rain falls, the color of the ground, the smell of alfalfa and bread. A town that smells like spilled honey."

"This town is full of echoes. It seems like they are caught in the cracks of the walls, or under the stones. When you are walking, it seems like they follow your steps. You hear crackling, and laughter. Some laughs are quite old, as though they are tired of laughing. And voices that are worn out from being used so long. You hear all this. Some day the time will come when these sounds fade away."

See Juan Rulfo, *Pedro Páramo* (Mexico City: Fondo de Cultura Económica, 1955).

154. Octavio Paz, "Nocturno de San Ildefonso," a poem expressing repentance for having been a Marxist, first published in *Plural* 36, September 1974, https://zonaoctaviopaz.com/detalle_conversacion/148/apuntes-sobre-nocturno-de-san-ildefonso. Translated into English by Betina Escudero, https://scholarworks.umt.edu/cgi/viewcontent.cgi?article=1620&context=cutbank.

> Good, we wanted the good:
> > to straighten the world.
> We didn't lack integrity:
> > we lacked humility
> We didn't want what we wanted with innocence.
> . . . . . . . . . . . . . . . . .
> > And the most vile: we were

> The audience that applauds or yawns in our seat.
> The guilt that doesn't know its own guilt,
>
> Innocence,
>
> was the major guilt.

155. Mariam Barghouti, "Bulldozing Palestine, One Village at a Time," *Al Jazeera*, July 10, 2018, https://www.aljazeera.com/opinions/2018/7/10/bulldozing-palestine-one-village-at-a-time.

156. See Visualizing Palestine, https://visualizingpalestine.org/visuals/segregated-roads-west-bank; Ahmad Al-Bazz, "In the West Bank, Segregated Roads Displace Palestinians," *Al Jazeera*, March 31, 2022.

157. See Jean Genet, *Quatre heures à Chattilah* (Paris: Éditions Tanger, 1982).

158. Toi Staff, "Prominent Jewish BDS Activist Denied Entry to Israel," July 2, 2018, *Times of Israel*, https://www.timesofisrael.com/prominent-jewish-bds-activist-denied-entry-to-israel; "La excoordinadora del movimiento BDS en Europa es repatriada a España," *El periódico*, October 9, 2022, https://www.elperiodico.com/es/politica/20221009/excoordinadora-movimiento-bds-europa-repatriada-77026419; Areeb Ulla, "British Muslims Detained in Israel and Kicked Off Flight Home," *Middle East Eye*, July 2, 2016, https://www.middleeasteye.net/news/british-muslims-detained-israel-and-kicked-flight-home; "Israel Refuses Entry to US Muslims," *Recordnet*, June 17, 2002, https://www.recordnet.com/story/news/2002/06/17/israel-refuses-entry-to-u/50754555007; "Israel Deports Pop Star Cat Stevens," *ABC News*, July 13, 2000, https://abcnews.go.com/International/story?id=83179.

159. Mahmoud Darwish, *No te excuses (La ta'tadiru 'an ma fa'alta)*, trans. Luz Gómez García (Beirut: Riad El-Rayyes, 2004).

160. Mark Fisher, *Ghosts of My Life: Writings on Depression, Hauntology and Lost Futures* (London: Zero Books, 2014).

161. Translated from the Hebrew by Jonathan A. Lipnick, "What Shall I Tell You, Good Bird?," *Holy Land Studies Blog*, Israel Biblical Studies, January 16, 2017, https://blog.israelbiblicalstudies.com/holy-land-studies/bialiks-to-the-bird.

162. Danny Sadeh, "Israel Investing NIS 11 Million in LGBT Tourism," *Ynetnews*, April 2, 2016, https://www.ynetnews.com/articles/0,7340,L-4786418,00.html.

163. "State Business: Israel's Misappropriation of Land in the West Bank through Settler Violence," B'Tselem, The Israeli Information Center for Human Rights in the Occupied Territories, November 2021, https://www.btselem.org/publications/202111_state_business.

164. John Berger, *Hold Everything Dear: Dispatches on Survival and Resistance* (London: Verso, 2007).

165. "Israel/Gaza: Operation 'Cast Lead'—22 Days of Death and Destruction," Amnesty International, July 2, 2009, https://www.amnesty.org/en/wp-content/uploads/2021/07/mde150212009eng.pdf.

166. Eyal Weizman, *The Least of All Possible Evils: A Short History of Humanitarian Violence* (London: Verso, 2011).

167. "Fatalities during Operation Cast Lead," B'Tselem, https://www.btselem.org/statistics/fatalities/during-cast-lead/by-date-of-event.

168. Sheera Frenkel, "Goldstone Retracts Part of U.N. Report on Gaza," *NPR*, April 3, 2011, https://www.npr.org/2011/04/03/135093832/goldstone-retracts-part-of-u-n-report-on-gaza; Conal Urquhart, "The Goldstone Report: A History," *Guardian*, April 14, 2011, https://www.theguardian.com/world/2011/apr/14/goldstone-report-history.

169. Henry Jenkins, "Avatar Activism," *Mondediplo*, September 2010, https://mondediplo.com/2010/09/15avatar.

170. "Background on the Demonstrations in Bil'in," B'Tselem, January 2, 2013, https://www.btselem.org/demonstrations/bilin.

171. Rory McCarthy, "Non-violent Protests against West Bank Barrier Turn Increasingly Dangerous," *Guardian*, April 27, 2009, https://www.theguardian.com/world/2009/apr/27/israel-security-barrier-protests.

172. Akiva Eldar, "Bil'in Sues 2 Canadian Firms for Building in West Bank Settlement," *Haaretz*, July 10, 2008, https://www.haaretz.com/2008-07-10/ty-article/bilin-sues-2-canadian-firms-for-building-in-west-bank-settlement/0000017f-dfa0-df7c-a5ff-dffae3170000.

173. Noam Chomsky, "'Exterminate All the Brutes': Gaza 2009," Based on a talk at the Center for International Studies, Massachusetts Institute of Technology, January 19 2009. Earlier versions appeared on ZNet and in *Spokesman* (England), no. 103 (2009), January 19, 2009, https://chomsky.info/20090119.

174. Jonathan Watts, "Belo Monte, Brazil: The Tribes Living in the Shadow of a Megadam," *Guardian*, December 16, 2014, https://www.theguardian.com/environment/2014/dec/16/belo-monte-brazil-tribes-living-in-shadow-megadam.

175. Silvia Emanuelli, "'La Parota' Hydroelectric Dam Project: The Impacts of Mega-Projects on the Right to Land and Housing," DPH: Diálogos, propuestas, historias para una Ciudadanía Mundial, 2006, http://base.d-p-h.info/es/fiches/dph/fiche-dph-6933.html.

176. Ignacio Pérez Vega, "Piden al Gobierno de Jalisco apoyo para resarcir daños a habitants de Temacapulín, Acasico y Palmarejo," *UDGTV*,

October 20, 2022, https://udgtv.com/noticias/jalisco/piden-gobierno-jalisco-apoyo-resarcir-danos-habitantes-temacapulin-acasico-palmarejo.

177.  Arundhati Roy, "Walking with the Comrades," *Outlook India*, April 26, 2017, https://www.outlookindia.com/magazine/story/walking-with-the-comrades/264738.

178.  Roy, "Walking with the Comrades."

179.  Noam Chomsky, "Exterminate all the Brutes."

180.  Slavoj Žižek, "Avatar: Return of the Natives," *New Statesman*, March 4, 2010, https://zizek.uk/avatar-return-of-the-natives.

181.  "Brazil Court Approves Building of Amazon Dam," *Al Jazeera*, November 10, 2011, https://www.aljazeera.com/news/2011/11/10/brazil-court-approves-building-of-amazon-dam.

182.  Jean Baudrillard, *Why Hasn't Everything Already Disappeared?* (New York: Seagull Books, 2009).

183.  "Brazil's President Signs 'Death Sentence' for Amazonian River," *Survival International News*, August 27, 2010, https://www.survivalinternational.org/news/6416.

184.  Invisible Committee, *L'insurrection qui vient* (Paris: La Fabrique, 2008).

# BIBLIOGRAPHY

Abu-Lughod, Leila, and Ahmad Sa'di, editors. *Nakba: Palestine 1948, and the Claims of Memory*. New York: Columbia University Press, 2007.

Adorno, Theodor. *Aesthetic Theory*. Translated by C. Lenhardt. Minneapolis: University of Minnesota Press, 1998.

Adorno, Theodor. *Minima Moralia: Reflections from Damaged Life*. Translated by E. F. N. Jephcott. New York: Verso, 1974.

Agamben, Giorgio. *Homo Sacer: Sovereign Power and Bare Life*. Translated by Daniel Heller-Roazen. Stanford: Stanford University Press, 1998.

———. *Image et mémoire: Écrits sur l'image, la danse et le cinéma*. Paris: Desclée de Brouwer, 2004.

———. *Remnants of Auschwitz*. New York: Zone Books, 2002.

Amin, Samir. *Le développement inégal: Essai sur les formations sociales du capitalisme périphérique*. Paris: Minuit, 1973.

Anidjar, Gil. *The Jew, the Arab: A History of the Enemy*. Stanford: Stanford University Press, 2003.

Arendt, Hannah. *On Violence*. New York: Harcourt, 1970.

———. *Promise of Politics*. New York: Shocken, 2007.

———. *Sobre la violencia*. Madrid: Alianza, 2013.

———. *What Is Politics*. Barcelona: Paidós, 2005.

Azoulay, Ariella. *The Civil Contract of Photography*. New York: Zone, 2009.

Badiou, Alain. *Being and Event*. London: Continuum, 2007.

Barthes, Roland. *Image, Music, Text*. New York: Hill and Wang, 1977.

Bataille, Georges. *The Unfinished System of Nonknowledge*. Translated by Michelle and Stuart Kendall. Minneapolis: University of Minnesota Press, 2001.

Baudrillard, Jean. *The Gulf War Did Not Take Place.* Translated by Paul Patton. Bloomington: Indiana University Press, 1995.

———. "No Reprieve for Sarajevo." Translated by Patrice Riemens. *Libération*, January 8, 1994.

———. "The Spirit of Terrorism." Translated by Rachel Bioul. *Le Monde*, November 2, 2001.

Benhabib, Seyla. "The Legitimacy of the Human Rights." *Daedalus* 137, no. 3 (Summer 2008): 94–104.

Benjamin, Walter. "The Author as Producer." *New Left Review* 1, no. 62 (July-August 1970).

———. "Critique of Violence," in *Selected Writings*, vol. 1, 1913–1926, edited by Michael William Jennings et al. Cambridge, MA: Belknap Press, 1996.

———. *Das Passagen-Werk.* Frankfurt: Suhrkamp, 1982.

———. *The Origin of German Tragic Drama.* London: Verso, 2003.

Benthall, Jonathan. *Disasters, Relief and the Media.* London: I. B. Tauris, 1993.

Berger, John. *Hold Everything Dear: Dispatches on Survival and Resistance.* London: Verso, 2007.

Bichler, Shimshon, and Jonathan Nitzan. *The Global Political Economy of Israel.* London: Pluto Press, 2002.

Boltanski, Luc. *La Souffrance à distance: Morale humanitaire, medias et politique.* Paris: Métailie, 1993.

Butler, Judith. *Precarious Life: The Power of Mourning and Violence.* London: Verso, 2006.

Chaliand, Gérard. *La Résistance Palestinienne.* Paris: Seuil, 1970.

Chief Seattle. "Chief Seattle's Thoughts." https://user.ceng.metu.edu.tr/~ucoluk/yazin/seattle.html.

Coetzee, J. M. *Iron Age.* London: Random House, 1990.

Cohen-Halimi, Michèle, and Francis Cohen. "Juifs, martyrs, kamikazes: La monstreuse capture; question à Jean-Luc Godard." *Les Temps Modernes*, no. 629 (November 2004–February 2005).

Committee on the Exercise of the Inalienable Rights of the Palestinian People. *The Status of Jerusalem.* New York: United Nations, 1997. https://www.un.org/unispal/wp-content/uploads/2016/07/The-Status-of-Jerusalem-English-199708.pdf.

Darwish, Mahmoud. *The Adam of Two Edens.* Translated by Munir Akash and Daniel Moore. Syracuse: Syracuse University Press, 2001.

———. *The Butterfly's Burden.* Translated by Faudy Joudah. Port Townsend, WA: Copper Canyon Press, 2006.

————. *Memory for Forgetfulness, August, Beirut 1982.* Translated by Ibrahim Muhawi. Berkeley: University of California Press, 1995.

————. *No te excuses (La ta'tadiru 'an ma fa'alta).* Translated by Luz Gómez García. Beirut: Riad El-Rayyes, 2004.

————. *Now As You Awaken.* Translated by Omnia Amin and Rick London. Pacifica, CA: Big Bridge Press, 2006.

————. *La Palestine comme métaphore.* Paris: Actes Sud, 1997.

Deleuze, Gilles. *Purparlers (1972–1990).* Paris: Les Éditions de minuit, 1990.

Dussel, Enrique. *Philosophy of Liberation.* Translated by Aquilina Martinez. Eugene, OR: Wipf and Stock, 2003.

Eliot, T. S. *The Waste Land.* New York: Horace Liveright, 1922.

Fanon, Frantz. *The Wretched of the Earth.* New York: Grove Press, 1967.

Finkelstein, Norman. *Image and Reality of the Israel-Palestine Conflict.* London: Verso, 2006.

Fisher, Mark. *Ghosts of My Life: Writings on Depression, Hauntology and Lost Futures.* London: Zero Books, 2014.

Fo, Dario. *Le commedie di Dario Fo.* Torino: Einaudi, 1977.

Foucault, Michel. *The Birth of Biopolitics: Lectures at the College de France, 1978–1979.* New York: Palgrave, 2008.

Genet, Jean. *Captif amoreux.* Paris : Gallimard, 1986.

————. *L'ennemi déclaré: Textes et entretiens.* Paris: Gallimard, 1991.

————. *Prisoner of Love.* New York: Wesleyan University Press, 1992.

————. "Quatre Heures a Chattila." *Revue d'études palestiniennes*, special issue dedicated to Genet and Palestine, January 1983.

————. "Une rencontre avec Jean Genet." *Revue d'études palestiniennes* 21 (November 1986).

Goytisolo, Juan. *Cuadernos de Sarajevo.* Madrid: Aguilar, 1993.

Graham, Stephen. "Lessons in Urbicide." *New Left Review* 19 (January-February 2003): 63–77.

Habiby, Emile. *The Secret Life of Saeed: The Pessoptimist.* New York: Interlink, 2001.

Harvey, David. *Spaces of Capital: Towards a Critical Geography.* Edinburgh: Edinburgh University Press, 2001.

Hobbes, Thomas. "War of All against All" (1651). Marxist Internet Archive, http://www.marxists.org/reference/subject/philosophy/works/en/decive1.htm.

Ignatieff, Michael. *The Rights Revolution.* Toronto: House of Anansi Press, 2000.

Invisible Committee. *L'insurrection qui vient.* Paris: La Fabrique, 2008.

Jameson, Fredric. *Postmodernism, or the Cultural Logic of Late Capitalism.* Durham, NC: Duke University Press, 1991.

Kanafani, Ghassan. *Men in the Sun*. Translated by Hilary Kilpatrick. New York: Lynne Rienner, 1999.

Kant, Immanuel. *Kant: Political Writings*. Cambridge: Cambridge University Press, 1991.

Khankan, Nathalie. *Quiet Orient Riot*. Oakland, CA: Omnidawn, 2020.

Khouri, Elias. *Gate of the Sun*. New York: Picador, 2007.

Klein, Naomi. *The Shock Doctrine: The Rise of Disaster Capitalism*. Toronto: Knopf, 2007.

Kraus, Chris. *Aliens and Anorexia*. New York: Semiotext(e), 2000.

Kraus, Chris, and Sylvère Lotringer, eds. *Hatred of Capitalism: A Semiotext(e) Reader*. Los Angeles: Semiotext(e), 2001.

Lévinas, Emmanuel. *Entre nous: Essays on Thinking of the Other*. Translated by Barbara Harshav and Michael Smith. New York: Columbia University Press, 2000.

Loewenstein, Antony. *The Palestinian Laboratory: How Israel Exports the Technology of Occupation Around the World*. Melbourne and London: Scribe, 2023.

Lucretius, *On the Nature of Things*, Trans. Cyril Bailey. Oxford: Clarendon Press, 1948.

Lyotard, Jean-François. *The Inhuman: Reflections on Time*. Cambridge: Polity Press, 1993.

Massumi, Brian. "Fear (The Spectrum Said)." *Positions: East Asia Cultures Critique* 13, no. 1 (2005): 31–48.

Nizan, Paul. *Aden Arabie*. Paris: Gallimard, 1931.

Pappé, Ilan. *Out of the Frame: The Struggle for Academic Freedom in Israel*. London: Pluto Press, 2010.

Pessoa, Fernando. *The Book of Disquiet*. New York: New Directions, 2017.

Prashad, Vijay. *The Darker Nations, A People's History of the Third World*. London: New Press, 2007.

Rabinowitz, Paula. *They Must Be Represented*. London: Verso, 1994.

Rancière, Jacques. *The Politics of Aesthetics: The Distribution of the Sensible*. Translated by Gabriel Rockhill. London and New York: Verso, 2004.

Rulfo, Juan. *Pedro Páramo*. Mexico City: Fondo de Cultura Económica, 1955.

Said, Edward. *Covering Islam: How the Media and the Experts Determine How We See the Rest of the World*. New York: Vintage, 1989.

———. *Orientalism*. New York: Vintage, 1979.

———. *The Politics of Dispossession*. New York: Vintage, 1995.

———. "The Public Role of Writers and Intellectuals." Deakin Lecture, Melbourne, May, 19, 2001. In *The Public Intellectual*, edited by Helen Small. Oxford: Blackwell, 2002. https://onlinelibrary.wiley.com/doi/10.1002/9780470775967.ch1.

———. *The Question of Palestine*. New York: Vintage, 1992.

Said, Edward, with Jean Mohr. *After the Last Sky: Palestinian Lives*. New York: Columbia University Press, 1998.

Sanbar, Elias. *Figures du Palestinien: Identité des origines, identité du devenir*. Paris: Gallimard, 2004.

———. *Les Palestiniens: Photographie d'une terre et de son peuple de 1839 à nos jours*. Paris: Hazan, 2004.

———. "Vingt et un ans après." *Traffic*, no. 1 (1991).

Sayigh, Rosemarie. *Palestinians: From Peasants to Revolutionaries*. London: Zed, 1979.

Sontag, Susan. Interview with Evan Chan, "Against Postmodernism: A Conversation With Susan Sontag." (2001). http://www.iath.virginia.edu/pmc/text-only/issue.901/12.1chan.txt.

———. *On Photography* (1977). New York: Picador, 2001.

———. *Regarding the Pain of Others*. New York: Farrar, Straus, and Giroux, 2004.

———. *Styles of Radical Will* (1969). New York: Picador, 2002.

———. *Where the Stress Falls*. New York: Farrar, Straus and Giroux, 2001.

Soueif, Ahadaf. *Mezzaterra: Fragments from the Common Ground*. London: Bloomsbury, 2004.

Weil, Simone. *La Condition ouvrière*. Paris: Gallimard, 1951.

———. *Écrits historiques et politiques*. Paris: Gallimard, 1960.

———. *Gravity and Grace*. London: Routledge, 2002.

———. "Lettre à Brenanos" (1948). https://www.bombasgens.com/wp-content/uploads/2020/04/Weil_Carta-a-Georges-Bernanos.pdf

———. *Notes sur la suppression générale des partis politiques*. 1947. Paris: Climats, 2006.

———. *Oppression and Liberty*. 1955. London: Routledge, 2001.

Weizman, Eyal. *The Conflict Shoreline*. Erasure. Göttingen: Steidl Verlag, 2016.

———. *Hollow Land: Israel's Architecture of Occupation*. London: Verso, 2007.

———. *The Least of All Possible Evils: A Short History of Humanitarian Violence*. London: Verso, 2011.

———. "Walking through Walls." *Radical Philosophy* 136 (March-April 2006). https://www.radicalphilosophy.com/article/walking-through-walls.

Weizman, Eyal, with Alessandro Petti and Sandi Hilal. Brochure for the exhibition and project in BOZAR, Brussels, from October 31, 2008, to April 1, 2009. www.decolonizing.ps/visitors.pdf.

Weizman, Eyal, with Fasal Sheikh. *The Conflict Shoreline: Colonization as Climate Change in the Negev Desert*. New York: Steidl and Cabinet Books, 2014.

Žižek, Slavoj. "NATO, the Left Hand of God." Nettime, June 29, 1999. https://
    nettime.org/Lists-Archives/nettime-l-9906/msg00184.html.
———. "Smashing the Neighbor's Face." Lacan.com, 2005. http://www.lacan.com/
    zizsmash.htm.
———. *Visión de Paralaje*. Buenos Aires: Fondo de Cultura Económica, 2006.
———. *Welcome to the Desert of the Real.* London: Verso, 2002.

# ACKNOWLEDGMENTS

This book is dedicated to my other hearts here and elsewhere: Lizzy Cancino, Layla García Emmelhainz, Eshrat and Javan Erfanian, Bruce Parsons, Tina and Peter Metschar, Margaret Schlubach-Rüping, Maria y Janne Vehreschild, John Greyson, John Paul Ricco, Rebecca Comay, Peter Fitting, Alice and Michel Toledano, Maria Gabriela Rangel, Romi Mikulinsky, b. h. Yael , Elle Flanders, Tamira Sawatzky, Majd Abdel Hamid and his parents, Muhannad Abdel-Hamid and Maha Tamim, Kifah and Khaled Fanni, Azmi, Shadi Habib Allah, Reem Schilleh, Sally Abu Bakr, Sonia Nimr, Khadijeh Habsbaneh, Yousef Majm Al Din, Nora Adwan, Nora Akawi, Maisa, Nathalie Khankan, Huda al Imam, and Silvia Gruner. To admirable people who have ceaselessly fought against the occupation, such as Haggai Matar, Neta Golan, Huwaida Arraf, and Juliano Mer-Khamis among others. Finally, to Fabio Rodríguez de la Flor, who invited me in 2011 to the University of Salamanca to read fragments of these chronicles, to María Fernanda Álvarez Pérez, my editor for this book in Spanish, and to the team behind the English edition: Zachary Gresham, Joell Smith-Borne, Gianna Mosser, Ignacio Sánchez Prado, and Jeremy Rehwaldt.

www.ingramcontent.com/pod-product-compliance
Lightning Source LLC
Chambersburg PA
CBHW030358270326
41926CB00009B/1162